We Thought You Would Never Ask

Finding Balance and Sanctuary in the Aquarian Age
A Transcript of Angelic Guidance

RQM Press
Jamestown, RI 02835

We Thought You Would Never Ask
Finding Balance and Sanctuary in the Aquarian Age - *A Transcript of Angelic Guidance*

By B. E. Schlubach

First Edition May 2019
Second Edition January 2021
Copyright 2019, 2021 by B.E. Schlubach

Cover Art by Judy Kinzel at Purple Tree Studio: purpletreeart.com
Book Design by Haley Cwynar: haleycwynar.com
Aquarius constellation image by Mara-ba, 88 Constellations
htttp:// supercoloring.com/coloring-pages/aquarius-constellation
Licensed under Creative Commons Attribution-Share Alike 4.0 license

Published and distributed in the United States by RQM Press.
Printed in the United States of America
By The Country Press
Lakeville, MA

First edition ISBN 978-0-578-21325-5
Second edition ISBN 978-0-578-79715-1

For additional copies of this book, please visit our website at
www.rqmpress.com

RQM Press
P.O. Box 363
Jamestown, RI 02835 USA

For Guru Singh.
And in memory of Gertrud, my finest teacher.

Table of Contents

Author's Note

With the exception of a few friends, family, and teachers in the yoga community, all names in this narrative have been changed, and personalities and locations masked out of respect for privacy.

I use the conventional English noun "angel" throughout as a handle or descriptor. By their own definition, angels are *"beings of love and light who transcend time and space."*

Communicating with the angels in writing happened to be the format I was open to, as I only had mild to neutral associations with the concept of angelic energy. Luckily – perhaps miraculously – I did not have to clear culturally-laden ideas about angels first, when I started this journal.

In recent years, it has become common for many spiritual teachers, writers, and other public communicators to include disclaimers or clarify their use of spiritual language, such as descriptions of deities, unseen beings, other dimensions, and universal energies. These clarifications are helpful to neutralize misperceptions about such abstract yet personally felt ideas, opinions or knowing.

Therefore, please note that all terms in this book describe spiritual and universal energies; and make no reference to religion or religious practices (which are human constructs). The yogic teachings I received provide a neutral definition of God or cosmic energy as that which "generates, organizes, and destroys." If the conventional word, "angel" does not work for you, please feel free to substitute another, such as "divine, loving presence."

The spirit guide and angel answers are universal: they are for you. If you happen to relate to any of the situations, emotions, or incidents, then please consider trying the guidance suggestions on your own. Otherwise, please just enjoy the ins and outs of the sharing of my personal story. The trajectory of events acted as building blocks for my own "primer" of growth, and so I share them with you here.

As of this writing, I still do not tangibly hear, see, feel or sense the angels in any other mode (not even a whisper), unless I am in a sacred space where the vibration is high, and even then it's simply an energy rush. Currently, it is a clear-cut, stable relationship in written format only. When the time is right, if ever, I know other sensory variations will show up in organic ways.

I respect the many talented, intuitive people who are already in contact with unseen benevolent energies and guides, and have shared their wisdom publicly, in many formats. I make no claims to be an expert or assert how or why these energies work. I can only share my personal experiences.

A note on the format: the guide or angelic answers are in italics, and my responses are in regular print. My side has been edited for brevity, but the angelic responses have not been altered. I have omitted inserting my name at the beginning of every responding paragraph for the sake of visual simplicity. The angel and guide answers may have spelling, punctuation and other anomalies – in my casual diary exchanges, it just came out that way, so I put it down as it came through. There may also be occasional inconsistencies in opening salutations and sign-offs.

Apart from my spirit guide and angelic communication, the other healing modalities, disciplines and practices mentioned in this book are my personal choices. This narrative does not advocate one therapy or modality over another. However, in my experience, kundalini yoga as taught by Yogi Bhajan* was an effective system for healing, physical fitness, psycho-emotional cleansing and re-patterning mental habits. This extraordinary spiritual technology changed my life.

Yogi Bhajan spoke of the human soul as the only part of our energy systems which could "defeat the defeat," where the cultivated qualities

---

*Yogi Bhajan (1929-2004), the yoga master who brought kundalini yoga to the West in the 1960s. He declared: "I have come to create teachers, not to gather students. I have come by my Guru's grace to serve those souls who shall serve the Aquarian Age."

of courage, hope and willingness become the key to overcoming human frailties and challenges. This overcoming, this prevailing, this victory, occurs on the fulcrum of our choices, which can only be made in the moment.

Sometimes this lifelong campaign of choosing to overcome-in-the-moment is subterranean, sometimes it bursts into activity. Much of the time, we don't know it is happening.

But when we wake up and decide to direct the campaign to defeat the defeat, the awareness comes that *we have backup.*

Barbara - 1960's New York City

Introduction

Remember, the entrance door to the sanctuary is inside you.
– RUMI

It is said that every author writes the book they wish had been available for reading in their time. For me, this is that book. This is the story of my private journey down the proverbial rabbit hole, in the form of a journal which took me by the hand and showed me that there is no "para" in paranormal. When I began it, I had no idea my private journals might one day be published, so throughout the entries I was purely open and trusting, pouring my pain onto the page with no holds barred.

This book covers a period of four years when I was going through particularly intense personal changes. It traces the long, slow journey from a shattered state of body, mind and spirit, towards healing, wholeness, and the beginnings of personal power retrieval. Of necessity the beginning steps I had to take were extremely basic, and these steps are offered here as an illustration of organic spiritual growth.

This book had its genesis in two parts: first, the accumulated challenging events of my life over five decades, which forced me on a quest for healing and relief from my daily experience of psychological and emotional pain. The second part came as a divine download, which was assigned to me at age 54.

The journal entries to follow offer a demonstration from my personal perspective: they juxtapose my human, emotionally reactive situations and questions with the clarity, kindness and compassionately guided answers, relayed from divine perspective. The call-and-response demonstrates what an enormous gulf there is between the two – and that there is simply no way that party A (the human) could possibly have written the response from party B (the Other-Side-guide). As the journal progresses, these juxtapositions trace my growth and the gradual falling away of my reactive states.

I am a Libra – the sign of the scales – and I cannot bear being off balance. I spent years with my nose metaphorically pressed up against the thick glass of healing practices and modalities, staring in at what I perceived as the special ones. It seemed to me that only they could be members of the Beautiful-and-the-Healed Club. I was frequently frustrated by the earnest messages out on the spiritual-literature airwaves, whose cosmic truths sometimes seemed unattainable, and which were certainly not applicable to me. Now, perhaps that was my perception, true – but why did it take so long to shift it? Why did it have to be that hard? This frustration became a quiet motivating force in writing this book.

The photograph heading this chapter is of myself as a little girl at three or four years old, and was taken by my father, Eric L. Schlubach. What is not shown, is the continued foreground of a seesaw, on a playground in 1960's New York City.

As I wrote this book, the theme of balance came up again and again, until I realized that I truly *was* that little girl on the seesaw, tipping back and forth on the fulcrum of the finite and the Infinite, with unseen guidance *just* out of sight. I now know why I have loved this photo above all others ever taken in my life, and I would like to think this explains the mildly-ecstatic-with-a-whiff-of-alarm expression on my face. The word see-saw comes from the French, this/that: *çi-ça.* I learned that in this pact with the divine, it is up to me (and you, and all humans) to overcome our belief that "I'm only human." As the divine exchanges energies with us to bridge the gap, we can choose to tilt the seesaw, so that both sides receive what they need. In other words, in writing this book I was floored (bump! there she goes, down again) to find that this simple metaphor cracked the code of my existence.

A genesis is a germination. I had no way of knowing that what began as a curious experiment, and deepened into a diary, a dialogue, and an intricate partnership in communicating, listening, willingness and healing, would one day become this book. I found that many spiritual themes which wove into the journal entries defied cataloging, and so I let it be what it wanted to be. Yet some threads can be picked out for following, which I highlight to give you some ways to approach this book.

Firstly, these diaries became a pragmatic, tangible form I could refer back to, for proof of angelic and divine support. The reassurance of the connection and the format, answered so many of my personal, driving questions, that after a few years, my mind, body and soul truly calmed as the fears drained away. The questions became fewer and fewer in an organic replacement process, when intuition, faith, trust and (occasionally) patience became my ingrained choice of response.

Secondly, this support and proof became a kind of angelic self-psychotherapy, where I could participate actively in my own healing (and it's *free...*). Every tiny action taken toward responsibility for my own healing, every intimate impulse towards self-initiation, was rewarded a thousand-fold. Each tiny action or decision I took, reinforced the foundation I was unknowingly building, so the theme of self-initiation is also a key theme in the book.

For myself, I can trace any progress on my spiritual path directly to many moments of grace over the years. A cluster of such moments of grace occurred in my thirties, when I absorbed, internalized, and began practicing the following simple, powerful affirmations:

"I am willing to change and grow."

"I am responsible for my choices. I am responsible for my healing. I am responsible for my life."

"I am committed to healing: healing to the source of the pain."

"What do I need to learn from this?"

These have been the bedrock of my spiritual life, and whenever I am stuck, it's always, always, back to basics.

Thirdly, these diaries became a sacred container of neutrality, safety, and sanctuary. In this, they echoed the spiritual name which I received during my kundalini yoga teacher training: *Sarandayal Kaur*, which means: "Lioness of God who creates a sanctuary of kindness and compassion, where she and others may know peace and protection." Writing in my journal, and the accrual of the entries, was not only a healing process, it was communication, it was communion, it was infallible refuge, and it became my personal testament to creating inner peace.

We cannot heal, make good choices, or progress as humans at any level, until we feel safe. Spiritual practices are designed to foster this state so that we can make a better choice, tip the scales, shift into greater awareness, and then build our own mental, emotional, physical and spiritual safe-spaces. My hope is that as you read, either for pleasure, curiosity, or a desire to shift to a higher place, you may extract and apply these demonstrations and principles in your own life, and experience their benefits.

We don't know what we don't know, and some of us may not be aware that we need or crave a safe space in which to grow. I once had an illuminating conversation with a senior yoga teacher after she had read a sample of this book. I was surprised when she said to me, *"I didn't know I could ask."*

"Ah," I thought. "So it's not just me!"

And so, I offer you the experiential journey of my angelically-coached journal entries as a place of refuge and rebalance. If as you read, you hold this sense of safety, and it touches your heart, calms you somehow, or sparks your own willingness to take the next – undoubtedly scary – step in your own life, then I am glad for your company on the journey. The journal-journey may rarely make sense, as the random events of my life zig and zag (just as yours do) so be prepared for the analytical mind to demand something to clutch at, or to insist on measurable results. In this reading, and in your life, come back to the container, the tangible form which holds the wisdom of the answers, and reassure your mind, that it is *okay*. And keep walking, breathing, trusting, praying, allowing, accepting – ad *infinitum*, for so it is that we are...Infinite.

Barbara E. Schlubach
(Sarandayal Kaur)
February 2019

A Letter From the Angels

prim·er (prĭm′ər) n.

1. An elementary textbook for teaching children to read.

2. A book that covers the basic elements of a subject.

It is us, the Angels.

Beloved Readers,

Joyous greetings — we are standing by to pour onto the page through Barbara's willing transcription. This is a joy and an honor, to reach out to you! First of all, know that you are very very loved on this side. We open and close all communications with this information because it is something most humans do not hear nearly enough, and when they do hear it, they have trouble believing it. So we rain it down upon them, knowing that it will soak in eventually. Dearest readers, thank you for embracing these messages! No, Barbara is not altering what comes out — she has been doing this for many years now and she stands aside as we come through. So this message is entirely for you, beloved reader!

The book she is undertaking as a partnership with us is an important work. We are using her to get our message of love and light through to humans. Throughout her diary form she has turned to us over and over again with questions, pain, hurt, and puzzlement over ordinary human problems. We always respond with as much support as will flow through at that given session. Sometimes, when she is very clear (and not too sleepy!) — we can blaze forth our love in complex language that transmits joy to her energy system. Naturally, this can be a little overwhelming and she does not understand it either. But she patiently, willingly transcribes whatever comes through, and it stands on record, as proof for her (and we hope, eventually, the world) of how much Divine love can transmute pain. Yet you are made of flesh and blood, and must live out your existences in time and space (which we are not bound by), so this makes for some dense energy barriers that take time to work through. So it is with human understanding, and the need for things to "make sense" on your earthbound plane. We are trying to bridge that. Once the book is finished*, you will see that there are many episodes and instances where our angel language is very plain and direct,

*This letter was written in August 2015.

and answers questions with clear expressions. Yet contained in these, is always the larger picture, and so there will be a very healthy mix of understandable, and not-understandable, situations and language. And this is fine, and all shall be well, for as the human species evolves in this Aquarian Age, consciousness will keep up with the evolution and such primers as this book, shall be — will be — child's play in years to come.

Beloved reader, does this help? Although we have simplified our language in this writing, and are addressing you directly, we know that you can tell that this is most definitely not Barbara writing. This is a key point of the book — the extreme difference between what issues forth from the human mind onto paper or screen; and what issues forth from angelic voices and thought forms. Hold these puzzles in your heart not in your mind, and ask us for help — all day, every day. Just ask! We would love nothing better than to fly to your aid. It is an entirely personal, private relationship. But we need the initiating call for help, to assist. Dearest reader, we send you blessings of peace, health, and joy, and wrap your family in our Divine embrace. Until we meet again — and you know we shall — we embrace thee with all love and blessings.

The Angels

Chapter 1: The Seed Is Sown

Know that you are not alone
And that the darkness has purpose.

– JOHN O'DONOHUE, *TO BLESS THE SPACE BETWEEN US*

The Assignment

The creative spark which ignited the flame for this book was struck in September 2014.

I had been a committed practitioner of kundalini yoga for over a decade, and in the spring of 2014, I graduated from kundalini yoga teacher training, Level I (KYTT). In this yogic tradition, my spiritual name and guiding light in my destiny as a teacher is *Sarandayal Kaur.** The transformational teacher training course peeled me like an onion, held a mirror up to the peeled spots, and then said "FIX THIS. No cosmetic blemish-concealers permitted." In the euphoric weeks after graduation, I felt like a rubber glove that had been spiritually pulled inside out, inflated, deflated and reversed.

During the summer months that followed, I continued to attend intensive workshops and classes, eager to continue the healing roll I was on. That September, the revered kundalini yoga master Guru Singh was scheduled to teach at the local yoga studio where I had done my teacher training. This was not to be missed, so I signed up, and attended the Monday night session. After the class, Guru Singh was surrounded by students asking questions. I lingered behind, hoping

---

*Defined in Introduction.

to greet him and share a personal experience. By some miracle, the crowd cleared away as the students drifted off to get some yogi tea. I approached Guru Singh, thanked him for the class, and then began to tell a brief story which epitomized one of the points he had made about the innocence of children and teenagers, and their openness to spiritual energy. My story involved a recent angel oracle card reading[*] I had done for two teenage girls, their first exposure to angelic energy; and the speechless awe we three had been reduced to when Presence poured through so strongly, that during the session I was physically shaking from the strength of it, and the girls reported that the room was full of light.

Guru Singh was gazing mildly at me, and listening politely, but when I concluded my story, he asked me a few questions: *Did I communicate with the angels? Yes*, I answered, *I write to them. I have ring binders full of writings.* I gazed back at him, sensing something was about to happen. In spite of knowing better, having been in and around kundalini yogis, teachers, and yoga studios for years and knowing that one behaves with conscious respect, or one's projection boomerangs uncomfortably, I was naive enough to think I was merely sharing a relevant anecdote with this powerful master that he might appreciate. *What was I thinking?* (That was the problem: thinking uses the linear, left-brain, rational mind.) Oh, my.

Guru Singh closed his eyes, appearing to roll them up to the focal point at the crown of his head, breathed deeply for a moment or two, opened his eyes, gazed firmly at me and spoke:

> *The angels appreciate your communication. You have a great gift.*
> *Your assignment is to write a book about your angel writings.*

I was kneeling before him, rapt with attention, and when this downloaded angelic bolt zapped me, I tried to maintain my composure, but I am fairly sure I just gaped. Inside, my ego was

---

*Healing with The Angels Oracle Cards, by Doreen Virtue.

going crazy, protesting, denying, rejecting, inventing a million stories about the complete impossibility of executing such a ridiculous assignment (What was I thinking? *Say no, Barbara, say no! you can't do that! Run, Barbara, run.* You want me to WHAT?).

One does not decline a Divine Assignment. I was busted.

I gulped, nodded, and verbally choked out "yes," but more importantly, my gaze locked with Guru Singh's all-knowing, kindly and imperative eyes; and inside, my soul said YES, visually completing the contract. My soul was tap dancing and singing "We've finally been given our marching orders!" but I was too terrified to notice. The pact signed and sealed, it was up to me to deliver now. Guru Singh motioned to Tom, one of the co-owners of the yoga studio, and he came over. He gestured to me, "Parmatma, she is going to write a book about angels. Keep an eye on her."

I thanked Guru Singh, made a *namaste* obeisance, rose and walked away, stunned and mentally spluttering. What had I just agreed to? How could I possibly? My writings to the angels were intensely, excruciatingly private. *How the...?* Yet, there was no going back, no refusing the task.

A line from The Lord of the Rings reverberated in my head:

"Never meddle in the affairs of wizards, for they are subtle..."

Together with the classic Laurel and Hardy line,

"This is a fine mess you've gotten us into, Stan."

The Threshold

The word "threshold" was related to the word thresh, which was the separation of the grain from the husk or straw when oats were flailed. It also includes the notions of entrance, crossing, border, and beginnings. To cross a threshold is to leave behind the husk and arrive at the grain...A threshold is not simply an accidental line that happens to separate one region from another. It is an intense frontier that divides a world of feeling from another.

– JOHN O'DONOHUE, *TO BLESS THE SPACE BETWEEN US*

By the time I was 50, the accumulated issues of my life had melded into something akin to spiritual leukemia. I presented a reasonably pulled-together façade to the world, but inside I felt one-dimensional, like a cardboard cutout. As a consequence, over the years my quest for healing had evolved into a lifestyle, and I would spend my weekends reading self-help books, trolling local libraries and second-hand book stores for the next title to leap into my hand.

On a frigid, snowy night in February 2011, I found myself reading a book about inner happiness.* It was a Saturday evening, and though I envisioned normal human beings doing sociable things like joining friends for drinks or enjoying a dinner party, this was not for me. I curled up quietly with my new title to see what answers might surface. My bedroom was cozy, and I felt safe. I remember clearly that I was feeling rested, calm, neutral, and slightly curious, but with no mental or emotional agenda.

Note these conditions: I was *willing*. I was *able*. I was *showing up*. I was *neutral*. And I was *fearless*, because the simple act of reading was well within my ability level and comfort zone.

Leafing through the pages, I read a number of the human interest stories, skimmed the rest of the book, and then noticed some of the exercises that were offered.

*Happy For No Reason, by Marci Shimoff

My eye lit upon one exercise: writing your question to the universe, and simply free-writing whatever answer came to you. All it called for was a writing pad and a pen.

I thought, *"That's a cinch! I can do THAT."*

I have been a diary-writer, ardent correspondent, and faithful letter-writer since childhood. For me, correspondence is like breathing. The simplicity of the exercise reassured me, and I did not feel intimidated by Weighty Concepts or the need to Have a Profound Experience while visualizing stars, planets, and the great cosmic waltz. No, it was just my old friend, white ring-binder paper, blue-lined, comfortable, tangible and ordinary.

At the time, one of the questions I was mulling over in my life, was trying to decide whether or not to return to the same resort in Europe, which I had visited in 2010 for a delightful 50th birthday getaway with some girlfriends. The cost, vacation time needed, and effort required to travel there, daunted me, so I mentally waffled back and forth. Despite years of practicing abundance affirmations, I still had a healthy level of anxiety around finances and the limits of my salary. I decided that this should be the question I posed to the Universe.

As I hand-wrote my first entry in blue ink, on a piece of white, three-hole ring-binder paper on 2/26/11, I was completely unsuspecting that this would lead me down the most outrageous path of my life:

"Please offer me guidance about whether or not I should make my reservation to return to Club Med Kemer in September. I am torn – I feel extreme resistance – so I need help deciding whether this is a trip I am supposed to take or not."

Silence.

"Ah," I thought, "it doesn't work. Phew, off the hook. Let me try something else."

5

Then...these odd words floated into my mind, utterly illogical, and therefore, I realized, they must be not-me, in other words, the answer. Staving off the deep craving to analyze, I flowed, allowed, remained neutral, and feeling very peculiar as I almost sensed this stream come down my arm and through the pen, transcribed:

*"tum tum tiddly tum piddly diddly tum. Open your eyes and write. Whatever comes into your head or heart or mind or body flowing word by word challenge is not an option silence is golden by fair means or foul seek and ye shall find in fair weather and foul singing in cadences follow the rhythm of the heart inconsequential here is your answer grateful don't edit just write closed faint stronger keep going almost there continuing hand over foot and mouth reaching for sunlight growing grabbing going crabbing welcome Turkey warm and fuzzy deep well happy go lucky glad and grateful take chance sheltered cheer up heart in throat relax grope grab all the gusto you can trust the process **just go**"*

I dropped the pen, astonished. This was real, this was most definitely not-me, this rhyming, associative gobbledygook. And, it *worked*. It gave me an answer: *"Just go!"* I was intrigued, hooked, awed. This was my kind of exercise. Somehow I had willingly, willfully and by chance, struck upon the right conditions for this "hearing." I recognized somehow, that this required "my" standing aside, not editing, not judging, and just transcribing impersonally, no matter how absurd the stream of word-bits seemed. The limitations of the English language force me to use words like "voice," "hearing" and "heard" but at no time was the stream auditory. It bypassed the physiology of the inner ear.

Thrilled with the success of the experiment, and deeply curious, I promptly wrote another question:

"Last year I had a healing session with Dr. John W. You know him, yes? Shall I make another appointment? What issues shall I bring up with him?"

The answer stream flowed:

"Tick tock hickory dock it's the clock make it stop Rhyme or reason in season no treason. Flow slow go dough mow po fo lo low low intsy itsy bitsy eensy teensy.

Go. Learn experience vulnerable be heart kind wonderful grateful listen talk explore simply
be its okay you are fine don't cry honey we love you sadness hurts we know its going to get
better soon we miss you keep going you can hear us now and that makes it so much better
easier we're here never forget go see John never regret grow grow grow you are lovely and
fine help is on the way lonely not too much longer we love you dearie it's going to be okay
sleep now, in peace write soon Love, Mommy and Papa"

At this, I burst into tears. My parents had both passed away when I was
in my twenties, and I had had to develop a fairly thick survival skin
to get on with my life, in their absence and without their guidance.
Their memory was deeply buried, and I rarely thought of them. I was
definitely *not* editing, manipulating or affecting the stream that came
through my pen. This level of proof was necessary to me, and continued
to be one of the attributes of the writing sessions that I continued to
test long after I became accustomed to the answer stream. The absence
of punctuation was unthinkably foreign to my ever-editing English-
major mind, another indicator that this was non-linear and intuitive
streaming. The tone and tenor of this language – kind, praising, loving,
positive, and supportive – contrasted so sharply with my critical inner
self-dialogue, that it also constituted proof which I continued to find
uncomfortable and outlandish (*who, **me**? Why are they being so nice to me?*
*Don't they **know**?*) for many years.

Deeply hooked, I continued writing questions and transcribing the
surfacing word-stream. I began to sense a pattern – that the gobbledygook
and rhyming nonsense was a kind of threshold which had to be crossed,
to begin the communication and two-way exchange, like static on a
walkie-talkie prior to the call-sign. I then posed a question about my
brother, whose money problems sometimes distressed me. This,
coupled with my question about who I was writing to, generated
more initial gobbledygook and rhyming nonsense. The answer
came, with a new level of clarity and comprehension, indicating
that I was learning fast, hearing better, and trusting more, even just
within the half hour or so I had been writing:

"Happy to help. So glad to meet you. This is a thorny issue. Wisdom is forthcoming. All will be made clear. Do not despair. Please be kind even though it is hard sometimes. He is hurt and your criticism doesn't help. He will find his way eventually. You can't do anything about it. Back off, be wise, be patient, yes I know it's difficult. You must lead the way through grace. You are doing so well don't falter now. We love you and bless you."

From a dull, non-descript, quiet winter's eve, this was turning into an emotional rollercoaster, and the hottest Saturday night date of my life. I slowly began to realize, "I'm *not* alone."

No, I'm REALLY not alone.

And, there *ARE* answers! And I'm not alone-I'm not-alone-**I'm-not-alone!"**

Overwhelmed, and trying to reach out in my clueless state, to these mysterious energies or beings, I attempted a few more questions, inviting a "benevolent spirit" to write to me. The resulting stream was garbled and confused. It seemed there were many voices, jostling for attention. I had no idea whom or what I had contacted. I quickly caught on that this was a party line, thanked them, and signed off.

It was enough for one night. I went to bed, exhilarated and changed. A grand turning point had quietly occurred in my life. And so it was to be, from that moment forward, I was to learn, slowly, entry by entry, communication by communication, that I had Guidance, specific, loving, outrageous, standing by always, *Guidance*. The rest — which was yet to come — became an exercise in fluency, like practicing French verb conjugations; and an exercise in cautiously, tentatively flexing these bizarre portals in my awareness.

Could You Tell Me How to Grow?

But I fear my story fatigues you. I would like to learn.
Could you tell me how to grow, or is it unconveyed, like melody or witchcraft?
– EMILY DICKINSON

Following the thrilling first session on February 26, I continued my efforts at communicating across this non-physical barrier, using pen and paper. All of my entries were written in longhand (except when occasionally typed at work). I had no idea who or what I was trying to connect with, I was just stretching and reaching with my mind. I was wide open and eager to be a human pen-pal for whatever was on the other side. My long-ingrained habits of dating all diary entries stood me in good stead, and with complete hindsight now, I realize that the trajectory this etheric correspondence was to take, *was guided from the first* into definite form – so that even your reading it now, is part of the continuum (let that one sink in…). My head was buzzing with curiosity, and I peppered "them" with questions, writing:

"I invite one benevolent spirit, angel or voice to communicate with me. Please guide my pen, open my channels, and help me to hear you. Who are you?"

I received and wrote down a mix of answers, one in Italian, from someone named Robert; another one which started *"Jostling for position…"* and continued on in jumbled nonsense. I let these ramble out, but could see they were leading nowhere. Already I was learning to discern, choose, and stop or start the internal flow at will. I kept trying, patiently, to stay open to whatever came through.

On February 27th, I wrote:
"My dear visitors – if you are there! I have no question to pose to

you, but if you would like to communicate, I am here and willing. Love, Barbara"

The other-world, threshold nonsense began as I transcribed with scrawled speed:

Humpa tumpa tumpetty tum silver medal gold in the sun gleeful pleaful bargain made bad endless friendless empty and sad joyful toyful will it be plaything claything fiddledee dee... begone spy princess into the night find succor in a padded hall where footfall never rankles glass slipper catch fall in the place where words well up rhyming trickster that is I oh clueless one be off to have some fun in the shade ready made under glade be not afraid.

This is not working now.

Good night. Who-who

This mystical, poetic stream struck me as pretty harmless, and it was sufficiently absurd that it didn't seem to matter if I missed a few words or misunderstood who or what came through. I was curious, but had no labels yet for whatever was responding through my "hearing." Who *was* this – could it be this was a spirit guide, a compassionate being who had passed on, whose Other-side mission was to guide, protect, nudge and escort a human throughout their lifetime? I didn't know, but I felt compelled to find out.

My second entry for that day read:

"Hello, I hope you don't mind if I keep coming back with questions – it's so thrilling to have communication. I do not take it for granted – I hope you know that. As I am new to this and do not know the protocol, please educate me. I would like to know who my spirit guide is and to be in touch with that guide. I ask in all humility. Thank you!"

Fiddle faddle piddle paddle mumpty bumpty goo. Loosey twosey pusey woosey udderly ibbidy boo...we are we we are one in the sun just begun to learn and understand hold your heart throw no dart sinking in the sand elementary cause rudimentary elegant are we Place the spade already made fabulous we three...join the rest for this fair test Welladay alack Smile you will beside the hill if anything you lack Clarity you see answers for to be riddles nothing lack Grateful grateful never hateful loveliness you are Smile my sweet and once we meet you'll wish upon a star. Love, Beloved.

Oh, my ears and whiskers, said the White Rabbit*…within hours of the first entry, I was deeply embroiled in a secret double life of the mind, body and spirit. I was about to experience a vocabulary word in its most literal sense: *duality*.

From my many readings of spiritual and self-help books, I knew that duality meant the two sides of all creation: our tangible earth-plane world, which is so convincing that we think it is real; and All-that-Is, Divine Oneness, Spirit, or God – whatever you would like to call it. It is the dimension where all else resides, which is not of the Earth plane. Well, I was in touch with it – and We were both pretty excited about it. Finally, *contact*, my first own, private contact, after years of reading about everyone else's mystical experiences in books. And yet, due to the organic, approachable nature of the way it was unfolding for me, although it was a little odd and astonishing, it did not seem like a mystical experience. Very cunning, this agent of Divinity – It knew I had to be carefully wooed, so as not to scare me off. I was so fragile at this point in my life, that anything too overwhelming would have made me slam the journal shut. Here, though, on the page, a strong personality was suddenly coming through, and making its presence felt. It was more than in my mind, as an intellectual word-stream; it was *there* with me, in the room.

Again on 2/27/11, I wrote:
"Oh my new friends, thank you! You have changed my life by coming into it. I have company. Here is my thought/feeling. I sense you are playful and fun, love to jest and rhyme. I am ready to stop being so deadly earnest and adult, and go back into the world to play. I'd like to take Latin or salsa ballroom dance lessons, so I can laugh and move and groove. Please advise me which studio in my area might be best to try."

*A reference to Alice in Wonderland.

Tootsy pootsy ribbon and rye kiss the girls and make them cry…when hardly deals you too Conceals the lack thereto consider where and why Before you leap or jump consider no more frump puddles never dry Insatiable glisten river for to listen incongruous am I Beloved heart I need to speak a simple creed albeit somewhat dry listen and then lunch follow up the hunch merrily berrily ringing in derrily silence for to try Beyond that I cannot tell ye merry maid of where you dwell Beloved heart I must now part be well be well be well
John

John? Who was John? It didn't matter; I was charmed and caught. There was no resisting this poetic presence, it spoke to every former-lifetime cell in my body. This, I *heard*.

Yet, it was all too new, and I still didn't know who or what I was dealing with, so in a more anxious, prosaic vein I continued: "I have an electric bill of $210 due two days before my paycheck will be in my account. I can either cover it with some juggling from accounts, or I can risk having less than $35 in my bank account until March 4th. Please guide me on the best way to handle this. Thank you!"

Umpty tumpty tiddly pum doodle absolam babsolom jiggledy flum …the threshold verbiage was still ongoing, but shortening. After six lines, suddenly it ran clear:

Hello again. Not at all, don't mention it. Let me see, bill payment. Timely bill payment. A sticky one, what? Tell you what. Trust what happens this week. Go ahead and mail the bank check. You're in for a pleasant surprise. Life is good, don't you think? Such fun to help you out. Ah, my dear, we will come to that later. Yes, dear, easy on the emotions, it clouds the channels. You're doing beautifully, and we're glad to communicate too. Write soon! Love, The Presence

Whoa…a voice, a personality, a clear message, AND a specific answer. Breakthrough. These entries have no time of day on them, but I recall that I wrote this late at night, and was once again steeped in an emotional cocktail of overwhelmed confusion, awe, and incredulousness. There was nothing to do, but go to bed.[*]

[*]*The check cleared.*

The next day, February 28th, eager to keep testing the airwaves but still naive about who I was communicating with, I covered my bases by addressing them generally:

"Greetings, my friends and spirit guides – thank you so much for your company and your presence. It is so astonishing not to feel alone and afraid anymore.

The question I have been carrying in my heart for so many years – and this is a big one – is where did my deep inner joy, my soul, go? Why did it fly away? I miss it – it is part of me, and it has been gone for so long.* When will it come back? Oh thank you thank you for any light you can shed. Have I said thank you?"

Scoliosis poliosis sentrap puppity poo lagame sagame dipping whippity loo... Sad you are and sad you be joy not found upon a tree Long ago and far away sadness came out to play search no more in love you dwell in happiness seeking you shall swell Nasty critters flew away nasty critters stay away brave and bold and fearless be you shall find happiness on a tree Lords and ladies all do dance sunshine falling in a glance Lightly lightly follow my lead smiling bravely planting a seed Joy shall be yours Joy shall be free Joy shall come creeping in wheresoever you be

Beloved Prankster

I was fragile, I was vulnerable, I was trusting, and I was wide open. The presence was *wooing* me. I *felt* it.

Dear Beloved Prankster:
I love you
You love me
What kind of poetry
Is best for thee?

Simphop wimhop tinkety too lisping pisping drinking goo elbow in and elbow out lean and shout grab your partner do si do careful not to tread on toe...Simple minds like simple fare

---

*At age 33 I experienced an emotional trauma which caused soul-loss, and in that moment I experienced some kind of life-force-being fleeing out of the top of my head. I had no idea what happened to me, but from that point forward could rarely feel emotions, and was essentially dead inside. I became skilled at masking my numbness. It would be almost 30 years before I was restored and re-integrated.

find me here find me there Listen loud and listen soft Listen quietly in a loft Adore thee I do Sweet Barbie Bee Find me some poems and I'll follow thee. Beloved Prankster

This was my lifeline – I had to follow it wherever it led. The sense of intimacy was outrageous, and warning bells were going off in my head – as well as a deeply adult disdain for the pure sappiness of it. The free use of endearments left me mentally queasy. What was this weird dance with whatever it was, a spirit guide? The hook was set, the partnership was agreed to. It was utterly irrational. Welcome to duality, Barbara.

I wrote back: "It's a deal!"

From this point forward, I began to have a daily running, internal "conversation" with the spirit guide John, who had slipped under my emotional radar. I began to sense that he and I had a strong past life connection, which linked us emotionally. I have never been particularly intrigued by past life studies, but had read in many books that they were a normal part of our human/divine experience. This philosophy made sense to me at a visceral level.

The guidance which came through was always silent. It was not so much a signal or a sound, it was more as though pure consciousness streamed from my pen-tip to the page – or leapt ahead of the typed letters on screen. The question-and-answer format became crucial, as I was to learn: a human posing a question creates an energy which must be responded to, so a question is a catalyst for contact. My hyper-politeness and innocence were my way of coping with this bizarre, unknown energy, since I had no idea what I was dealing with. Yet, with other-side help, over time I fell instinctively into a format of *ask, believe and trust, let go,* and say *thank you.* I subsequently learned, that this is exactly what it takes – and is all that it takes.

March 1, 2011
Hello again. It's evening and I'm a little tired, but I'd like to try communicating if possible. Please have patience, and thank you very much for hearing me.

Today I spent $700 on new front brakes for my car. It was quite necessary, and I am so grateful to be able to drive safely again, but this is a tough hit in the bank account. I feel as though I do nothing but struggle to make ends meet, with big bill after big bill. I can squeeze by, but I think there has got to be a better way. How can I be open to more abundance? Thank you for your advice.

Pleasant night, no? Hello there, happy March. Finance problems, eh? I can tell you're tired tonight and weary from a long day of running around. Let's think about it, and let's talk tomorrow when we're both feeling perkier. These things require smarts and clear thinking. Toodle loo!
John

The success of these initial conversations was exciting, and I couldn't wait to write again the next day:

March 2, 2011
Dear John,
Today was terrific. Did you have something to do with that? Sunshine and smiles all around, abundance in the air.

Hello my love how are you. Been doing research, have you? Of course you have. I trust you to follow your heart and excellent common sense. Now, where were we? Talking about finances, I believe. Hm. Please take that lottery ticket away. Waste of money — I told you so. We have much more creative ways of bringing wealth. Patience, my sweet. Post me another question about your money issues. Be specific, if you can. You need help figuring out how to buy a new car, right? Details, details. A Porsche won't do — too flash, but thanks for the thought. Yes dearie, I am indeed. Calme toi, I'm perfectly harmless. Right you are, my heart. You and me, kid. So nice to see you smile. That's the ticket. You're getting it now. Any other questions?

Dear John,
My question is about Mehmet.* Did I know him in a previous life – is that why there was mutually deep recognition? I don't want to spoil things for myself by predicting the future (*smart girl*) but it would help

---

*A handsome, kind man I had met on vacation, and whom I was mooning over, now safely back home.

me to know if I have just invented this romance in my head, or if his looks and intent were genuine. I'm driving myself a little crazy.

Silence

John?

I'm thinking. Mehmet is an old soul. Yes, you knew him, once upon a long time ago. He is as sweet, genuine and true as any you will meet. He does, however, happen to have that effect on a lot of women. He is also a charmer. Never lose sight of this — Carla was right (she's a smart lass, by the way, and a kind one. You have a very good friend in her.). No you did not invent the romance. You are sensible enough to struggle against conditioning yourself into false feelings. The mutual recognition is very strong and easily mistaken for love. If you ever saw him again, yes, you might have a romance, and it would be **very** good for you. I am so sorry for your long dry spell, my darling, but you did have a lot of healing to do. Truly, I am here to help you through it. That is why I am a rogue and a rake. I will steer you straight. Terrifying, yes. Necessary for growth, yes. Can you do it? Yes. Fortunately, you and I make a good team, you have a lovely smile, and you're a beautiful flirt. We will banish that serious face very soon o po-faced one. Fear not, I am with you ever. Does that answer your question?*

Do you have a Scots accent?

Aye lass, that I do. Your beloved, John.

The next set of problems I ran past my new friend John had to do with a family crisis over selling some jointly-owned real estate in Florida, of which I was one-sixth owner with my brother, sister, and two cousins. The property in question was 40 acres of mangrove wetlands in southwest Florida we had inherited from my mother and my aunt (my aunt and uncle had committed double suicide in 2004, and their two sons were in such pain that all communication with them was toxic). The property had been passed down like an untouchable hot potato, and had remained unsold for at least five decades and was now on its third generation, breeding ill-will and recrimination. I had become the lightning rod for many of the vicious emails, and was hurting.

---

*A lifelong friend from college days.

Dear John,

Good morning! Things are clearer on paper – I am learning this. Thank you so much for your company, the conversation, and the poetry. You're getting through, bless your heart.

Please help me with the following. I need to print out, sign and fax the Florida contract back to the realtor, but am resisting. The whole Florida property problem is the biggest snarl in my life. Can you give me some comforting advice about handling this, and all of my mixed-up emotions?

Good morning dearie. Trying this at work? Good show. I'm always here for you. I can feel your heart when you smile, so keep smiling, my love. Big snarl, yes. We are due for some long conversations. For now, just know that you're doing your best. Let your cousin handle it – this is his path, and it is a rough one. Your sister – well, that is another iceberg tip. Fax the contracts to the realtor – he is caught in the middle of the crossfire and doing his best, too. When the right buyer comes – and he/she will – it will be such a relief you won't believe you ever hesitated for a second. We have time to deal with this. Your sister's fear is a big ball of anxiety she is projecting – but you know that. Keep your distance, pay the bills, deep breath, and take each step. The sun will come out soon. I love you, my heart – John.

What would I do without you?

Sleep alone!

March 4, 2011
Dear John,
How do I really know that the words that are welling up – not a voice, or anything audible – how do I really know that it is you, my spirit guide, and not some psychological, emotional trick projection of my brain, wherein I cleverly answer myself?

So where were we? wondering if I'm real, a genuine spirit guide, not some trick brain projection. A good question, actually, you are right to doubt. There are plenty of malign spirits out there which would absolutely take charge of your brain. But how to reassure you, as proof is not really possible. You have faith and patience, that is good. This gets us to the first level. You are open and willing — this permits the channels to be open. You have been practicing surrender — this is excellent. In short, you get what you deserve — you have met us halfway, so do not think it is all up to us. I can tell you're a little uncomfortable or unsure of how to handle the fact that I have a personality, and that we're developing a rapport — to use a polite word which has made you smile. Twinkly girl, I adore thee. But see — here is a good example — the hint of a thought flitted across your mind that you projected some of that...I'm thinking. I run into this with every human, haven't surmounted it yet. Physical proof is not advisable — we'd both be uncomfortable.

Can I strengthen my presence? Possibly. You can also keep working with me, and this process, and trusting the flow. You have noticed —yes, that was quite deliberate — that when I am silent, or absent, you notice it/feel it/miss it. You have picked up on it when I've been moody or grim. You have a higher degree of sensitivity than you think you do, even if you don't see your chakra colors, can't see your third eye, or sense our presence.

What if we tried an experiment, and I deliberately project an answer instead of listening for you?

"Try it" — that could be me, or that could be you.

Okay. You're silent now. Hold on – if you will please just refrain for a moment, let me try to fill in your answer. "okay, dearie." No, that is not right, you don't say "okay." However, the sensation of "me" versus "you" is very close. Over to you.

I need another question to keep going.

Did you help me play Scrabble tonight? How can I involve your help more clearly – and do you mind if I do?

Lass, that's what I am here for. You don't need to try to please me. I have fun when you have fun.

Can we do things together?

I can think of many things we can do together.

I think I am beginning to be grateful that you are disembodied. What a week. Thank you, for everything.

Poetry, now? Yes, we are meant to be, you and me as you see lucky we luverly three.

John, please tell me if I muddy the channel or start projecting onto your answer?

Yes ma'm, indeed...
Beloved, John

March 10, 2011

Dear John, as you know, I am very sad and discouraged tonight. I would be grateful for your help and advice. I am computing all of my expenses and I have a shortfall of about $1,000. I am just so weary of feeling like I can never make ends meet, no matter how I try. Please offer some guidance.

Lass lass lass the sadder you are the harder to reach me. I know you're trying so hard everything you know under the sun. I am here for you, you know that. No rhyming tonight, just straight talk. Then after maybe we'll have a bit of teasing to sweeten you up again. I cannot bear it when you are so sad. I picked you up off the floor before — did you feel it? Could I would I carry you off and heal it. Wise little lassie, change and grow, change and grow this you know tis better so.

To the question at hand — your financial shortfall. There's an ache in your heart which is blocking you. Write, lass, write. Strange to say it is your challenge to overcome the sadness, the weariness of trying so hard, the discouragement — when you conquer these, you feel ease. When you feel ease, it all flows. When it all flows, money grows. So see if you can release the fears and tears and sadness rise above it learn to love it find the good focus only on it. Trying lass I feel you trying. And the surrender too. So sorely puzzled are you.

Heart of glass let it pass oh weary one oh dreary one I'll chuck your chin I'll make you grin I'll fill you in — breathe, that's right my sweet. On days like today you forget to breathe.

Could we please get back to how I can cover all these expenses?

*Two separate issues, not needing tissues. First the actual fees or costs, reality of it is hard to cover hover lover bovver stover. Second issue is your feelings about these. Be dispassionate not passionate. Find the strength overcome nearly done one more test then such a rest **promise**.*

Give yourself a bridge loan from your bank. Quick, easy, solved. Release anxiety piety saiety deity about paying yourself back. It's coming in the running over there on a chair silly bear mend the tear better now? Silly cow no offense meant just fun intent oh my heart come back now. Beloved bothered and bewildered

Prankster John

(same night)

Dear John,

Thank you so much for your support, you are a miracle in my life. I feel like a stumbling puppy who goes face first, tangling her paws, looks up and says "help me." Not much difference, is there?

Oh, you're much smarter.

Thanks.

It's more serious than that, you're getting inklings here and there. You're not yet ready for the fare — we'll take it one stumble, one fumble at a time thank god for rhyming rhyme keeping it light to spread the light showing that we care.

Is it possible for me to get too attached?

Too attached — what is that? Fear of hurt? It's all or naught, this is not sport. Caught oh yes you and I are truly caught, a glorious florious morious thing rejoice in the catching the hatching the patching the latching kingly king and queenly queen we have our place in the scene Little by little I'll gain thy trust little by little fear turns to rust and flakes away plakes away cakes away must!

Funny old you, funny old thou, believe in thyself, that's an order now. I love it when you giggle higgle siggle.

You know my questions before I ask them but you also know I must phrase them. Are there other spirit guides besides you who would like to communicate with me? I would like to be open to other Light Beings who are out there – wherever you are.

It's serious delirious merious perious...other light beings — spirit guides — yes there are. This is a talk for another time, another place many a face out there in space. Popular

*you'd be my lass up a tree give it some time and then in due time as you grew stronger
longer monger —*

Open you'll be
Receptive yes breathe
Holding your breath is a slow death
Deeep deep deep you go
With a ho ho ho ho
Lass o mine we're fading fine to bed with both of us.

March 11, 2011
Dear John,

My question is, can you please tell me about my brother? This is
serious, as you know how much I worry about him, plus the full cocktail
of family emotions. Please tell me something about my brother's spirit
guide that will reassure me, and take away my guilt and fear.

...in a mess need to bless when far away star away.
His spirit guide cannot hide. He is strong he is long he is merry with a song He zigs and he
zags round your brother's crags He troubles his mind and rarely does find an avenue for
completion He's dealing with doubt he's dealing with fear — oh my dear, so much fear — and
he chips away sips away as best he can. Your brother is a special case. He is highly watched
over and protected. At some level he knows this, too, which is why he says to you: "I'm
okay" *and means it. His financial woes are designed to break him open like a bank (nice*
image don't you think) so he will fall on his knees and thank.

It makes so much sense when you put it that way. Here is the biggest
question, please – I am confused and reluctant to lend him money.
If he asks again, I will probably say no. Please give me some advice –
I am so troubled.

Oh my heart, sweet heart we will solve that so easily. Smile away, chile away. I cannot tell thee
whether to give or not, that is a choice. It hurts terribly to see a family member on their knees.
Your wrath hardens his path. Send him joy, send him love, send him abundance in thy prayers.

Say no if thou must, but do it with trust that love will buoy him up.

In other words, say no with a loving intention and attitude?

Yes, exactly.

Then I must work on releasing my anger at his irresponsible behavior. It's so hard when I tried to give him a lifeline, a way to cope, I guess you could call it "enough rope."

Aye, enough rope to hang himself — figuratively of course. We think we are doing well for them, sell for them earnestly pearnestly dell for them, yet so misguided it is.

John, this is what I really do not understand. If someone is metaphorically sinking in quicksand and there is a rope or a stick to extend to them, then yes, of course you throw it to them. Don't you?

Only if they ask for it. It's all in the asking. If he is sinking but doesn't see it, doesn't want help, then yes, you stand by and watch. It hurts us too, very painful, in fact.

But if he keeps borrowing money and not repaying it, then I am just feeding his habit. So when do I draw the line?

You are coming to boundary-setting a little late with him. The first time you do it always feels painful, strange and wrong because you are bucking all of your conditioning and tribal loyalty plus coping with guilt at knowing your action could cause harm. But you were right — absolutely right — to point out to him that his issues have caused harm, too, down the years. He has had so few mirrors held up to him, you see, being solitary. The few that are shown to him — by your sister and you — he can look away from and avoid.

That is excellently clear, thank you so much, John. Let's start the day...

I continued writing to John every day, sharing every single detail that confused or baffled me. I wrote to him as I sat at my desk at work, and this was a practice in sanity and miracles which was the only thing that kept me going. I submitted every item that ruffled my feathers even slightly. I was still fragile and fearful; at some level, I recognized my neurotic inner messiness, but was helpless to do any more than try to manage it incident by incident, emotion by emotion. Writing to John, and his sensible, teasing, teaching answers, calmed me down, gave me an outlet, showed me perspective, and almost always solved the problem at hand. This was especially the case with the dozens of issues I had to deal with daily in my job, dispatching maintenance calls for a company which owned historic buildings. I was often overwhelmed, and had little recourse to advice from colleagues. Here is one such example of many, as I edged my way back to a saner, more stable perspective:

March 17, 2011, at the office throughout the day...
John,
Here is the issue of the day, an ongoing one. Why does the issue of delinquent clients irritate me so? Between a slack administration and the residents who are taking advantage of it, I get seriously annoyed. Help me, please.

Over here lass, and always here. You are troubled because in some part of you, you recognize that you could be more charitable in your heart, and forgive them their trespasses. You have some guilt because of it. Yet your sense of fair play and integrity tells you that tolerating the non-paying clients is also wrong, thus you have conflicting emotions. You are very concerned to do the right thing, which in your case is to execute the instructions given to you, and take your cues from the officers of the corporation. It is their decision and their responsibility to pursue or not pursue these situations. If it harms them, it is on their shoulders. That's it, lass, deep breath. Your best course of action is to keep breathing deeply, think of me as often as you can, practice those letting go exercises if you need to. If it is any help, your senior supervisors know you're right (Me: Do they? Really?!) *but their boundary-setting is not as keenly defined as yours. Nor do they really comprehend how much extra work this makes for you and the accountant.*

Thank you so much for the perspective. One more sprint and we're home.

I'm here to keep you on the ball. 15 more minutes — let's see what you can do.

Chapter II: Breaking the Shell

Proof is not necessary in the realm of perception.
– PENNY KELLY, THE ELVES OF LILY HILL FARM

We Thought You Would Never Ask

This extraordinary invisible companionship – which, it dawned on me later, was very much *The Ghost and Mrs. Muir** – was not only loving, supporting, sensible, and accurate – it also tolerated every last bit of outpourings that I knew were tedious, and self-absorbed – which meant that I could lean on it as often as I wanted, as hard as I wanted, and *know I would never fall*. It provided astonishingly detailed practical, in-the-moment advice, tailored to "little old me." A mere two months after commencing the experiment across the divide, I was deeply absorbed in a healing process which picked up speed, depth, and intensity with every communication. Furthermore, I rapidly discovered that the Unseen Guides' communications were always fascinating, because the spiritual depth was flawless and unanswerable. It came from Source, period. Oh, did I have a *lot* to learn.

During this intense period I attempted some first efforts to communicate with angels. February's breakthrough to this unknown dimension sent me into high gear. I suddenly remembered a course offered at a local yoga studio about angelic communication. I signed up for it eagerly, and it validated everything I was going through, not only with reference to spirit guides, but regarding other levels of non-physical Beings as well. I learned that what I was doing was

---

*A novel published in 1945 by R. A. Dick about a widow living in a haunted seaside house, who develops a loving relationship with the resident ghost, a former sea captain (played by Gene Tierney and Rex Harrison in the 1959 movie). Also made into an American TV series.

called automatic dictation (not automatic writing), and that most people are dominant in one form of sensory reception, but some are capable of receiving messages through vision, sounds, feelings, or knowing. The workshop teacher, Stephanie, was to play a pivotal role in my healing a short time later.*

As much as I loved my correspondence with John, eventually I sensed some limitations to his guidance, and often the mental intimacy of a personality was uncomfortable. I was experimenting with all forms. Now armed with a little more information about who and what I was writing to, thanks to the angel communication class, from time to time I began to write, quite simply, to the "Angels." I knew there were many kinds of angels, of many hierarchies, culminating in the most well-known of all, the Archangels Michael, Gabriel, Raphael, Jophiel, Uriel, and Metatron. I knew so little at this point, and was sufficiently intimidated by the vastness of it, that I kept it simple. Subsequently, I also learned that angels do not actually "speak" although they may appear to in these journal entries. Rather, angels *vibrate*, so that the thoughts which filtered through my human consciousness arrive as English language "words," "sentences," etc.

March 17, 2011
Dear Angels,
I have just finished reading *Angelspeake*† for the second time and I have some questions. Please tell me if there is a group of you, separate from my spirit guide John, and what your group name is.

You are tired now, it is late. We can come to you and answer your questions, but you would do better to ask us in the morning. There are many many many of us, and we love and adore you. Please sleep now!

Thank you my angels! I will indeed write in the morning.

*After eight years, I had finally diagnosed my daily exhaustion as "energy interference," a shamanic term. Stephanie would help me clear this parasitic energy out of my body.
†The Angelspeake Book of Prayer and Healing by Barbara Mark and Trudy Griswold

March 18, 2011, 8:00 am
Dear Angels,
Good morning, here I am! I would like to repeat my question from last night. Please tell me, is there a group of you, and do you have a name for your collective body?

Oh, we are laughing. We thought you would never ask. We want so badly to be in touch with you, you have such a gift. We love and bless your every step (yes, even the $700 brake bill, that was to keep you safe). We do have a name so that you can always call on us and refer to us. We would love it if you start writing to us when you are at the office, as well as to John. Our name is Heavenly Choir. That's it, straight and simple. We may suggest other names to you as we go to make it easier on you. Now, sweet girl, it is time for you to do your kundalini yoga, and the rest of it.

Heavenly Choir, thank you so much! Am I correct that I sense you to my left, sort of eight feet up?

We are actually everywhere, and if in human form would overflow the room. But to give you a point of reference to address, yes that spot will do.

May I please ask one more question?

Yes!

Can you please tell me if I am clairaudient or clairsentient?* I'm pretty sure I am not clairvoyant.

You are clairsentient. Your gifts are muffled and new right now, sleepy muscles to flex. Work with us every day (we know you'll work with John!) and we will help you tune those muscles. Please enjoy your day, we love you, bless you and guide you!

Thank you!

Friday, March 18, 2011
A poem from John, sent on a stressful day at work:

*Clairsentient: heightened perception of sounds or feelings. A psychic ability which occurs in different degrees.

27

If you're going to seethe
It's better to breathe
Rather than teethe
Just breathe
When your mind is wreathing
Try breathing
When the world is stale
Just inhale
A moi, a moi, a moi
*Ensemble nous sommes encore une fois**
Darling!

March 22, 2011 (at the office)
Oh, J…I am in such a grumpy mood. What is this about? Even that walk on the beach didn't help. Talk to me…please!

It's so good of you to call on me. When you forget to do that, you slip into little holes in your day. Normal, yes, but we're working on strengthening the connection. You have the right idea — when you feel blue, do something nice for someone else. Your blues feel a little more deep-seated. Could be a delayed effect from Sunday's treatment. Flow, flow, flow. Smile for me, trust me, and let's keep moving. What next, lass?

Something easy…I'll put away the property keys, clear the decks.

Much better, lass!

March 24, 2011, 10:00 pm
Dear John,
I am very blue tonight. I've tried everything – going for a walk, playing sentimental music, calling my friend Josh to express condolences, yoga postures by the fire. Nothing works. What is wrong with me? I don't even know if you're there, I am that sad.

*To me, to me, to me; We are together once again.

When you are sad and oh so blue you simply don't know what's happening to you You think I'm here you think I'm not; too sad to care heart in a knot. Grumpy dumpy lumpy pass, shake the blues, that's my lass. Change and grow, reach for the light try again do what's right. Overcome and overwork, overstretch and overshirk. Listen on my sad little girl, answers will come when you're in a whirl. They never come when sad you be for that you have to turn to me. If I had arms I'd hold them wide enfold you to my loving side. Beating heart within my breast says down pen now, let's have a rest. Always ever late at night, you try too hard and cannot write...or think or smile for me. Come lass, away lass, come to me. Love, John

And so it went, day after day, thought by thought and breath by breath: intimate, caring, and healing, coaxing me forward into healthier choices and states of mind. I threw everything at them that came my way during the day, trusting that one of these guidance forms would jump in and answer. It was never linear or tidy. The conversations and exchanges grew more fluent and specific, and eventually, after about nine months, I turned to John less and less, and began simply writing to "Dear Angels." Until that time, I was never quite sure who could answer my question best, so in some places I switch back and forth, or write to both.

As I wrote, the proof I needed did not come all at once, as I politely – and sometimes not so politely – argued back with the John or the angels. Proof became a slow realization, as the rained-down kindness gently soaked my consciousness in healthier thought patterns, and de-escalated my near constant state of fight or flight. On the numerous occasions when there was no direct, tangible outcome for my requests, I began to see that the outcome would come along later, and would be more beautiful than I imagined. Most of the time, though, I was extremely impatient and at the mercy of my linear mind, which *wanted* immediate results – so I had to school my expectations and reactions over and over and over. And over. Most of the time, though, I was just baffled by the gap between my immediate, practical need, and the strange phrasing of the guidance. It would be years before I learned to simply observe and trust this sizeable gap between the rational, left-brain demands for logical results; and the softer, intuitive knowing of the right brain.

March 23, 2011 (at the office)
Dear John,
Help! All hell has broken loose – broken copier, director needing copies of the public park re-design survey, my supervisor needing copier, my needing copier…copier tech just left after supposedly fixing it…yikes!

You know what to do. Breathe and do the next thing. Oh, and focus. Stay seated, make a list, stay centered. Plow through. We like a challenge!

… finally a lull, with the copier working. Success! Please tell me what to do next. Oh, about that new duty they just landed on me, of taking care of the extra property – what a pain. I guess I wasn't too gracious about accepting that, was I?

I think you knew better, could have shown more willingness — which would have reflected better on you with an overworked and harassed boss. Take it on without grumble, execute it flawlessly, and something good will come of it. Yes, I know your colleague is aggressive in carving out more and more resources for her staff — that's what a good manager does. I understand — you resent the housekeeping aspect, as it appears menial. But you signed on to this company, so you get to accept the responsibilities they throw at you. Cast it in the best light possible — what errands can you feather into your trip to make it worthwhile? It may be a peaceful opportunity at the Farm…the crews go out there all the time without complaint. Bring your lunch and sit in the sunshine. It will be fine, smile and be pleasant, hold back your comments.

March 24, 2011
Dear John,
So far away – am I that distracted? I don't seem to be getting any better at strengthening this connection.

But I am here...fortunately we have all day to try. Don't beat yourself up. Distraction is natural. Try a little meditation break a couple of times during the day. And — ?

Breathe! I'm ready to start...

Do try to stay with one thing and finish it, not interrupt thy little self and jump around.

I could use a hug. It's funny the way people scamper around here like frantic little bunnies (pretending not to be frantic little bunnies). I don't want to be a frantic little bunny.

Over here and listening dear. Channel clear and nothing to fear. Ask away every day. Get thee clear and all shall be thine. Lovely oh lovely lass of mine. Back to work...

Monday, March 28, 2011
Hello John,
I seem to be having another emotional storm system moving through. Feeling so serious and grim. Can't even come up with something to ask you about. You're probably not there...that's okay. I've been so cold to you, wouldn't surprise me if you sheered off.

Heavens lass, can't reach you at all you're so blue. Wondering if it's a side effect of that healer you visited. He may have rumpled up some long sleeping emotions.

Oh my sweet, don't turn away now. The darkest hour is always just before the dawn. I suppose I should count myself lucky even to get through this much to you. We'll ride this out together, if you want. At least you're writing to me now — thought you'd never start.

It's just that this whole relationship is so outlandish – neither here nor there, shadowboxing with my imagination, no proof except my changing emotions, and those are unreliable. You and your celestial friends have all the foreknowledge, all the aces, on your side, and I get to flail around and hit brick walls at 60 mph, then not know what to do about it. Is this supposed to be training for a real live human relationship of the "I can't live with you, I can't live without you" variety? Don't mind me, I'm just mentally thrashing.

I do mind ye, I mind ye very much. You are my ewe lamb and in my keeping. Your ills are my ills. I don't know if you're ready for the metaphysical discussion that would answer your questions — at least, not here, not now. Yes, you have been at this point before, many times in your life, and you always figured out what to do before.

I feel like I'm going in circles, never advancing, always coming back to the same point. I ping-pong back and forth between trying hard and then surrendering, and even in surrendering there has to be a tiny point of volition, so I'm trying there too, but that accomplishes nothing. I feel boxed in with no viable option. I can't even shrug my shoulders and say "I don't care! It doesn't matter!" without getting a mental nip from you about how unhealthy this attitude is and what it leads to (and acknowledge, as always, that you are right.) I tell you though, if this is a foretaste of what a relationship with a man is, I reject it. Easier to be single for the rest of my days.

This is a lot to answer, and I am not sure I have any answers that would satisfy you. Will you do this for me? Get yourself a nice, tall glass of water. Then let's settle down and do some minor administrative work. Let's stay busy for the next couple of hours and see where you are then. I don't suppose you're interested in knowing that a lot of people out there love you and would love to have the chance to tell you so, if you let them in? No, you're not up for it, too blue. Inhale and exhale for me, drink some water, and please keep turning to me. I feel your sadness and fear so keenly. You and I need a long walk in the sunshine or by starlight — maybe tonight? See how you feel. Now off you go, lass, please!

(later)
Made it so far. Nothing serious accomplished but I feel a little better. Why does being blue/depressed feel more gritty, substantial, real and solid than being happy, peaceful, light? Or is that just years of wrong-headed conditioning? Don't answer that, just thinking aloud.

You need a lot of grounding today. Almost there — straight home and then for some meditation in your sunny blue room. That chocolate is sending you into sugar orbit, but no fear, lass, it was what you wanted at the time. Recognize that at this point in the day you are tired, fragmented, frayed, bored, and stale. Let's get through and go home!

There's nothing to add to that – always right, coach.

Tues March 29, 2011, 8:40 pm
Dear John,
I am all over the map in my moods, emotions, and energy levels. Fantastic tai chi las night, a quick walk under the stars, then dropped like a 10-lb brick. Today bright, clear, full of energy. I guess the storm system has moved through. Am still working on the subtlety of connecting to you – this is important – tell me if these conditions are right:

- Being in a neutral state of mind

- Having zero expectations

- Not yearning for you or straining after the connection

- Breathing into my heart, and projecting from my heart, not the mind

- Peacefulness – a silent/peaceful/sunny environment has a completely different feel – it clicks right in

- Just breathing, period

- Taking care of physical discomfort that distracts me

Sorry – that was long-winded but I had to write it down because I am serious about figuring this out.
Goodnight, John…

March 31, 2011
John,
I am back at the keyboard and ready to converse. Good morning!

So long away, so far! Yes yes yes neutral state of mind, and breathing into your heart. Keep to as much stillness as you can. Ah, I can feel your gratitude. It's our morning hook up — so much better than a cup of coffee.

I am starting to realize that this is quite a luxury, being in this state of connectedness. I say hello with my heart, literally. It feels as though it is greeting you.

Better and better yet. The Angelspeake class you took was excellent, some very wonderful new discovering people attending. The angels LOVE this class, that is why Gabriel was there. You can call on him, too you know – don't be shy just because they are "celebrities" or their names have historical weight in the human time frame. And the miracles, oh we are rubbing our hands with glee because we cannot wait to shower them on you. I like this phrase you use, "learning curve", and yes it has been steep for you, but you've tackled it like a trooper, no shying away for my proud courageous lassie. Your "double life" will grow more intense if you want it to. Your biggest issue is making the time for the connection and the exchange. We can work on this. Some cold rainy days this spring could be put to good use — can't be in the garden, so stay indoors with your writing pad and me, and all your celestial friends.

Right then, just a few quick words and let's get out of here...everything on your desk can wait. You are starting to stretch too thin and need to get back to taking care of yourself. The priority next week is to start yoga again. Let us worry about finances. Yoga and meditation for thee, and a long walk. Let's go!
John

April 1, 2011
From John: *Miracles abound all around on the ground in the air have a care find their mark in the park come to you and coming true never blue we're watching you growth and joy using prayer multilayer.... Family harmony it's a dharmony Worried we feel you are, watching you from a star. Brother sister cousins and fear all mixed up and no one near. Let them go, let them flee, sadness–making is not for thee. Cherish hope, lots of rope, property sells, ringing all bells. Miracle maybe Florida fraybe. Give to us, this great big muss. Give it away, with it we'll play. Little girl blue we're calling to you leave it behind joy you will find. Patience and faith a true heart maith. Doesn't rhyme out of time over to you.*

April 3, 2011
Dear Angels, Help! I know I need to buy a new car soon...this will be my first time ever attempting to buy a brand new one on my own. I am anxious about how to cope with the details and auto dealers!

Please help me find a way to make this purchase quickly, easily, fearlessly, and without going into debt. I've read that this process is about the 99% of creation that happens before manifestation.

Here are my needs:

What I do not want: I don't want an out of date car which breaks down and costs me money.

What I do want: I require, desire and deserve a beautiful, new car, well-designed, safe, elegant, sporty and functional, which suits my practical and aesthetic desires, and which comes to me easily, affordably, quickly, with the help and guidance of my angels.

Angel Asking List for Purchase of 2011 White VW Jetta (or something better)

- Please help me obtain the best possible price for my existing car.

- Please help me marshal my assets to put down as much as possible on this car.

- Please help me obtain the lowest possible financing so that I can afford this.

- Please send me the most talented negotiator to help me obtain the best price for this car.

Love, Barbara

Monday, April 4, 2011
John: Hitting Monday morning with a bump. All's well, we have it in hand. Miracles, remember? Let's tackle what is on your plate. I am here by your side and we're going to have fun.

You have a strange idea of fun.

Agreed! But think of it this way — with you at the computer, you are in near constant contact with us, which we love. You're starting to get the hang of asking all time, all the time, all the time, especially with transmuting negative thoughts. Can you feel it working?

I'd say that was a miracle. I am so intrigued by this process. Thank you and all the angels for taking away the nervousness and discomfort.

That's it then – onward and upward. Here's a request for the angels: Please help me transmute my financial fears into confidence. Thank you!

Stay with me lass — we go through this every afternoon when you get tired and frazzled, and start to assess everything that hasn't been done in the day. Let's focus on the positives: first you do have the money to cover your taxes, and the timing allows you to spread it out. Secondly, all your major winter bills are behind you — you're home free, and they'll be lower from now on. Third you did a very smart thing in setting up that line of credit, and if you can just consolidate your credit card debt, you won't feel as scattered. Last, look at the abundance that is flowing in — the gift of jewelry from your cousin, and the extra incentive check next week. Perhaps tomorrow we'll start the financial overview you need. Don't forget to add back the outgoing sums, and turn the outflow around. Please go to bed early tonight — you are at your best in the morning, and we need you smiling and gorgeous. Good work today!

Nothing Will Be Truly Difficult: My First Encounter with Archangel Michael

By this time I had been communicating with John and the angels for about two months. My personal life logistics and emotional issues overwhelmed me, but no matter what, this lifeline of answer-streams seemed to pick up where my thinking left off, whether my question was specific and pragmatic, or general and open-ended. Whenever my questions were boiling up inside me, all I had to do was pick up the pen and guidance came through. It was never, ever what I expected, and oftentimes the practical solution which flowed through, was simply to calm me down. I had to stay in the moment, and that was enough. It was not a logical process, but it worked.

April 6, 2011
Dear Archangel Michael,
I am honored that you are here, thank you. Please tell me what you would like to guide me or advise me about.

Archangel Michael: Clarity. You seek clarity. Clarity, healing, answers — you are a true seeker. We love this and are here to help. We feel your puzzlement when clear answers are not forthcoming. These morning sessions will be important places to get answers because this is when you are clearest. You can try evenings but then you are very fuzzy with fatigue. Besides, the mornings are so beautiful now! We will help you to wake up early. Regarding finances, sprint just a little longer with us. We love you too much to let you keep struggling. Wasn't that pearl necklace you received beautiful? That was no coincidence. Timing dear — you will see it all around you now.

Regarding your family property, this is indeed woeful, but we like a good challenge. You now know two excellent tools: 1) prayer; and 2) ask to have negativity transmuted into love or positive thoughts. And the continual asking — have fun with that. Ask for someone to take you out to dinner, and we will send you someone who will!

Regarding paying for yoga class, we know you perceive a lack of resources. Ask us for them! You had a very good idea to make an asking list, just so that you remember everything. Please start that today. Your happiness is our joy. We feed on it!

Do you know what I love about you and all the angels? Once the guidance/ advice descends, it's like being hit on the head with a loving 2 x 4 – "of course! she says to herself." So thank you – and for making me laugh.

Archangel Michael: Oh, beautiful child, we have not yet begun to set you on the road of abundance and joy. Nothing will be truly difficult from now on. Keep surrendering your ego so that your channel becomes clearer. And now, my dear child, darling girl and light of our eyes, please rise and do yoga. We surround you and support you!
Love from Michael and all the Angels, with especial love from John!

The Comfort of Old Habit

April 9, 2011
Dear John,
Tonight, sitting in bed after a light-and-energy filled day, suddenly I feel so blue. Tonight is our six-week anniversary. I feel as though we

have been on a long road together. Why do I hurt so?

John: Darling girl, your sadness is natural. In your non-sad moments you know this — that as the damaged parts of you start to heal, the "crud" comes loose and floats up. Stirring up old patterns is not always an easy road. Shift your focus, change the channel. Hold recent memories in mind that are of peace and light. Choose better thoughts. Is there a reason you are holding on to the sadness or pain — is there comfort there, the comfort of old habit? You know what to do.

Is it true that as my energy shifts, I will feel/sense you less and less? The angels have hinted that our relationship will fade. This is strange and also sad to me, and I am struggling with it occasionally.

*This is why you were asked to surrender the relationship with me. Yes, I will become fainter in shape/outline/ presence to you, but stronger in other ways. Your perception of other angels is strengthening — we were thrilled you could feel us flocking in when you played Spem in Allium.**

Thank you, angels...

Monday, April 11, 2011, 1:30 pm
Dear Angels,
By the way, thank you and all the angels so much for reaching me with snatches of tunes and songs – especially overhead in stores. This is a great way to get my attention – then I know you're there, at my side, and it reminds me to come out of my self-absorbed sadness. I was so blue when I went into the supermarket, but then because I am more in the habit of listening now, the first thing I heard was *You've Got A Friend* by Carole King. I stood under a speaker and let the message flow over me. What sweet relief! My contact with you is the richest reward, and I just want to remember it moment to moment. Is there anything else, John?

Kiss these italics goodbye for today!

---

*A Renaissance choral work for forty voices, by Thomas Tallis. Spem in Allium is Latin for "Hope in the Air." I found that this exquisite music was an angel attractor.

April 12, 2011

Dear John,

Here I am, little girl blue. Why is it that when I am in the dumps you are more present to me – I feel your concern – than when I am happy? I'll never figure this relationship out – at least until I'm on the same side as you – which is probably why it's designed that way. I am allowed to kvetch, aren't I?

John: We're starting to know this place well — this point at which I remind you that you always grow through it, always bounce back, always have us, are never alone, and have lots and lots of tools to choose from (breathe, pray, meditate, release, affirmations, EFT†) …but what you really need and want is a big old hug, my poor lass, the one thing I can't give you. Aye, that's one design flaw humans have — they can't hug themselves too effectively.

You're right – I need and want a hug, wahhh! Sometimes I just get tired of having to be so damn adult and parenting myself. Want to curl up into a ball and let someone else do the fixing for a change.

Which is why, lass, part of my job here is to urge you on to finding a mate, a partner, a friend in this life. Oh, do I feel you pushing against that thought! Too hard, you say, too painful, too much work, too much to put up with, too many imperfections, too much criticism and intolerance. It doesn't have to be that way. We need to work on those beliefs and limiting thoughts. For now, my darling, know that I am giving you a virtual hug to the best of my ability, and if you will find the lyrics to "Mamma Mia," that might cheer both of us up. Let's go for a walk, get thee some lunch, and buy that Ricky Martin CD at the Music Box if they have it. What do you say?

I'm having trouble cutting and pasting the lyrics. Maybe we should write our own lyrics.

I like that idea!

Back again, lunched and bunched and munched, still low and blue, nothing do to but work away. Stand by…I have to log off now.

---

†Emotional Freedom Technique, an acupressure tapping method which releases tension and emotions.

Wednesday, April 13, 2011
Dear John and Angel friends,
I can't imagine how it appears to you from your side, watching me go up and down in my moods like a thermometer. Maybe you just stand by and watch with compassion, since you know the outcome and what I must go through…"Will our heroine ever get better, improve at switching out of her mindless mindset, the ego-and-list-driven projective state that passes for reality? Only the angels know for sure!"

Oh, sorry everyone, did you want to tell me something? Just amusing myself here.

You know lass, I really think that using those muscle-tension release balls to massage your tightness are working wonder on your tension. It has plummeted…keep using them! Soon you'll be back in my non-arms.

Having a non-romance with a non-entity? How well we understand each other. As long as you don't start non-adoring me. Things could become non-pretty then.

How could I ever non-adore you?

(same day)
Dear Angels,
Tomorrow night is the company's gala opening at the historic house museum. I will be working hard and will be very distracted, but will you be there with me?

*Angels: Go and glow, be as beautiful as you know, feel your sparkle and your wit. Feel at home, **get used to it!** Feel the position, come into your own. Know your power, blossom like a flower. Invoke your family, invoke divinity, invoke your grace. Yes yes yes — play inspiring music that gives you joy — let it flow out your pores and the evening is yours. We shall be there, floating down the stair, hovering here and there, enjoying sight and sound, you'll see us if you look around. Be prepared to shine, Barbara dear, the night is thine!*

Love to you and heavenly blessings, the Heavenly Choir who sing to you with love, guidance, protection and prayers!

(same day, later)

As you know I have started writing down a list of my life problems in an "angel asking list." Can you please tell me, are these things I need to ask more than once, every day, at certain times, or what? It's a very long list.

*Angels: Your list is our list we love lists we'll unroll it unravel it dispatch it match hatch it bewitch it twitch it flitch it and pitch it. No, no need to ask more than once though if it comforts you, go right ahead. Best to be rested, clear, neutral, happy, specific when you ask. Our timing may not match yours but close enough....we know no limits. List every detail you want and we'll guide you home. You're already catching on, that if we think you should have something better, your concept won't pan out, then the lightbulb will go off that you could think **BIGGER**. And oh yes, a white car, an Angelmobile, is what we'd like to ride in with you. Please make that list for your new car soon, and have fun. We're watching, and guiding, and praying. Dear girl, you're surfacing — bumpy ride, we know — but you're getting gasps of oxygen. Ask for more! What is outrageous to even consider? Ask!*

Another question, please. How often would you like me to play *Spem in Allium*? I was blown away by your Presences. It felt like a dovecote at feeding time.

Heavenly Choir: Tee hee funny expression, Yes, we enjoyed that and flocked in. Whatever you wish, dear — any elevated music like that will bring us in. Try it — try more!

April 14, 2011
Dear John,
Your airwaves are barely coming through. Is there something I could be doing better? It is almost as though your personality is fading. I understand if you don't have time for metaphysics right now.

John: Funny lass, I always have time for metaphysics, it's our specialty. Can you bide with the situation and trust just a little longer? I know, I know we are faint and not crystal to each other. Your energy is changing all the time these days, and this is part of the equation. When you are feeling especially far away, re-read some of your entries. This is an excellent thing you have done, it constitutes proof for you.

I noticed that the Heavenly Choir came through like gangbusters last night. Should I be turning to them every day, as well as you?

Yes, please do. They just love helping you so much, and you are so willing to listen and try their guidance. Whereas with me…

Oh, yes? You mean you get a bit of push-back and attitude? Imagine that. Now, for tonight, please help me to shine and tune into all the angels everywhere.

We are at your service…

Thank you, my friends.

Friday, April 15, 2011
Yikes, just spoke with the mechanic and the new axle is going to cost me $280. I am starting to hemorrhage cash on this car. Please transmute my fearful thoughts.

John: There's a silver lining to this, though you can't see it now. You've hit your wall, you know it, and it's time for action. You cannot keep this car any longer. You're ready to move on. This will be our best weekend yet. Set aside lots of time for meditation, prayer, reflection asking, study, and walks. Work with us. We can change your life, and we will. This is where we roll up our sleeves. Watch it happen. For now, deep breath, keep moving, drink water, and finish up what is on your desk. Please go easy on caffeine, greasy food, and sweets this weekend — we need you to run crystal clear. Can you find the strength to say no to Chinese food tonight? Think about what you need to do for yourself, rather than what you'd like to do for yourself.

Okay, I think I can do it – let me summon my resolve. Thank you for encouraging me – my willpower can always use the bolstering. By the way, I am seeing Jettas everywhere now – it's a nice car, isn't it?

Yes, and just the thing for you. Don't be tempted by cheap — stay the course.

Monday, April 18, 2011, 3:00 pm
Dear John,
Again, feeling low and blue today. This is ridiculous – I have so many

reasons to be grateful, so much good to focus on, and somehow the effort doesn't stick. Any advice?

John: This is a moment by moment thing, and it doesn't help you to say that "things will be better tomorrow" or "it's all part of the plan." I know, my sweet — you're so very tired of being tough and independent, taking care of yourself, all by yourself, all the time. You just want a little margin to your life, a little more income, a few less problems. You're getting stale and you need a change of scenery and some stimulation, away from your cares, but it probably won't happen soon. You'll have to keep working on finding joy in the little things and restoring yourself every day. The truth is, you're in the middle of a sea change, hence the ups and downs. At some level you know this, and just have to ride them out. This is why we encourage you to play music — it's the best and fastest mood changer you could wish for. You are juggling dozens of logistics and don't realize how overwhelming it all is, because it has become normal. Can you find one good thing about today?...What, didn't that brisk walk first thing this morning give you a lift? In spite of the cold and the wind, you had color in your cheeks, lass. I'm trying to get you outside as much as possible, to ground you. Thy little head gets full of sad fancies, we need to blot those out with time spent in nature. How about a walk by the light of the full moon tonight?

Chapter III: The Cry For Help

Hope, help, healing are here.

– THE ANGELS

On April 22nd, I entered a dark night of the soul. My journal entry from this evening is a radioactive wail of self-pity and vicious sarcasm directed at the angels. The despair was total – I could not hear them, nor was I sure I wanted to hear them. The few responses I allowed in, I immediately batted back in a scrawl snarling with rage and loathing. The desire to self-destruct seemed like the most real sensation I had ever known, and the possession sapped my will, so although the angels told me I had a choice, I couldn't get to that place. It was a night of deepest evil. Above all, I was furious with the angels that they could not heal my despair and pull me out of the vortex of profanity and hatred. "What good do you do me," I mentally screamed at them, "and why bother working with you if in my deepest moment of human need, you cannot get through?"

How do you make a sane, willed decision when you are consumed by what Eckhart Tolle* calls the "pain body," which takes over your functions? How do you reverse the deadly mental trend, the inner stoicism that begins as a private virtue, but evolves into a self-directed sledgehammer? The message I had internalized over the years was that I just had to be tough, tougher, toughest, because no one was going to care or help me out of my intangible, undiscussable situations. For me, this attitude had spiraled into self-loathing, which would then establish itself as a new, lower "normal."

---

*Eckart Tolle, spiritual teacher and author of The Power of Now. He defines the pain body as: "This accumulated pain is a negative energy field that occupies your body and mind. If you look on it as an invisible entity in its own right, you are getting quite close to the truth. It's the emotional pain-body. It has two modes of being, dormant and active...the pain-body, when it has taken you over, will create a situation in your life that reflects back its own energy frequency for it to feed on. Pain can only feed on pain. Pain cannot feed on joy. It finds it quite indigestible."

I have healed from this dark-side struggle, but I continue to think about these questions. It took me six years before I had the courage to face this entry from 4/22/11 again, and could read it with enough neutrality and compassion to transcribe it in typed form.

Then, as I wrote this book, I avoided dealing with this passage until the very end of the editorial process in November 2018. I did not want to face it, yet I knew I had to include some of it to satisfy readers' curiosity. More significantly, I had to include it for a higher reason: the lessons it contained might help another human traverse their own dark night of the soul. The phrase from the angels that decided the issue was:

It might save lives.

And so, in a present-day, explanatory leap forward in the time sequence of this journal, I turned to the angels and asked them to reinterpret this incident with the passage below.

A Battle of Dark and Light

November 18, 2018
Dear Angels,
It's the Dark Night of the Soul entry. It's so painful, I don't see how I can include it in the book. What really happened on that night? How can we hold this in the highest vibration of love, and also solve this entry?

Beloved heart,
This is a beautiful day, and a beautiful moment. This is your magnificence as a human being, in coming full circle, to complete a cycle of energy, healing, love and light — of this magnitude — in the same lifetime. As you join us here on the page to compose this, all fuses —you become one of us (cold nose tip and all!). You do not feel it, you do not know it, you do not even sense it, but the room is now quite full of angel presence, for you have invited us here with your heart, your searching questions, your need for resolution, and —yes! These

finely complex human situations which we so dearly love to assist with. For this we live. Let us go carefully here, there is much to examine and flow back to you regarding this incident of April 22, 2011: your ultimate turning point.

*What happened on that night, when your fears rose up in such massive form, that it blocked you from hearing us, and sent you spiraling into despair? You know now, with distance, that it was a pure battle of Dark and Light within you, and you gave voice to the Darkness, and that is what is recorded in your journal. In the midst of that battle, you had no perspective, no resources, and gave way to what was loudest in your mind. Yes, it sapped your free will — and yet, know it or not, the very act of trying to reach us in that entry, was enough to break the back of the energy — for the act of writing kept you in the moment. Remaining in the moment gave you — and Us — enough of a sliver of an entry to come through. Please transcribe these responses, the proof is important. We were there all along, we never left you, and what happened ultimately, is that you wrote out the entirety of the pain body energy, and **purged it**. It could not bear the Light which you were reaching for, from deep inside your soul. Your surface experience of this was crucifying, and we held you as you writhed in pain. These extreme tests are by design, and no rational thought will ever grasp their divine origin or purpose.*

*The successive weeks, months, and years of entries continued to flush out more and more of these negative or low energies, and your journal is a miraculous testament to this process of coming into more and more light — by choice, by asking for help, by changing habits and patterns, by surrendering what is old and stale, and by continually flowing on a river of willingness, faith, trust, hope and self-initiation. Flowing into the light, with us as your guides, until you stand in the sun, laughing with joy! For this will indeed, be the ultimate destination, when you leap off from your ultimate turning point. We love you **SO**. Heart of ours and angel child, eagle of divinity, fly free! Go now, and choose from those entries of April 22nd with compassion, and hold this sacred space for your readers. You are now entrusted with this sanctuary.*

Escorting you with wings of light and radiant choruses of joy,
The Angels

With this present-day introduction, I share with you here some compassionately selected excerpts from April 22, 2011.

Friday, April 22, 2011

Misery. A cold spring night, and I cannot get warm, emotionally or physically. There's a damp spring chill outside – tonight, the Friday before Easter. I have cranked up the propane fireplace and both electric baseboards. I have two pairs of pants on and am wearing the ear-warming band under my microfiber fleece hoodie. I have a silk scarf at my neck and have polished off two glasses of red wine – I think Spanish cabernet, or something. I cannot get warm. I am depressed, angry, miserable, self-pitying. I have kept it at bay all week, but now I am giving in to it. I loathe myself and keep thinking, "WHO THE FUCK CARES? IT DOES NOT MATTER. I AM WORTHLESS." I have shut out the Angels and am desperately sad. I am so angry and confused – I loathe everything around me, my life, everything. Bolting down chocolate today with full knowledge of what crap it is.

So, go on, Angels. Give me answers. I challenge you. Just this once, I am going to let you in. You want to communicate? Oh, or don't you bother when people are distressed and angry? *OOOh nooo, can't do that, channels aren't clear. Oh, well! Let them stew.* Right?

(silence)

Yes, just as I thought. So sanctimonious you can't help someone who's really in trouble! Can't get through. What's the matter – a little negative energy scaring you away? Here's your chance. Surprise me.

Angels: Go on, write it. Do you think we're not here? Yes, negative energy makes it hard to get through.

You know, you don't have to do this. I know how busy you must be with Easter coming up. No point in wasting your time on someone self-pitying and destructive like me.

Angels: We've been waiting for this to happen.

Well, aren't you proud of yourselves. You can predict everything I'm going to do or say, right? So why bother?

Angels: We really do want to talk to you. We really do miss you.

And what about John?

John: Here, lass.

And what is the point? Anyone?

Angels: (silence)

John: So sad, so angry.

No shit.

John: You've had a hard week.

So?

John: We've been watching and waiting.

Yes, I know. I had to work to shut you out.

John: You're too angry to hear our answer.

Oh, bravo! More patronizing solutions. "Poor human, so angry. Can't help herself."

John: This is a power struggle.

No shit. They don't mention this in any of the literature. It's all sweetness and love, celestial light, always.

John: What do you want?

I told you. I want straight answers. I want to stop feeling manipulated and patronized. I want consistency. If this is a power struggle, I have no bargaining power, no collateral. I need distance and perspective. Living in my head is warping my reality. I really, really need not to be so ashamed of my flaws. I've become completely self-conscious. It's horrible. Your perfection is really annoying, you know.

John: What would you like me to do for you?

THAT'S THE POINT. You cannot do anything for me because I am worthless. You cannot help me. God cannot help me. You don't have any solution for despair. Nothing is working anymore.

Trying doesn't work.
Surrender doesn't work.
Self-inquiry doesn't work.
Love might work, but since I have none of that in my life, then I'm out of luck.

That's it. I'm done.

I can be as angry as I please. What do you care? You'll just pat me on the head like you always do. So what?

Angels: We are not patronizing you. You cannot patronize something you love.

Okay, here is my question. Why is the idea of suicide so attractive?

Angels: it is a form of rebellion. You feel the world is indifferent to you and want to test it to see if anyone cares.

You know, considering I've blocked you all for almost a week, you're not too chatty now. Am I boring you? Shall I shut you out again?

Angels: it's your choice. We stand by and wait for you.

Give Us That One Chance

April 27, 2011
Dear Angels,
This is really hard for me. I am still sad, confused, angry. I feel fucked up. I am very unsure of letting you in, since it puts me on such a rollercoaster ride. I am only writing now because you, Archangel Gabriel, asked me to this morning. If there is something you would like to tell me I will listen.

Angels: Please ask a question.

What would you like to tell me tonight?

Please write… do not hesitate or fear. We love you and support you. Growth is painful. Please ask us to help you release your dark feelings of inadequacy shame, and self-loathing.

I'm stuck. I go round and round in a tight little circle, and the loathing is so great I convince myself that there is no help, and that reaching out is impossible. There is something about self-pity which is strongly self-reinforcing. Here it goes again – the raging loop in my head, which is so convincing that I believe it: "oh, who **CARES**? It doesn't matter!" So what would be your antidote for this?

The human ego is devious and throws up many blocks. Bear in mind that we are patient and vigilant — when we see an opening, we appear to you. Give us that one chance.

Why am I so desperately sad?

You are changing more and faster than you know. The old shell is falling away — this is a loss of identity which hurts and confuses. Share it with us!

How?

Just like this, right now. Tell us, and maybe we would ask you to pray or meditate. You do know what to do, but as you say, the self-pity is self-reinforcing.

But I don't feel any better now, even after sharing with you. I'm sorry – I'm exhausted and falling asleep. I have to stop now.

Good night, sweet Barbara! Be not sad, we will lift this from you, Try not to repeat that thought "who-cares-it-doesn't-matter" — it really hurts you more than you know. Sleep well, darling girl! And thank you for writing!

Good night, angels. Thank you for listening and responding.

April 28, 2011, 9:07 pm
Dear Angels,
What a perfectly AWFUL day. Insane from one end to the other – jittery, pressurized, harassed, beleaguered, and to cap it off, that that bitchy woman sniping at me about her damn refund when I was so exhausted and unhappy and stressed, and just couldn't cope one more minute. Then coming home and trying to meditate, trying to do EFT, having a glass of wine, going for a walk, and still feeling like shit, angry, helpless, and looping in negativity.

So, that's it, here I am. What would you like to tell me tonight, if you can get past this anger? And I even feel too sad to come up with a question for you.

Angels: We're here.

All right – I'm asking. Please take away my sadness, anger, confusion, hurt, despair, and sense of self-loathing. Can you and will you do that?

Angels: Yes, we will.

Can you do it soon? I swear I'm going to snap at someone or take someone's head off.

Let's look at this clearly. There are multiple situations going on. First: personal change and growth. Second: heavy work load, high pressure and extreme demands at work.

Third: private worries about managing finances. Fourth: extreme desire to be in your garden and extreme frustration at not having more time to work on projects. Fifth: not enough vacation or free time. You work hard! Even with all of your best efforts, there is only so much pampering you can fit into little moments of the day. So recognize your overload, and how much you do. Appreciate it. Be in awe of your complex juggling act. Please try not to compare yourself to others. You yourself know that given more resources, you could fly as high as the rest.

You recognize walls when you hit them — that these are the extremes which generate change. You hit one today and it got your thinking, "hm, do I really want to stay in this crazy position?" Please don't fear transition — we are here to launch you higher and higher. You have friends everywhere and are well-known and respected. Let us help remind you of how wonderful you are!

Please do not worry about expressing yourself freely and honestly when you are grouchy or "feeling like shit." This is good! This is refreshing! this is honest. The old "must-be-a-good-girl-all-the-time" is falling away. Don't you feel liberated?

You know, I do. As soon as I blasted off mentally about that, something lifted – or maybe that was you helping me. I am not going to tackle it here, but this is a problem that intrigues me – the overriding sense I get from the spiritual-yogi-life-culture which promotes everything as being blissful, dreamy, cheerful, loving, etc. Where is the space in that for any negative emotions, which are just as right and natural and need to be expressed? Then, buying into that cultural mindset so much that one feels guilty if not peaceful and blissful, because the media says we must be so. HA. Well, I'm certainly hitting my dark side.

But here's my problem: I didn't turn to you today, though I knew better, but was so full of dark feelings I got stuck in them – then the work situation just compounded on itself. What can I do, and what is my lifeline?

First, take yourself OUT of the situation physically, if you can. Go sit in your car, and breathe. You know what to do then. A walk might help but you don't want to further overstimulate yourself. You were flying on coffee today and not enough breakfast — if a, *then b, as you say. Set your intention: what result would you prefer? Take precautions and plan. **Write to us**. We know it's hard to keep private, and find the time. Here is an encouraging thought: you're already in the habit, it is simply a tool you had put down and misplaced. Look for it, pick it up again.*

Can you help me with my perpetual irritation at people who park in the wrong parking spot in the company lot?

Just ask us to remove it. Poof! Not worth the waste of your precious energy!

Thank you. Can you help me get out of bed at 7:30 tomorrow morning so I can hit the yoga mat early? That would be miraculous.

Yes, we are happy to. We feel your sleepiness, good night, dear girl.

Thank you very much. Good night, angels.

Sunday May 1, 2011
Dear Angels,
Please tell me what is going on – I am slightly horrified that I drove half an hour to the yoga studio for the movie screening, only to find it closed because it was held yesterday! This is the second time this weekend I've had a major memory lapse. I am baffled – please throw some light on these incidents.

Angels: Dear girl, you simply have too much on your mind.

Can you help me with this on a daily basis? I mean, if I ask you every day to remind me of my appointments, will you help me? I can't anticipate every single thing I need to ask for.

Nor should you! Yes, we can help you. This is why we encourage ongoing conversation. Yes — that's it — bring your attention fully to us, and practice constantly. These unanticipated results are fine and good. We will help you past the disappointments. Ask us to transmute your low feelings. Please, bring us into your life and give us things to do! We have your attention now, after all, don't we?

Yes, and I feel my human failings all the time now. Very well: Angels, please transmute my disappointment and dismay at my memory lapses. And please help me to remember to ask you to remind me every day. This is a hard way to learn, on such a lovely day.

We love you and support you, always.

Thank you, Angels...

Give the Organization to Us

Tuesday, May 3, 2011, 9:40 pm
Dear Angels,
No matter how fast I move, blitzing through things, I never seem to be able to get into bed by 8:30. Yes, I know – hippo yawn – I am beyond exhausted. I moved through today at high speed, focused and checking off my lists...when I would rather have spent most of the day in bed with a book. Why, angels, is my life so frantic now? It isn't reasonable – I cannot keep this up. The lists just keep unrolling. I feel like I stopped having fun years ago. Please help me find more free time in my life to relax and play. PLEASE.

Angels: Your breathing is improving, and you can feel it. This is good. Poor girl, don't fall asleep on us! It is good to have your attention, tired as you are. Today was spectacular for you and we were winging you through it – could you feel us? We answered your request to get it all done, and get it all done you did. Though it is a bit much on you. You asked about the interpretation of the 'Children' card. Yes, we sent this. You uncovered a long-buried side of yourself at Club Med, and oh, we enjoyed that so much. Please start playing again! This is an essential part of your nature. We want you to fill your life with laughter, dance song and play – just as you want to, too. We hear you – how, when, is this possible with your packed-full life? Give the organization to us. You have already made the request for a more efficient life – let us help you. Keep the stream of requests coming – work with us. Every time you find an inefficiency, ask us to streamline it. We will find pockets of time for you so you can explore playfulness again.

I would love to do that. I have to say, I am skeptical, but I have no choice since I feel like I am up against a wall right now. Thank you, angels. Now, about my car – *help*. More broken pieces, more hemorrhaging cash. Please tell me what to do, fast. It's hard to live with an unsafe car and financial uncertainty.

*We hear your cry for help. You have two choices: you can keep spending money here and there to keep your current car going (which will mean that you can sell it with a clear conscience and use those repairs as selling points), or you can act right now, take the path of least resistance, trade in the car, spend a little more than necessary on the VW, and not optimize the sale of your stocks. Your friend gave you good advice — hold out for a higher price. The truth is you need to come into a clear, restful patch where you can analyze your situation clearly, with abundant time to make a wise decision and act with deliberation. This can be the case for you if you give it another 4–5 months. Trust your sense of this, and trust us. Your finances are already on the mend, and abundance is coming. **Really**. It's going to be a great summer.*

I know you have your own sense of divine timing but the waiting stirs up so much anxiety. Could you please send me some extra cash right now to cover this bill? Thank you!

Good night, dear child we have already sent help and more is on the way. Sleep in peace!

This is the Point of the Test: Pull Out All the Stops

May 6, 2011
Dear Angels,
I am just a mess tonight. Frantic day at work, with a VIP meeting all afternoon – no work done, just doing my Cinderella act schlepping up and down stairs with trays of tea, coffee, cookies and chocolate. I find it absolutely infuriating, and it always gives me fantasies of quitting in a lovely big melodramatic exit. Can't calm down, tried to meditate, had a glass of wine, listened to kundalini music, went for a long stomping walk – you know all this! Am still fuming in my head over work scenarios. Please help me detach, calm down, and stop projecting.

Angels: Have you tried EFT, dear?

Thank you. That helped a lot. Why didn't I do that starting at 9:00 am? I hate feeling so ramped that up my head feels like it is going to explode, and **nothing** calms me down. And worst of all, it blocks me completely from hearing you or John. Why does this happen to me over and over and over and OVER again, when I know better? It's as though all of the practices I've tried over the years never really sank in. Have I changed AT ALL? Am I just banging my head against a wall? What does it take?

This period is seriously testing you. The efficacy of the practices you talk about would not be as apparent in a calm phase of your life. This is the point of the test: pull out all the stops. Be more aware than ever. Have all your tools at your fingertips. Remember to use them. Make a list and carry it around if you need to.

Angels, I'm so tired, I could cry. I'm tired of sprinting and being frenetic. Is this another "contrast" situation that will bring me to a point of decision about my lifestyle?

It's possible — be open to it. We've talked about this before: transition. What would you rather do, be or have?

That's easy: more resources – more time, money, leisure and energy. I know my life is already quite, quite wonderful – and I try not to lose sight of that – but you're always saying I can ask for more, so I am. Please?

You're almost there. We will deliver. For now, the best thing you can do is to turn in, dear. We will help you sleep! Love, the Angels

May 13, 2011
Dear Angels,
The point of peace: sitting in my pale aqua-blue room with a cup of sweet chamomile tea and writing to you. The day is done; the week is done. How I love being here, right now. Finally, time to listen quietly and think. Not sure I am passing all my tests with flying colors, they are coming thick and fast.

What I am grateful for:

- Being somewhere where I can hear you.

- The new way my body feels now that I'm doing body-rolling. Relaxed connective tissue everywhere. My energy has doubled, and I feel lithe.

- That today was payday, in the nick of time. And I received the 3% increase, oh joy.

- The weekend is here, and I can pour myself into my garden.

- Warm (sort of) weather is here, and maybe the dreary grays are really gone.

- Great new books to pick up at the library.

- Looking forward to your help with getting efficiently through all my must-dos, so I can relax and play, enjoy and sit in my hammock.

- Having such a good life here in this coastal community.

Please Keep Asking

Wednesday May 8, 2011
Dear Angels,
I am wearing my ring tonight – I love the way it serves as a reminder to ask and to keep you present in my life. I have to remind myself to remind myself, like something out of a Jerry Lewis film. Angels, are you sending books to help me answer my questions? I feel as though there are serious messages here for me.

Angels: It is so easy to work with your exploring nature — you are gliding from lesson to lesson. Yes, these books contains some dense and profound teaching which intrigue you. Your soil is rich, seeds are being planted — let us water them so they can germinate. Your natural curiosity will take you where you need to go. The renewal of your meditation is the best thing yet — we applaud and cheer you for this.

I have to say, the last couple of days at work have had a very different quality to them – I feel calmer, more confident, and my attention and energy has been more consistent and less erratic. What a difference this makes in my performance. Something fantastic is being sped along, it's palpable: at work we released the public park redesign story to the press last night, and sure enough, today it was gleefully splashed all over the daily news. Yet I feel so calm – this is the eye of the hurricane, perhaps. We've managed every curve ball so well, it's almost like this project has powerful blessings. I just know there is some kind of angelic confluence helping the project team along. Am I right?

Now that you know us, you can feel us. There are indeed large forces at work sending continual streams of support. Your patroness is smiling down on you, and happy with your work. Please keep asking so that we can get down into the details with you. From now on it becomes crucial.

Angels, you are amazing. Yes, I do need your help, and yes, please guide my every move in upcoming days, especially please help me write the grant applications and a letter to the landscape designer about her proposed trees. If I can get those two hurdles accomplished, I can roll up my sleeves and be ready for anything. So – time for bed, I know – I have my ring and will remind myself tomorrow to ask, ask, ask. Thank you, angels!

Our pleasure, dear girl. Sweet dreams — and we love you!

Saturday May 21, 2011, 7:30 am
Dear Angels,
Well, I've listened to your gentle promptings, and I have to say, this is outrageous. It is utterly out of character, habit and inclination for me to wake up at 6:15 – earlier, even; meditate for 35 minutes, then prepare breakfast for myself the way I have just now. Yet here I am, having served myself breakfast in bed, on a tray: oatmeal with raisins, bananas and walnuts; a small dish of fresh strawberries, and a steaming cup of sweet jasmine tea, on a tray with a tea-cloth decorated with red hearts. So, dear angels, what is this about? Do you have a special announcement for me, or answers to all my problems? I'm sorry, I am

not being flippant – you know that – it's just that I am baffled by this New Me. Please tell me what you propose.

Good morning dear girl! It's a beautiful day and we don't want you to waste a minute. Your garden is calling to you. As for breakfast in bed, we are just responding to your request for more elegant domestic rituals. It is so gratifying for you – and this is a good place to start. We feel your need for elegance, and we want to help return more of that to your life. As for rising earlier, you know why that is happening: the meditation combined with the deep tissue massage and relaxation, plus a long walk last night. These sent you into a deep, refreshing sleep. Wouldn't you want to do this every night you can?

Yes I would – thank you. These subtle and effective things can really change my life, I see that. Isn't jasmine green tea the best?

It is indeed!

Sunday, May 22, 2011, 7:00 pm
Dear Angels,
Here we are again, lovely ones, on a quiet, cool, overcast Sunday. Brrr, it is cold today...but I am happily curled up with a glass of Merlot, calm and contented because of everything we have accomplished. I tackled everything I resisted – that was you, I know it. If it had been only me, I would still have a dirty house, messy business papers, plants begging to be transplanted and an undisturbed bicycle which had not been taken for a spin. This state is much preferable to chaos, confusion, weariness, tension and frantic zigzagging from one task to the next. So thank you, Angels.

I did want to write to you tonight to open the channel. Is there any guidance you would like to offer me now about anything, like preparing for work?

Angels: We just WAIT for this moment and we love it! Thank you for writing. How we adore to pour blessings and love on you. The more you open to receiving, the more we pour. The walk on the beach was delicious! Thank you for holding us in your thoughts, and pointing out the heart-shape of the cove, bay and rocks. You are seeing it now everywhere, dear child, as we intend you to. These are wonderful shifts in your perception. You are picking up steam now. Do you sense it? You are calmer, happier, have more consistent energy, and the mood swings are lessening. That was a bumpy time! It is past now, blessed child. We cannot commend you enough for your commitment to 40 days of meditation. This will change your life, and we will be right there with you.

Have no anxiety about preparing for next week. All is happening according to divine timing and we are your turbo-jet boosters. You can be the strong, centered, reassuring force in the office. Your colleagues have calm natures but are overburdened at home and do not have your array of calming tools. You make a great team. Your confidence — and your star — is rising. Enjoy this!

Thank you, Angels. I sense this shift, and it is a little strange, as I am more accustomed to being anxious. I have another question for you. I have read a book which gave me some insights and raised some questions; specifically, the author talks about the possibility of spirit guides and human dependence on them as a codependent relationship. If our relationship was codependent, would you tell me?

Angels: We are sending Archangel Michael to reassure you.

Archangel Michael: Dear child, it cannot be! I must tell you that I am laughing. You are our beloved child. We guide you. We do not control you. Your reliance on us can only bring blessings and more blessings. If it happened that a sad, lonely, damaged human being discovered a connection to us, and turned to us over and over and over again, until he or she became less sad, lonely, and damaged, how could that possibly be unhealthy? Eventually, as with a child learning to ride a bike, the training wheels fall away. Also, the communication becomes more subtle, instinctive, intuitive — as you are finding.

This author is human too, and though he has attained an extraordinary level of Beingness, in that instance the parallel was misguided. He may have been trying to point that woman back at her human relationships, which may have been codependent. Also, bragging about your spirit guide's counsel is a misuse of power, as a means of feeling better than the rest. Holier-than-thou, I think you call it. Quite common.

Michael, I wish you could stay with me always and just talk to me. How I love listening to you – thank you.

Archangel Michael: I like it here with you — we like it here. It is a delight to communicate. Please touch your reminding ring and ask again and again and again!

Choice, Choice, Choice

Sunday, May 29, 2011 11:15 pm
Dear John,
I seem to be in two positions at once – going against my best intentions, and then watching myself do it, like a car crash in slow motion. Last night I was invited to a delightful dinner party with some dear friends – although the host became unpleasantly drunk. But then, I came home and stayed up until 3 a.m. reading a book. As a result, today I was a physical mess, a mixture of fatigue and sludgy energy. I knew better, but I did it anyway. And then I had zero connection to you or the angels. Why do I do these things to myself?

John: Ha — you and your funny terms — sludgy is a good word for it. You value this connection highly enough that you are disturbed if you cannot make it quickly or easily. But as to preventing the occasional lapse or stumble, sweetheart, you are too hard on yourself. We do not ask you to be perfect and disciplined all the time. If you get enjoyment out of reading into the night, then it is good and fine. If the consequences are so unpleasant that you learn not to do it again, then it is this you must learn. Choice, choice, choice.

I know, but it is as though a contrary spirit gets into me, and shouts down or overrides the part that knows better and would prefer to go to bed early. Is recognizing that moment or series of moments, pure willpower? I feel as though I need more ammunition against the old, poor habits that occasionally return to plague me.

What you are slowly realizing is that you have difficulty reading books in moderation, that you tend to disappear into the pages, gobble them down like candy. Is this a salve for an old hurt, is it an old habit, or is it a tool for comforting yourself? Probe these things and you will find the answer. You already sense that you are growing out of the need to use books as a coping tool — and as you have found, they can be subtly sabotaging to your disciplined life.

61

But do not fret, dear heart! I love you, we love you, and it is time for deep, sweet sleep so we can get up and play tomorrow. Yes?

Yes...

Friday, June 3, 2011 9-something pm
Dear John and all the Angels,
What a day. Could my life be like this more and more and more?
I don't think I have ever had so much steady, calm, clarity or flow,
from the moment I woke up at 6:30 to this moment right now. I had
purely consistent, centeredness and focus throughout the day – with
a few lapses. It as extraordinary – as though you were ushering me
(which of course, you were). By all rights, *today*, which is the last day
before our BIG-BIG-BIG scary outrageous career-blowing press
conference with the celebrity architect on Monday, should have been
wacky, frantic, mind-numbing. But it wasn't. I felt miraculously
steady and focused, and just proceeded from one thing to the next.
My colleagues were frayed by the stress – especially at the end of
the day. I felt fine – better than ever! So, tell me, is this experience
something we can repeat?

*John and the Angels: Now you're getting it! Yes, of course we can repeat this — this is what
we plan for you. This is your state of healing and grace. Do you believe us now?*

I believe you, and thank you. This novel experience gives me a
benchmark to measure myself by. It was very odd to look at my two
colleagues – normally towers of calmness and strength – and to actually
feel calmer and more confident than they. Extraordinary the way things
fell into place today. Click, click, click, done. Today I was in an altered
state of non-distracted calm. I hope we can have more of that tomorrow.
Was there anything else you wanted to guide me about or tell me?

*Angels: We would like to sing you to sleep! Good night, sleep tight, see you in the
morning bright!*

Sunday, June 5, 2011, 11:10 am
Dear Angels,
Good morning! It is a beautiful day and I am about to go into my
garden and play. Unfortunately, I have some kind of severe muscle
spasm on my lower left back, right on my sacrum. Please guide me and
tell me what the best treatment is.

*Angels: Blessed child, we are so sorry for your hurt. Rest is best, but you have a busy day
ahead. It will slowly work itself out if you move gently. You might want to take an aspirin.
Heat applied directly is fine. You are doing everything right, darling girl, but sometimes
these things have a path. Don't forget, you have deep issues that are being released, so be
patient. And yes, we will help you to buy an excellent new bed!
Love, the Angels (who love you!)*

Break the Cycle, Seek the Solution

June 10, 2011, 8:40 pm
Dear Angels,
Tonight I definitely have a conflicting situation to ask you about. I am
delighted to be hosting the beautiful 17-year-old daughter of some
London friends, just for an overnight. As the big family dinner is that
same evening, I wrote to my elder cousin asking if I could bring Lucy
from London. She wrote back to say it wouldn't be fair to Lucy or
the family, and that she was "squeezing me in" as it was, anyway. I am
disappointed by this inhospitable response. Yes, I know – her dinner,
her right to decline extra guests. I am tired of always being in the wrong
where she is concerned. I need validation. I need an outlet, and I'd like
to present my side to my other cousin, Karen. Please advise me.

Angels: Can you clarify your question?

There are several layers here, I guess:

- Am I so wrong to be mildly offended;
- It dismays me that no other family members ever call her on her conditional hospitality;
- Was my response ill-judged? I mean, I was hurt when she made it clear that she didn't want me at her dinner anyway.

Does that help?

Angels: Complicated! With many layers! This is a feud of long standing, as you say, a power play. Your difficulty is that you have become enamored of the rebuttals and the defense positions, and the sense of being hard-done by, so that in every instance you do not seek a solution. You seek to prove her wrong in response. This way, it perpetuates eternally. You have to decide if you want to break the cycle. She will never change — until you do. You may not think so, but your response this time was much, much better — you can feel your detachment, which is so healthy! Yes, it is hurtful that she does not welcome you with open arms as a family member. She does require tribute and deference, and as you are not willing to play along, you are excluded. As you are a younger cousin you will never have status with her. As to the injustice over her treatment of you, let it be. Give it to us. We will set all right. Surrender it tomorrow morning (or even tonight). Oh, precious Barbara, child of ours, this is one of your pettiest, but greatest struggles.

Karen is a wise soul who will hear you lovingly and weigh things with her heart. Yes, talk to her if you need to. Try not to inflate the melodrama and the "I have been wronged" role that your ego will try to get you to play...do not gloat, it is harmful and mean. Take your cues from your cousins and their loving examples. Walk away if you cannot abide a situation...Create your own family connections. Visit your other cousins independently. Make the effort and you will be repaid. Strike out and be independent of your elder cousin. You may even create your own nucleus. Imagine how satisfying that would be!

Try to remember this in future dealings with your cousin: seek the solution, not the ego-gratifying retort. Walk away. Practice detachment. Restore your own family bonds — do not depend on her. Be an example to others who might want to break free of her influence. Offer hospitality the way you know it should be offered. Treat others with the courtesy and respect that she withholds. This is balance and law — you can live it, act it, create it.

I love this fantastic answer, thank you. Oh, yes, angels, please help me to do all these things. Is there any chance I could one day live in a big house again, so that I can have some family to stay? That would be very gratifying.

Of course! Ask, darling, ask!

Angels, thank you so much for your wisdom and calming answers. I knew you'd help me. I feel so much better now. I will say good night.

Good night, dear one. Sleep the sleep of the blessed, for truly you are, sweet child.

Saturday June 11, 2011, 6:00 pm
Dear Angels,
Thank you for guiding me through today. I sense you wanted me to write, so I am here and listening. Was there something you wished to relay?

Angels: You are so welcome, dear child. You are so sweet when you cock your head to one side to "listen" for us. Michael is here. He would like to tell you something.

Hello, Michael, thank you for your presence. I am still a little in awe of you. What would you like to tell me?

Archangel Michael: Blessings upon you, child. Yes, you deserve them and we love to shower them upon you, we are so grateful for your willingness to listen and write. We are moving through you more and more now. Please do not be shocked or surprised if big blessings start occurring. Your dear sweet channels run a little clearer every day, thanks to your meditating. Please keep that up! We hear and appreciate your longing for more yoga in your life — this is coming. If you are meant to attend the yoga workshop at Kripalu, the means will come to you. Do not fret about the family dinner. You sense that all will be well, as it shall be. All of your actions are guided now. You can make no mistakes. We cherish this connection more than you know, and will send grace to you and through you as we always do, but you will be able to feel it and know it now. Yes, it takes strength to be a conduit for pure love. We will build you up slowly and steadily. Surrender your belief in your undeserving state. It is that easy. Don't forget to keep doing your new car homework! We are having such pleasure setting this in motion and helping you.

At work I frequently voice my opinion too strongly or blurt out a tactless comment. My supervisor often makes stinging, passive-aggressive comments. Can you please help me hold my tongue and become more tactful? My penchant for humorous sarcasm overrides my better judgment, it seems. And I don't know what to do about my supervisor's acid tongue.

Archangel Michael: We are there at every encounter. Touch your remembering ring and ask for help. Yes, your colleague is occasionally jealous of your growing importance within the company and she does regret her one-liners. She has trouble with blurting things out, too. We will give you the courage to talk to her in a direct and kindly way — choosing a neutral time when nothing provoking has been said. Trust us, and ask.

Thank you, Michael! I hope I never, ever lose this sense of wonder and awe at the extraordinary guidance you give.

Archangel Michael: We surround you with love, and we bid you enjoy your tranquil evening!

June 22, 2011
Dear John,
Wednesday afternoon, feeling groggy but at the same time jumpy and unsettled. I need some back-to-basics training. I'm not getting much work done, just piffling around. So different from yesterday, when I put my head down and blasted through a lot of things. Oh, John, will I ever, ever have consistency? That's rhetorical, you don't have to answer that. Sigh. Anyway, here I am.

John: As long as you keep coming back to us, nothing else matters because we can put things right in a jiffy. Don't you feel better already? Practice a little stillness, 'tis true you are jumpy! Reduce your movements, close your eyes at every opportunity. Yes, even type with your eyes closed — yes, that's it. Now, did you have some questions for us?

Yes, of course I do. An old friend has left me a message saying he would like to come to stay next week, bringing his daughter. These friends can be high-octane and hard to deal with, and I don't

have the energy or resources to clean up my house to guest-ready
standard, only to have this hurricane-duo come through and make
a mess and exhaust me with their demands. I said I would call him
back tonight and let him know. What do you think?

*That is a pretty pile of reservations and resistance, true enough. These are all thought-
based, not heart-based reactions. What is the worst that could happen? Your rug might
get dirty. You'd be inconvenienced going to work for a day or two. They might annoy
you with cell phone use or leave dirty towels on the floor. What could you gain from it?
Pleasant memories, a connection re-established, friendship and laughter, a chance to
give a young girl another strong friend in a much needed chain of friends. And yes, you
know how much hospitality you accepted from his parents years ago, and this is weighed
in the balance. It is your decision.*

The other intangible factor is that I don't feel good about this the way
I felt good about welcoming Lucy. That was effortless and natural, and
everything went beautifully. Whereas, my heart sank when I heard my
friend's message. How much attention do I pay to this inner feeling?
I could overcome it, but it happens for good reason.

*As you say to yourself, above all you do not want to model other unkind people, right?
You are struggling to find the balance between generosity, hospitality, and your perceived
lack of resources. Give it to us! Ask! Let us help you grease the wheels and make sure
everything goes beautifully. Trust us, we can make this fun and pleasant. Overcome your
anxiety, and magic can happen. And don't forget — the fatigue you feel this week, may
vanish next week, and energy could flow through you. You are shifting all the time.*

This is the answer I needed to hear. Very well, I'll give them the
green light and invite them to stay. Stand by for lots of asking. Can
we start with shifting my anxieties, and transmuting my reluctance
and resistant thinking into kindness, generosity, and genuine
hospitality? Oh, it is so good to be back in touch with you!

Breeze Therapy for Mediocre Thoughts

June 28, 2011
Dear John,
Toasty day today…AC is on but I'm not feeling sluggish – yet.
How nice to be wide awake and ready to roll. In spite of all my good
intentions and mental notes to myself, I've gotten out of the habit of
writing to you. I seem to keep struggling to establish this discipline.
Here's a thought: will you please help me keep up the discipline of
writing to you and the angels?

John: You're looking very pretty today, lass. And I'm glad you're wearing your ring.
Torment not yourself about the variability of your attention to us. This is simply the nature
of your life and your humanness. Consistency will always be difficult to achieve. Accept
and enjoy your special nature! We love you for it no matter what phase you are in (or how
many times you are interrupted!).

You are so amazingly reassuring. I could just steep in your words and
thoughts. Thank you for that.

PHEW. What a day. Between the client crisis, the supervisor's
uncertainty and fear and need to talk it through, the delivery of the
dishwasher to the Smiths, the medical crisis of the curatorial intern,
who has gone into liver failure and is going to be flown to the Central
Clinic, and the mass confusion over the Flower Show booth takings
this past weekend and the problems with the credit card slips, I have
just been HAMMERED today. I can hardly breathe; just bolted lunch
and am as jittery as a cat. Oh, help! Could you just please take over
everything and solve it?

You're already there and you don't know it. You've got a cool breeze coming in the window,
the credit card slips have been done, you've forwarded all the service calls, and you're back
to communicating right here, right now. Isn't that wonderful?

Yes – it's all going to be fine, isn't it? What would I do without you? I am buoyed up, too by the thought of a bike ride out to the lighthouse tonight. What do you say?

I say let's hurry home and hop on...Just three more hours to cruise through, we'll smooth your way from here on in! Darling girl, let's walk outside right now in the fresh air.

...back at my desk and more crises. One of our property abutters on the park is known as a loose cannon, and does whatever he wants and backs it up with his millions. We are dancing on hot bricks here, trying to set up a board meeting immediately to bring him around to our point of view. Please help me remain detached, cool and logical, and not be so embroiled. What a bucking bronco this park project is.

What would you like to see happen?

I would like, please, for the Friday meeting to pull together effortlessly, with all parties willing and available. I would like for the directors to influence this gentleman in a positive way, and help him to see why this is a great project. I would like the curve balls to stop coming so I can just sit quietly at my desk and do ordinary things like write memos. Please.

We'll see what we can do, darling mine. Fret not, all is happening as it should. You and your supervisor make a good team, and there is nothing else you can do but handle situations one at a time.

Thank heavens for my earplugs, which allow me to concentrate amidst the traffic about 6 feet to my right and the fan and the yakking pedestrians and the blaring car radios. Is there an easier way to make a living, I wonder, or are all jobs like this?

You have a special path, love, and you're on it. No rest for the weary, just occasional hammock time. You have a lovely 3-day weekend coming up, and good friends to see on Thursday evening. Do you see where I'm steering you?

Yes, into positive thoughts, good things, gratitude, solutions, better options, calming thoughts. Right?

Right.

Ah, but without the contrast of all my woes, these would not seem so sweet, is that right?

Right.

You mean that my fantasy about 100% hammock time would leave me unhappy and listless? I'd like to try it anyway.

Later... Are there gremlins here? Fuses blew on the third floor, and my colleagues are climbing around in the basement to find the electrical box. I am trying to squeeze everything in, schedule security upgrades, deal with the client who is in the hospital with pneumonia, plus end of day admin. I have contrast in spades, and am about to crack from overload. Kiss that hammock fantasy goodbye. Or is this just a test to see if I can reprogram my thoughts to all positive things?

It's a test.

Gee, thanks. Please don't grade me, I don't want to know. But part of me does see the piled-up melodrama in today's events. Let me mull this over this evening as I actually sit in the hammock with some ice cream. With so many things going wrong – no, strike that. Every moment is fresh and invented anew. I will keep taking the test until I pass the test. How's that?

Sweetheart, my fair try-hard friend, you have no idea how adorable you are. You're doing beautifully. Keep the memory of this day as something to laugh to at in future. The more you handle, the more you can handle. Now, let's wrap up and get you out of here, and onto that bike. Breeze therapy for mediocre thoughts, yes?

Yes!

July 8, 2011, 10:10 am

Dear John,

Good morning! I am determined that this will be a better day than previous days this week. How is it that I start out so well, calm, cool and collected, and then it all just goes to pieces? Anyway, please help me stay centered throughout this workday. When I go back and read your advice from previous days, it just makes me smile. My biggest problem is loss of perspective. You set me right in no time. It's a lovely hot summer day, with heavy fog and mist along the shore. Right – am set up with my cup of jasmine tea, what shall I start on?

John: Good morning my dear girl, my lass. I love it when you write to me. The idea here is to help you change your habits of mind, and you're listening and learning. Yes, if you can get to a point of changing the perspective, making that shift yourself, you'll be happier and less fractured as you go. Also, your expectation that all will go smoothly or that your surroundings with be calm, simply because you need them to be, is unrealistic. It's a question of shifting with the circumstances, staying in constant flux and responding well, like a jet fighter pilot. Or, to use your metaphor, an Olympic ping pong player. You are very funny, my dear! It comes down to performance.

Friday, July 8, 2011, 8:30 pm

Dear John,

You know, it never occurred to me before now, but this is like texting, this constant exchange of thoughts. Angelic texting – I like that! Oh, John, the swim tonight was so blissful, like diving into chilled silk. Then sitting on the dock afterward in the deep fog and growing dusk – what a precious calm I experienced. It finally got me to a quiet state where I could sense you. This is where I want to be more of the time, this is my goal, this at-oneness with fog, mist, dusk and salty bay waters.

John: That was a good experience, not only for the pleasure of it, but so that you can now know a new level of preference, and seek it out more often. You are changing, lass – do you feel it? Thank you for writing, by the way. I cherish you, my love, haven't told you that in a while. You need to hear it all the time, especially if it makes you blush. You're falling asleep — enough now, to bed with you — and up with the robins tomorrow.

Friday, July 15, 2011, 12:50 pm
Dear John,
Here I am, ready to pick up where we left off, on a crazy Friday. Just had a 2-hour fundraising meeting – plus the usual insanity and sleeve-tugging and pesterment, can't even snatch 30 seconds to write my list. Why do I always assume that things will proceed quietly and in an orderly fashion, allowing me to really get work done? Instead, with this group it always feels like a stampede for the last grain of caviar. I don't know how to solve any of this. I am feeling tired, sad and overwhelmed. Can you please transmute my rotten feelings and help me chug through this boring list of tasks? I know, it's too much to ask. Never mind. Over to you (what a whiner I am today).

Well, not over to you. Just had about six interruptions, three-four phone calls, and someone in my office shoving a piece of paper under my nose. I am back to the old problem of being unable to do my work due to the nature of my work. It isn't funny anymore.

John: Sweetie, you need me worse than ever. You need US! Hand it over, ask ask ask ask. Back to basics, it's your only option (unless you want to escalate into a tighter coiled up state, which I don't think you do). Stay with me here: Breathe. Center. Still yourself. Close your eyes. Regroup. Now, take one thing at a time off your list. Clear off the easy things first. Hit the pause button with every tiny interruption. Try not to self-interrupt. Stay seated as much as possible. Shall we?

Yes, thank you. I need you. Could you and all the angels please also give me a little protective space, just for half an hour, and redirect phone calls and people walking into my office; I just need a respite so that I can get a purchase on the admin.

Oh, brilliant, you guys are brilliant. You've posted one of the paint crew at the front door of the office sanding and painting, so that the door can't be used at all. Now that's what I call a great solution. THANK YOU Angels!

Thursday, July 17, 2011, 12:45 pm
I feel like I'm losing ground. Keep getting blasted interruptions – mail delivery and the city assessor and a walk-in prospective client and random phone calls to book house tours and a hotel concierge is coming to pick up more tickets. Can you steer them all away? I am just so tired of being swamped all the time, and never being able to get down to doing the actual work.

John: Let's take inventory. The office is nice and cool, both your supervisors are out today, making the office calmer – you've got me by your side and you're already half done. It's just shy of one o'clock and you have the whole afternoon. I'll bet you can print out those leases in half an hour. That might even give you time to head out for a walk. That's it, deep breath, just brush away those annoyances like the mosquitoes they are. Your colleague will be gone soon and then you'll have the floor to yourself. You can do it!

I may also just put my phone on do-not-disturb – then I could shut the door...have got to get some uninterrupted time. Okay, here we go. Thank you!

Something Has Shifted

Sunday, July 24, 2011, 10:30 pm
Dear John,
What a long, lazy summer weekend it has been...yesterday after a swim it was too hot to move, so I stayed in the hammock most of the day. It's funny – this is my ultimate indulgence, but it isn't as gratifying as it used to be. Maybe the need it used to fill is diminishing.

John: Hello love, thank you for writing. Are you sure you want to write? You're pretty sleepy.

It reassures me, and I need the practice. Thank you very much for guiding me to purchase Tara Brach's *Radical Acceptance*. What a superlative book. I am learning from it slowly. How wonderful, that there are practices I can make note of and try out in "real life." But I wanted to say, I miss you. The frequency is falling off and the clarity is softening. Maybe it is pegged to my human need for help, or I am trusting more, so that I ask less. Enough of me, over to you. Was there anything you would like to tell me or guide me about?

John: Precious precious precious heart, adorable child, how I miss our frequent exchanges. You are happier and calmer now, more and more. You know and sense when things are shifting. You are paying attention, can you tell how much you have changed since we came into your life consciously on February 27? Yes, love, five months — a lifetime, isn't it? Keep up with the Tara Brach, we are reading over your shoulder. Marvelous things still to come. How we enjoy guiding you! My poor sweet, my only message to you is please hit the lights and lay down your sweet head.

Yessir, right away. Thank you for the message, I just needed to hear from you, xx

Friday July 29, 2011, 8:25 pm
Dear John,
It was an insane, but insane day at work, but something has shifted – it didn't bother me at all. I just rolled right along with it. We had a fund-raising meeting this morning which was horrific – a descent into witchiness. One of the committee started bluntly attacking my boss, in the most critical way, which should have shocked us, but it's as though the committee was ready to stone us, and the rest jumped in. My colleague was deeply upset – to the point of tears – because she thought there would be some small, tiny acknowledgement of the announcement of her resignation; some small, tiny acknowledgement of the amazing amount of professional, careful work she has poured into the fundraising project for five years. Not a peep from

the committee. Apart from one vocal contribution I made to the discussion, which sucked me into the maelstrom – I just observed. It was pretty outlandish. And of course, after the chaos of the meeting and the emotional outbursts, the rest of the day was shot and my colleagues were unsettled. Then we all wallowed in the melodrama quite happily.

The point being, I suppose, that to finally be settled in here at *home*, with soft peace and soft night and soft crickets chirping, is blissful and sane. I am *very, very* glad to be here right now, John, writing to you. I'm dumping the luggage of the day on this sheet, so I can get down to more important things. This "being human" is a bizarre journey and we are bizarre creatures. So, not a second to spare for you today, but that was a brilliant inspiration you gave me to 1) give my colleague a good, hard hug; and 2) buy her some chocolate. Those two gestures made the day for me. What would you like to tell me, John?

John: You are clear now love. Last night's kundalini yoga class was powerful. Thank you for asking us, and thank you for listening! Don't you feel different? Things may start happening faster and faster for you now. By the calendar it has only been five months since we've been communicating. Look at all that has happened! But you have something on you mind, I think, do you not?

Yes, John, I do. What had been an occasional thought or wish or wondering idea over the years, is now rising up more and more consistently: what if I opened a bookstore? What once seemed inconceivable, remote and frightening, now seems intriguing and possible. I keep eyeing commercial buildings for sale or rent. I keep think how peaceful it would be to be my own boss, and have a flexible schedule. I think how much fun it would be to have a snug little shop with a slow trickle of business, so I could be left in peace. A shop where I could bring a dog…a shop that would have to be stocked by occasional trips to England and forays into the hinterlands of the US. A shop with a conservatory attached filled with fragrant vines and blossoming flowers. This is all the upside, I know. The nitty-gritty, cold realities and finances would have to be faced as well. Dear John and the angels, let me phrase this more specifically for you: please tell me or offer guidance about my desire to open a second-hand bookstore. Can I do it and also make a reasonable living?

*John and the Angels: There is so much to say on this topic! We love you, adore you, support you! Of **course** you can successfully open a bookstore. You have us, don't you? This is a terrific idea! It has been brewing for a long time, you just needed confidence and a little more internal healing to take place. This is you, it will make you so happy, give you so much freedom, give you such a place in the community, provide such an outlet for your talents, open up your life in so many ways, and give you more control over your finances (believe it or not). What is wonderful is that you are in an excellent position to take this slowly, start nibbling around the edges of the idea here and there, do your research and make your business plan. After all, you didn't intend to work for that company forever, and this will be a graceful exit. All of your past experience will go into building this, and you've always known it. You have a thousand contacts in place from current and past careers — the rest is just timing and resources. And we're pretty good at those. Oh, darling girl, come out to play — it is time!*

I am speechless. I guess you have an opinion on the subject. This is the start, then, isn't it? I am bowled over by that outburst. Really, truly?

John and the Angels: Really truly!

The above exchange with the angels got my juices flowing, and I continued to brainstorm, but I had to shelve the idea until the spring of 2012, when it surfaced again, and I picked up the thread of my dream project then.

Isn't That the Point of Beacons?

Sunday, August 7, 2011, 7:15 pm
Dear John and the Angels,

I was so astonished when that hummingbird flew into my house and fluttered up against the skylight. Please tell me more about that – what a gift! Or was it Margaret's* advance guard, to say, she'd be on her way?

John: A hummingbird entering the house is a sign of peace and healing. And yes, it is Margaret's totem and spirit guide, bring blessings directly to you. Wait and see! Are we not enjoying weaving this magic fabric, in moments of love, surrender, clarity and truth? Reality comes in through the interstices, when you let the energy grid be as it prefers to be. All is self-correcting. Increase your seeking of the deep magic, decrease your dependence on the human constructs of fear and anxiety. Keep coming to us, asking us, praying and meditating. You are wise enough to understand that questioning only takes you so far — then it is time pick up with faith.

John, can you tell me more about my kundalini yoga practice? I adore kundalini yoga, it is a lifeline and a miracle – a practice whose mystical, physiological, spiritual accuracy strikes deep into my most secret places, and fills the empty holes with love, healing, and hope. Yet when I am before someone as advanced a teacher as Margaret, I also feel humble, small, inadequate – because I think how much I would give to be a teacher just like her. Could I ever be so brave, beautiful, disciplined, transformed? When I call on the teacher within me (when we chant the opening *adi mantra*), it feels like a very dim, far away persona. So much of what Margaret speaks of is pure theory to me – how do I close the gap? She lives and breathes it, channels it, receives it – I just want to be like her. Maybe this is not realistic, but isn't that the point of beacons?

John: This discussion of kundalini yoga and its teaching can be ongoing. Please ask us more, you are doing more beautifully than you know, it's just your human impatience and conditioning for speedy results, leads you to disappointing expectations. Nor has your practice been altogether wholehearted or consistent — a true commitment would take you towards it in leaps and bounds. Talk to Jessie, talk to other teachers in community — recommit! Ask us for the discipline, let us help you become "happy, healthy, and holy." You have the foundation, you just need a little more clarity and the clearing of some resistance. Yes, you can be a teacher. Yes, you can achieve what Margaret has. Yes, you can soar into this world of kundalini. Observe and accept your hesitation to embrace the culture and lifestyle. What is holding you back?

*My first kundalini yoga teacher, whose radiant teaching changed my life.

I want it but am uncertain – my motives are not strong enough. Yes, I will write to you again about this to examine my motives – that would be amazing.

Saturday August 27, 2011, 1:15 am

Dear John and the Angels,

Here we are, some weeks later, and things are still topsy-turvy. No houseguests, but instead Hurricane Irene, who has been slowly boiling northward for the past 7 days. The meteorologists are beside themselves with detached professional hysteria: finally, a real storm! When I went back and re-read last week's entry, it seemed so long ago, a different world. It has been rainy and overcast all day, but not much wind, and maybe 95% humidity. Now I'm awake and sitting in bed listening to the crickets and the breezy bursts in the maples – wind that will start to increase and hold steady by morning. Who knows if it will be a category 1 or just a tropical storm. However, Manhattan has been evacuated, and transit is not running. Do you have any suggestions or guidance for me for riding out the storm?

Angels: We were guiding you all day today – could you feel us? That is why you were so calm and efficient. Isn't it a nice feeling to have clarity and act on it directly? We love flowing through you, All is well. There is much to be enjoyed in this situation as you have already thought — spending special time with friends and family, cementing another happy memory. The storm is merely another vehicle (as you say) to bring out contrast and test people. It would be a good day to spend extra time in your morning practice, praying, meditating, exercising and thinking of others. Send your prayers out, they are needed. Write to us again tomorrow night and let us have a wonderful long session. For now, dear child please sink into a deep, sweet sleep.

Thank you my darling friends for your guidance and protection. Good night...

Friday, September 9, 2011
Dear John and the Angels,
You just sent this day to test me, didn't you? Today is the big
fundraising event at Longlawn – so here at the office we are all
frantically compiling last minute lists and double-checking payment,
names, etc. I am feeling, not so much harassed as a little irritable
(please help me accept this and transmute it).

To make our day doubly joyful, today the city public workers are
ripping out the sidewalks, inches from our historic 200-year old
building, with massive thumping heavy equipment which grinds
and clashes with metal upon metal, shrieking, banging, screeching,
bashing. BANG, BANG, BANG. So delightful, so charming. Earplugs
are no use, but at least I have them. So please angels, tell me happy
things and help me overcome these silly distractions.

Angels: Sweet girl, all is well and all shall be well. The test comes in your choice of reactions.
Your humor is an excellent way to parry these challenges, and it will uplift those around
you. Be resourceful. What can you do elsewhere in the office? Walk away from your desk.
Find another place to work. Run an errand. Ask your supervisor Mindy if you can do
anything for her. Accepting the circumstances means working with them in a creative way.
You are worthy of this, you can rise to it. Yes, the tests are coming at you one-two-three-
four, as fast as you can field them. Thank you so much for turning to us and asking for help.
We appreciate that you want to do better in your life, moment to moment. Trust that this is
indeed happening. Lovely one, you are more precious than you realize, and we are working
to bring this into your awareness. Joy is just around the corner. We are with you now,
tonight, and every moment. Keep asking in sticky moments, and give it all away.

4:20 and the day just happened! Off to get dressed, and to the event.
Thank you angels, for guiding and protecting me. Please help me to
be pleasant, cheerful, welcoming and professional tonight, and to
maybe even enjoy myself.

Chapter IV: Emerging

"The moment you touch your soul, you become fearless."
– YOGI BHAJAN

A Worn-Out Old Coat

Tuesday, September 20, 2011
Dear Angels,
The countdown has begun – here it is Tuesday evening and tomorrow is my final morning at work before I leave for vacation in Turkey on Thursday. I feel strangely detached and calm – as though there are things I really ought to be anxious about, but am too overwhelmed to even approach anxiety. As you know I have spent days washing, drying, ironing, laying out, and staging my clothing for the trip, turning the guest bedroom into a packing room. Even though I did this same trip last year and am coasting on that rehearsal, I still think there must be one more thing to do, purchase, or finish. Please help me in these final days – is there anything I have overlooked?

Angels: Calm your fears, child. Last year you did not know you had us. This year you do! Whenever something goes smoothly, that is us. Whenever no mistakes occur, that is us. Whenever all is remembered with calmness, precision and careful thoughtfulness, we are there. You keep reaching for your old travel anxiety like a worn-out old coat. It is deeply embedded — but it will fade more with each peaceful travel experience. Throw it away like the old coat that it is! Your life is unrolling before you in bright new vistas, and we share the joyous journey with you. Such opportunities for asking us!

Dearest Barbara, we love you so much and adore the way you write to us all the time with questions. We feel your doubt, hesitation, and insecurity about whether this process is "real." You are a partner in the reality – you rise to meet us. The stronger your belief, the stronger the effect of our blessings. Blessed child, we embrace you! Precious one, please just go to bed and rest. You have a big day of packing tomorrow. We love you!

Your Joy Is Your Birthright

Sunday, October 9, 2011, 10:45 am
Dear John and the Angels,
A peaceful Sunday in October – and it's my birthday! The day is already extraordinary. We are having a heatwave, and the outdoor temperature must be in the 70's. Bright, hot sunshine is pouring down (I'm outside) and a mockingbird was singing sweetly not too long ago. A year ago I was in Kemer, Turkey, celebrating with Anni, Fany, Nicole, Lale, Patricia and Yasemin. I feel like a different person – as though I've been cracked open and the joy is starting to leak in.

I have been musing on the nature of grace, how it is delivered to us in moments we can remember and cherish, if we are present enough. I have one such memory from Kemer, which makes me glow. For some reason the sight, sound, sense, my state of openness – fused into a sweetness that I can go back to, visit, and replay. Did the person involved know he was delivering grace? No, he was just going about his ordinary job, being himself. Which means that grace flows through us whether or not we know it, that it is an alchemy which requires a giver and a receiver, and that it can be experienced over and over. Well, I don't know if you all would call it grace, but that's what it felt like to me.

And TODAY – today is so exquisite that only a fool could miss how chock full of grace it is. I am open to everything!

Oh! There's that mockingbird again.

John and the Angels: Truly, you could sit here for the entire length of the day just enjoying the peace, sunshine birds, and beauty of the weather. We would love to spend the day with you! If you make a little effort, you can get the few necessary tasks out of the way quickly — then you are free to appreciate every passing moment. You are a beautiful child of light and grace yourself, an instrument of joy and giver of beauty. We need you on this earth to help us do our job. We appreciate your openness so much! Your life is unfolding in magical ways. Continue to release your fears and trust us and this wondrous process. All the angels are singing for you now, all of your dear departed ones are blessing you. There is nothing more you need to do or worry about. Go forth and play, knowing we are at your side. Your joy is your birthright, and it is returning to you. You need not stretch to understand what passes — you are a conduit. Let all flow through you, let all bless you. Beloved girl, heart of ours, we love you more than ever and are sending angel magic to you for your birthday. Ask us as you go, and keep us in your heart. Cherish the friends — you already do, we know — who send you love today. Happiest of happy birthdays, dear Barbara!
Eternal Love and Blessings,
John, the Angels, and the Heavenly Choir!

October 17, 2011, 3:55 pm
Dear John and the Angels,
There is one thing I don't understand: how do people begin to cope, who aren't in touch with their angels? I think I would have lost my mind this past year – and it's still a distinct possibility. Today, for example, I was so pleased to have gotten my old carcass of a car to the tire store...but this year I will have easily spent $2,000 on my car. It's like a second mortgage payment. You have my attention: I'm listening. Please tell me what I need to do next, and what the best solution is to my temporary car-less state.

John and the Angels: It's all practice for more positive habits of mind. The list you came up with as you stood outside the gas station waiting for the taxi — excellent! Just like the rust on your car, you have to chip away at the rusty habits of mind which incline you toward sadness, negativity, or ego-centered dramas. Only positive energy solves things. So please, work with us! What positive list can you come up with about purchasing a new car?

Let's work on it tonight, it could be fun. We love these opportunities to manifest in your life, even though you see it as a hitch or a problem. Poor sweet, you could use a hug, couldn't you? Let's really used this incident to dive deep — meditate tonight, bring up your fears and release them, work through some of your resistance to things automotive. They really are miracles of engineering, you know, and a huge blessing of abundance and privilege in your life.

So is that all it is, just pure habit, when I reach for the "oh-no-groan--woe-is-me" attitude? The difficulty is that it is so easy to slip into mentally, it feels like the normal, natural response. I mean, how many people who have automotive challenges say, "how wonderful! My brakes are shot! How wonderful! I just ran out of gas!" I mean, we are allowed a little consternation, aren't we? Or does positivity become so habitual that the "bad" things happen less and less?

John and the Angels: We are laughing at you! Do you know how funny you are? Delightful Barbara, we cherish your humor. Here's what we say: try it. Try a 180-degree change of attitude the next time something "bad" happens. Stand it on its head. Laugh. Yes, state, claim that it is a terrific thing, you just can't see why yet. See what that shifts. See these things as Chaplinesque, with a happy-ever-after ending.

But we need contrast...so when I attain nirvana and am always sublimely positive and serene about everything, will there be no contrast left in my life?

John and the Angels: Well, it isn't too likely, but you can lessen the degree of contrast — how about that? We're on the case! We love you too much to let you down. It's time you were in something fun, sporty and safe, dear child. Love, John and the Angels — with celestial hugs until tonight.

I was mentally begging and asking for your help today – to transmute my fears, to solve the car problem – which you did. But in the interim of waiting I was still seething with insecurity, fear and uncertainty. That was so *scary*. And I am so relieved to have my car back, with new and better tires, to drive home on a rainy night, in safety and confidence. Thank you angels, for saving the day. Can we please just get on an even keel now, pleez?

Silence.

Well, either you're not ready to talk about it, or it's too difficult a question.

John and the Angels: Sweet lass, how we laugh at you! As if you could ever a) keep us out; or b) ask too difficult a question. Ah, we feel your gratitude at being safe and sound — lovely! We know you are puzzled by the oddity of this tire problem. It is one jigsaw piece in a much larger puzzle which we can't fill in for you now. It happened because it had to happen, and you were the agent it came through, that is all. Would you remember this incident, and use it again as a reason to trust us in all things, even in dark moments of uncertainty? We pulled you out as fast as we could. Another time, you might want to shower blessings on the mechanics and salespeople — that helps, too.

But I was deep in fear, and forms and degrees of anxiety, with zero presence of mind. So I could have made better choices about my reactions and all those embedded triggers. I feel like such a neophyte, though – it's a huge leap to change old patterned ways of thinking. I see your point, that I can shower blessings in perceived "negative" situations just as well as in perceived "positive" situations. Hmm. I was too selfishly engrossed in worries to give anyone another thought. Was there anything else you'd like me to learn from this incident?

John and the Angels: No, truly you are doing well as you reach for us more and more and more. You learn fast, and you actively want to change and receive guidance and answers. As you learn to manage these unreal states of distress, your angel hearing will strengthen. So all is well, we love you more than ever — oh yes we do — and we love this teamwork! For us it is fun and exciting.

Funny angels, this is teamwork I could never have dreamed of. And we hop all over the map together, in and out of emotions, situation, solutions, life, like giant fleas. Or – what metaphor would you choose?

Angels: Oh, bullfrogs, we think. How about bunnies? Or toads? Or grasshoppers? Lovely! Fun!

Thank you again, Angels, for keeping me safe and solving the car problem.

Sunday, October 23, 2011

Dear John and the Angels,

I think Heaven must be exactly like my bed after a long hard day: white, warm, cozy, peaceful, silent, *safe*. Just had a long hot soak in the tub with some balsam fir oil, followed by curling up under the duvet in my fluffy white spa bathrobe with a mug of hot cocoa spiked with peppermint schnapps. Mmmm!…I have re-read the *Angelspeake Book of Prayer and Healing* and I always find something new in it. What do you do, how do you respond, if a human asks you a question in a rude or demanding way? What if someone phrases a question as "Give it to me, dammit!" or "I want it now!" with an aggressive or rude intention?

Silence.

Don't tell me I've stumped you.

Angels: Sweet child, sometimes the thoughts and answers come through a little slowly. You enjoy our conversations so much that you want to chat and be open all the time — this is so wonderful. We really love you, you know. You will start to feel it soon — we know you are occasionally sad because for you, so far, our reassurances have been words only, with no corresponding emotional sensation inside of you. Oh, but that will change as you do, just a little longer now. Thank you for being patient. You have had many dark, sad, lonely hours and this has come to feel "normal" for you, so it does not occur to you to change it. The cavalry is on its way!

As for your question, what do we do, or how do we respond to "rude" humans? This is not an issue, as we do not judge, and these human reactions are transparently fear-based, which only excites our compassion. Anger and "rudeness" go right through us, they are not real. But do we answer the prayers and grant the requests? Only if it is in their best and highest good. There is never a literal, direct manifestation if the intention is based in greed or unkindness. But this is a very good question, as many millions of people ask for things they think they want, but which may slow their spiritual growth. This is their choice, however.

A Conversation with Swami Kripalu*

October 30, 2011, 12:20 pm
Meditation room on 4th floor of Kripalu Center for Yoga
Dear Swami Kripalu,

Almost a year has passed since I first sat here and felt your presence.
It has been a long near-year, and I feel like a different person, so
much has happened. But throughout it all I have held the intention
of returning here to communicate with you. This is a precious
moment. Here I am. Swami Kripalu, what would you like to tell me?

*Swami Kripalu: That's it, excellent, always begin all things with a beautiful smile, which wells
up out of the true beauty in your heart. Thank you for writing to me. You have felt my presence
throughout the weekend, you have invoked me, you have asked for my help, you have showered
others with blessings, you have asked to be awakened. This is all, this is everything, this is your
gift to me. All will flow from this. You need do nothing more. Beloved child of light, continue to
walk with the angels and seek their help and blessings. Nothing is impossible to you now, for you
have put your foot upon the path of true courage in exploring the tender radiance of your heart.
Know I am always available to guide you — indeed, it is my greatest privilege to be called upon
for assistance! All, all, all will come. This extraordinary blessing of radical communication will
guide you truly. Share it with as many people as you can — yes, even write to the senior staff at
Kripalu. Do you not think they know this already, for they, too, hold me in their hearts.*

*Go, now, child, and enjoy your delicious luncheon, sweet tea and savor this physical world! It is
so brief, and your experience of it matters. Dive deep, drink long, love profoundly, bless always.*

With deepest love and blessings,
Swami Kripalu

P.S. Write to me when you are home. I do love to have a good conversation!

---

*Swami Kripalu, (1913-1981): One of the greatest yoga masters of the 20th Century; he was renowned for his practices
of Kundalini yoga and sahaj or spontaneous yoga, as well as for his core teachings about the power of Divine Love. His
influence led to the development of Kripalu yoga, and the establishment of the Kripalu Yoga Center in the Berkshires.

With All Heaven Behind You, How Can You Fail?

Friday, November 4, 2011, 10:40 pm
Dear Angels,
I am reading Tama Kieve's book *This Time I Dance!* It all sounds lovely
and encouraging and exhorting and supporting. But she was a young
20-something filled with passion. I am 51 and I've fought a lot of
battles. I did win through to my passion when I reached down deep,
found my courage and went to professional horticulture school at
age 38. I did it – I have been there. But all that faded and fled in
my forties, and I've been rudderless ever since. I am not sure I have
passion anymore, at my age.

So you tell me, because I just don't know. I am floating on a current of
stability and comfort, and enjoying it. But as for meaning, promise,
and heart's desire? What is it, where is it, will it ever show up in my life?
And you know what? If you don't answer, that wouldn't surprise me.
That would be an answer in itself. That's how mixed up I feel about this
"purpose" thing.

*Angels: Be not sad be not sad be not sad! Oh, we are here to the rescue! Not answer indeed!
We will come with troops and trumpets if need be....ah, nice clean fresh page to fill. We are
off and running. Now, darling heart of ours, please listen and pay attention — not that you
wouldn't —you are an excellent student. You want, yet you don't want. The comfort and
stability blunt the passion. You struggle to trust the material world. Invite Mara to tea.* As you
dissolve your fears, the passion and purpose will shine forth. We cannot tell you what it will be,
because that would spoil the ending. If all you have is faint flickers, trust those.*

I was hoping for something a little more specific than that. It's just
– those faint flickers don't seem terribly exciting – and certainly not
enough to leap into the void like the author did. And where do I start?
What do I do?

---

*A reference from the classical Buddhist teachings. Mara was a supernatural being who confronted Buddha with his
shadow sides of greed, hatred and delusion. Instead of resisting these dark energies, Buddha embraced them and
invited his 'enemy', Mara, to sit down and have tea.

You've written to us, haven't you? Then you have started. You've read Tama Kieve's book, haven't you? Then you have started. And did you not, just today, blurt out the word "bookstore" as a spontaneous confession to a near stranger? Have you not cherished secret dreams for years now, private fantasies? Then you have started.

Sleep now, sweetheart, our beloved. This is a brave thing to do! You have just confronted doubt and fear and resistance! And you've made a beginning! Tomorrow is a sparkly new day and a better time to scheme and dream —write to us and let us be partners in this venture. With all Heaven behind you, how can you fail? Love and sweet dreams,

The Angels

Tuesday, November 8, 2011, 8:40 pm
Dear Angels,
We are going through a really discouraging period at work. I have just laid out the angel oracle cards, with this question: "The project I am involved with at work seems to be going badly and my boss is becoming negative. What can I do to help it be a success?"

The cards turned up were: *Listening, Body Care, Nature, New Beginnings, Friendship, Focus.*

Can you shed a little more light for me please?

Angels: Thank you for your patience — we are here. The project you are involved with is large, significant, and complicated insofar as many people's destinies relate to it, not the least the celebrity architect and designer. Serious protective energy is being guided toward this project. Dark hours and energy variations are normal. You may want to monitor these more carefully, and call on us every time you perceive negativity. Shower it all with blessings, pray right at your desk, write to us, and yes, chant "aad guray nameh."* Absolutely, do it. Protection and guidance is there, but it helps to invoke it. You have the right instincts with your boss — helping him to switch out of his dark moods, trying to reason with him and counsel him against negativity. This is no time to hold back out of prudence. Say what needs to be said if you think it will change even a drop of negative energy.

*Aad guray nameh: a mantra in Gurmukhi; often used in kundalini yoga for protection and projection.

Trust your knowledge and instincts — there is a reason you were guided to be in this position now. We need you to hear our guidance and follow it — thus the card "Listening." The other interpretations will become clear as you go. Your boss depends on you, so stay clear and steady. This is a time of testing. Call on your friends and believe in what you know is right. Give your patroness on the board of directors a pep talk! You have all the tools you need, including the awareness to use them. Trust trust trust! Smile for us sweet Barbara, we are by your side always.

Thank you – you said exactly what I need to hear. Here is my second question of the evening, please. Last weekend I stopped off at the auto dealership for a quick look at some cars. The model that really took my attention is the 2012 VW Golf TDI in graphite blue, with manual transmission and heated seats. Oh, this is a pretty car, a sporty car, a 4-door I think I could really love. I am going to test drive it this weekend. Could this be it? It felt right – something about it clicked. The price tag is pretty high. So, angels, this is the big question – if this car is right for me, how can I afford it? Please help.

Angels: Ask us rather, "please help me obtain financing for this excellent auto!" Ask and ye shall receive, child of ours and precious one. If your heart desires it, then it is right. You have finally gotten clear — it is a good feeling isn't it? It simplifies everything. The remaining detail, then, is merely the money. This is easily done, and it will come together seamlessly, we promise. Start with the test drive, sit down again with your calculator, talk to your knowledgeable friends who can help you negotiate, and ask us for more! We just love helping you, have we mentioned that? Now, time for sweet dreams, lovely girl. We have work to do!

Love and sweet blessings, the Angels and Beloved John

Friday, November 11, 2011, 1:45
Dear Angels,
Back to the car-purchase drawing board – only it is more fun now, less fraught with fear. Last weekend I stopped into the auto dealership, and took a quick walk around the lot with one of the salespeople,

Richard. I just wanted to see what was there, test it against my gut instinct. I told the salesperson my list of preferences, and he walked me straight over to the Golfs and said, *"this is your car."* Gorgeous little 2012 beauty in graphite blue. Zing! Something inside me said, he's right! I'd had that feeling before, but there was always something lukewarm about it. This was the strongest and the clearest it has been. I've been thinking about it ever since. Angels, I think this is it:

The 2012 VW Golf TDI 4 door manual in graphite blue,
with heated front seats,
for somewhere around $25,000 or less

Can it be any more specific than that? It feels like me, my automotive heart's desire. Thus I am back to the drawing board, planning, scheming, pulling out my auto finance pockets and examining them. Dear angels, if this is it, please help me! The financing side isn't as scary and overwhelming as it was eight months ago, but I still don't see my way clearly.

I feel like I've come a long way – this auto purchase process has really has been a process – I see now it's more about other things in my life than about the end goal. It's a mirror, a backdrop against which I work things through. Oh wise angels, please talk to me now about car financing, and then we can go for that walk!

*Angels: You're the best and we adore you! You're learning how to come out and play with us! Come into our angelic sandbox and let's build sweet sandy castles on earth. O yes! (by the way, that might be enough caffeine for today). Regarding financing, you are right on track. Compile your notes, do your research, track stock prices, call auto financing institutions, for rates. The jigsaw puzzle is coming together. There will be wonderful surprises for you as the pieces fall into place faster and faster. Asking that friend for a loan? Hmmm — this is the lion's den. That is a last resort. You're almost there and we just have to ask you to trust, wait, and keep playing in the sandbox. The castle is almost ready to be unveiled. Oh, how we love you, our earthchild and angelfriend. And please, yes! Let us sit down and curl up later to brainstorm along the lines of your pipedream á la Tama Kieves. It's time to incubate, things are brewing and hatching and fermenting. All is **more than well**. Love love love love love to you.*

The Angels and Gorgeous John who misses you

Thank you, angels! **Wow.**

Courage Is Catching, So Is Joy

Monday, November 14, 2011, 9:15 pm
Dear John and The Angels,
It's another beautiful, soft, night with a hazy moon.
Please help solve the next set of problems…there is bad feeling
between me and my cousin in Florida. Nor am I talking to my
siblings, the other two-thirds of the property-tax pie. My cousin has
decided that I am to blame for everything that goes wrong with the
Florida property. I am terrified of his sarcastic emails to the family,
when he heaps blame and recrimination on me. I know he is wounded
and angry because his parents, my aunt and uncle, committed double
suicide a few years ago; but why me? He is irrational and caustic,
and charges like a mad bull. So please – I am just eaten up with this
ongoing toxic situation, which has gone on for years. How do I handle
the taxes, and stand up for myself?

Angels: Darling girl, you have so many life skills now, this is where you practice them:
acceptance — to dissolve the feelings of unworthiness, fear, and aversion. Meditation — to
help you breathe, center, focus, and become calm. EFT — to release immediate impulses and
emotional surges. Prayer — to send blessings of peace and forgiveness to your wounded cousin.
Please try these and see if the energy shifts. This is indeed a very severe energy snarl, and you
are central to helping unsnarl it. For now, only deal with the taxes — just write briefly and
ask that they be sent or faxed again. Keep all communications to a minimum. As things grow
*better, you may want to write a **kind** note to him asking him to please refrain from attacking*
you. Do it only when you are calm and centered. Notice your tendency to spiral into fearfulness
and generate stories. What are some ways you can recognize this trigger point and interrupt the
spiraling? You know how to do it, you just need that tiny moment of awareness. And of course,
you can always write to us but it may not be convenient in the moment.

You're right – I **do** have these skills. I **can** practice them. I have come a long way from the reactive person I was before. And this **does** feel like a tired, old story – trying to get its claws into my brain, trying to rev up my ego into the old patterns of anger and defensiveness. How amazing...there – I just tried to think of my cousin now and could only feel neutral. You know what is funny, Angels? I sat down to write to you with this ball of upset-ness in my mind and heart, sensing it would be a big melodramatic spill, woe-is-me. Yet – it didn't happen at all. Poof-it's-gone, is more like it. Wow. It really works. Does that mean there's hope for solving the Florida property-sale situation?

Angels: It is already loosening up, thanks to you. Keep praying and blessing at every opportunity. You have no idea what effect you are having. Courage is catching, so is joy. We are so proud and happy to help you solve these human sadnesses. Yes, dear one, we wish you into your snug bed so that you can be beautiful and bouncy for tomorrow. All good things are happening. We wrap you in our angel arms and sing you sweet lullabies. Goodnight, blessed child!

Love, The Angels and John

Turn It Over to Us

Saturday, November 19, 2011, 8:30 am
Dear Angels,
How delicious to have a weekend morning to sit propped up in bed, heating pad against back, weak sunlight struggling through the window. How fine to have time for this soft white stillness, when I am alert and awake, but give myself permission to go into sweet, deep immobility where sanctuary lies.

I am writing because in my pre-waking doze, I was sensing some color, maybe an angel presence, asking to be heard. Could you please send whomever wanted to communicate?

Angels: It is I, Michael. Thank you for patiently waiting and now writing. What a miracle to be able to enjoy you enjoying us. This is very very fine, lovely child, light of our eyes. Be not grave, we are not so stern! Your laughter and giggles carry messages too — this is only divine energy bubbling up through you and manifesting. Child, the days to come may be strange and far from ordinary. The skills you have learned can be used to manage too much as well as too little, the flood as well as the drought. Let it not carry you away, turn to us in all things. We need you as our agent on earth, for much good can be accomplished. We can help you skip through this world, spreading laughter, joy, beneficence, healing, kindness, love. What you experience as confusion is only a not-seeing — turn it over to us. What you experience as a not-happening is only your human time limitation — turn it over to us.

Michael, I am humbled by your wisdom and guidance. I am curious – the angels said that their magic works well when I take long, late evening walks, which I so love to do. Why is this?

Archangel Michael: You know the answer to this, dear child. Being out in nature, under the stars, breathing fresh night air, free from distractions and worries, is a purer state of being. There is an ancient part of all human beings which stems from the nomad instinct. It is greatly attenuated now, of course, but it is genetic. When you activate this by your long striding walks we can permeate your energy more easily. We experience your pleasure, the rhythm of the stride, your neutral state of mind. Walking brings you close to us because you are in your body, not your mind. We can help you heal on these walks — ask us! This is excellent partnership.

Thank you so much, Michael…one of my greatest bafflements in this process is that much of what I read, learn, am told by teachers – has to do with opening the heart. This means emotion, feeling. I think (ha – notice the verb) – I am very closed down. I don't have positive, compassionate swellings of loving feeling or emotions – or only around animals, really. With all of the healing I have done, this opened-heart stuff seems like a foreign language. I don't even sense the emotion when angels tell me repeatedly how much they love me. It's like being autistic. I don't know if this is good, bad, normal, or I shouldn't even worry about it.

Archangel Michael: Ah, child, this is (ha) the heart of the problem, indeed. Opening up those flood gates must be handled slowly, carefully, well. Yes, you have many defenses, which we could breach, but the time is not right and you are not ready. It's a process of building your entire energy system up to be strong enough to handle it. You are progressing faster than you know, and that you are even writing of it is a wonderful sign. Your healing happens in real time, with real things and creatures, and with your free will. You can choose to practice opening your heart in safe environments, little by little. Ask us for the courage it takes, as us for the opportunities, ask us for the guidance. Nothing more is necessary. We love you too much to let you stay shut down – there is so much richness to experience in your short life! It is very important! We use the tools at hand – if you perceive best through active thoughts, there go we. If you were visual, or auditory, there would we be. Now, child, shall we go hand in hand together into the day? It is lovely outside, and your garden beckons.

With pleasure – thank you so much, Michael!

....*No*, Wait.

November 28, 2011, 10:40 pm
Dear Angels,
The Monday workday after Thanksgiving – it wasn't too bad – evenly paced, nothing too annoying or overwhelming, just mop-up. That is, until the end of the day. The director had been out slaying dragons – complications arose over the park project regarding soil contamination. The director came into my office at 5:15 discouraged and negative, and said it seemed that the plug would be pulled on the project in light of the letter from the state authorities. I'm not going to go into the convolutions here, you know them – but what is frustrating me is that we are *so* close to getting approval for this project, and yet everyone is just collapsing before the finish line. I'm appalled by people's cowardice. I seem to be the last person standing who believes that this is a great project. HELP! Is this project really going to fail? I could accept if we made it to December 14 and the

council voted no, but to pull out before then seems to me the height of cowardly mediocrity. I am just spluttering. Can you please shed some light on why, after so many promising signs, this project is suddenly spiraling down in flames?

Angels: Dear girl, dear girl, dear girl. You know we can't give anything away, tell the future, give you hints about how this may turn out — but that is not really what you are asking. Once again in your life you are managing your disappointment, and assessing your level of expectation.

I just don't understand how it could all unravel so quickly. Were my expectations so unreasonable, my trust in the governing body so naïve? Oh, you know I am sage enough at this point to be accepting of any outcome, defeat in any form, but I am simply disgusted by the way this is trickling away in petty, stupid ways. If the state letter scotches it, we wouldn't have had a chance anyway, but I am....*no*, **wait**.

Okay, angels, you're waiting for me to stop whining and switch gears, right?

Instead of being disgusted, I can choose a better response. The expectations and disappointment don't really matter, it's the transmuting them, transcending them that does. In effect, I have worked through my own small-mindedness and am now turning to a larger source for answers and solutions. What would you like me to do, angels -- pray, shower blessings, meditate? My boss's negativity sits in the room like an anvil. He's chopping down this project all by himself. I don't know how to counter it. Any suggestions?

Angels: Bravo, dear child! Such a brilliant, fast learner. You worked it right through and you answered your own questions. The problem of the negativity is a good one, as it is indeed an energy field which you feel and which affects you. Perhaps tomorrow look up the Kundalini Research Institute and find a good mantra to spread positive energy and dispel darkness. Look up some of your mantras from class. Repeat them throughout the day if you think of it. Pray and ask us to transmute the negativity. Bring us in as often as you can. Yes, the project is in danger of failing. The outcome is not as important as the big effort we ask you to make right now, continually, to override or transcend or blast through the negative forces. You feel them affecting you — ACT! Perhaps the greatest danger now is that of *complacency. You are right, no one is fighting for this. It is that which will tip the balance. Trust your power to influence this for the better, no matter the outcome. You **know** what you **know**—don't expect others to understand or agree, but get stubborn about pursuing it. This will always serve you.*

Dear angels, thank you...how amazing, yet again, that the answer and the course of action and the intention always come clear. I am so glad I have you with me.

Now, to another question, and this one is for you, John. As you know, I watched a sweet, romantic film called *Leap Year* with an actor named Matthew Goode. He plays an aloof, poetic, somewhat smoldering and sardonic Irishman; his performance was riveting. And his romantic intensity made me think of you, which is disturbing. I don't like being disturbed! No, it's all numb and slumbering nicely, thank you very much. So, please, tell me John, what I am supposed to learn from this oddly, tingly, I-know-this-man feeling I get from the movie?

John: Oh lass. Lass, lass, lass. Would that it were you and me in the film. I miss you, miss our conversations, our walks, our intimacy. I'm always looking for a way to show my love, get through to you, find a medium to help you experience it. That's my job, you see — to pierce the numbness and the oh-too-comfortable-zone. So you and I do this dance together — you know it's happening and you resist or deflect it, or suddenly get too terribly busy and distracted. Hmm — think I wouldn't notice? Yet at the same time you are struggling to fulfill the demands of your human life — and those demands kidnap your attention and energy. But they also place you in the numb zone. You experienced a mild depression the other day when that zone was briefly disturbed, and you experienced the contrast: fear of change/growth/genuine feeling versus contraction/numbing/safety and comfort. The "never-mind-me-it's-okay" blues. You're so funny — you know, you think if you just live your life quietly enough, go along without hurting anyone or anyone taking notice, that the big walloping things like True TRUE love and Ultimate Destiny, Happiness and Joy will pass right over you and leave you comfortably huddled in your niche. But you're better and bigger than that. You heard your teacher Margaret — the soul keeps knocking at the door.

*So, yes, beloved, I am here, hovering, and would love nothing better than to get under your skin and appear to you in the guise of the character Declan. There's a fair amount of resemblance — you have excellent taste, my dear. The character of Declan disturbs you for good reason. But sweet, be not afraid, please. You are running from this and pushing it away. It can **heal** you. Take my hand, lass, let's work this through. I know your terrors, I know your beliefs of unworthiness. You know enough now to start gently examining these. Won't you let me help you?*

Nowhere to run, nowhere to hide. This is terrifying – so let's start with that. Because I don't think I deserve you or any of the angels. And here's a thought you've heard me think often enough: why – or what motive do I have, to find a real human male to love me, who may be flawed or require more compromises and tolerance than I am sure I have – why bother?

John: Because you need to grow your soul in this lifetime, and there's only one way to do it: plunge into relationships that are sometimes glorious, sometimes messy, sometimes maddening. A tidy life is a dull life, and you'd just have to do it over again in another life anyway. Take my hand, cherie, look into my eyes, and trust. See the pattern of attraction with the recent men in your life. Your soul is reaching out for something truly magnificent. Shall we, love?

But oh, I am so frightened. Man, this human trip is hard. John, we could go on all night but it is midnight, I must go to bed, really. Though I am feeling a little overwhelmed right now by the beauty and strength of your response. You see, that's just it – I don't know if I could handle the intensity of a John/Declan 1,000-watt emotional illumination directly on me. Give me a 20-watt bulb...oh, right, we're supposed to be working on that. Too much for one night – thank you dear John – and good night.

John: Thank you for letting me back in. The road is so sweet when we travel together. Keep me in your heart, lass?

I will do my best...the image of Declan really helps.

Tuesday, November 19, 2011, 10:30 pm
Dear John, dear Angels,
I managed to remember to do it, with your help! This morning, driving to work, I was softly chanting the *"sat siri, siri akal"** mantra, and then all day, even in the grocery store. Something shifted, something worked – will never know if that was it. But at the end of the day, the director came downstairs, wearily propped himself against the supply cabinet, and said, "Let me bring you up to speed. The project is back on." Oh, my heart soared! I had been semi-afraid all day – I would hear snatches of his deep voice in phone conversations and I barely kept the fears at bay – but for now, we're safe. The board of directors is going to let the city council go through with the vote. I don't understand all of this seesawing or why it has to occur, but it is *nerve-wracking.* My supervisor Mindy is funny – she is fiercely devoted to the boss and the hammering he is taking is making her anti-park, so she snipes at the project. I need to remember to stay out of her office. Thank you angels, for helping me to find, remember, and practice ways to stay strong.

Angels: Beloved heart and child of ours, all is well and all shall be well. Every day unfolds magically, and we hope to help you experience that magic again. You are an alchemist, creator, and we so appreciate your openness to our guidance. Sleep sweetly now so that you can be fresh and awake all day to create more magic with us!
Love, the Angels

The Well's Pretty Dry, Michael

Saturday, December 3, 2011, 9:40 pm
Dear Angels and John,
I have been in constant pain from this lower back spasm, so my thinking is fogged and my energy is low. Okay, Angels – I know. I should probably

*Sat siri, siri akal: In the kundalini yoga tradition, this is a mantra known as the Mantra for the Aquarian Age, which affirms that our essence is timeless and deathless.

go to a doctor about this, but I don't want to. I don't have a GP, it takes months to get an appointment, and I can't afford the time away from my desk. This is a big issue for me – the doctor thing, avoidance thereof. I have so much resistance I don't even want to ask for your help. How to ask when you are so bound up in avoidance, that you avoid the avoidance? So this isn't even really even an asking – I am opening up the lines and if there is anything you want me to know, please tell me. I hope it's good news, like "you will be perfectly healed tomorrow."

Silence.

Is there a communication time lag, or am I off the hook because you have nothing to tell me? Sorry, shouldn't be facetious.

Angels: It is I, Michael. You need me, beloved child. No pain, hurt, injury or sorrow is too little or too big for us. This is an entire package, which includes all of your resistance and unwillingness to look at what is wrong — do you not think it is so with many frightened humans? This is why we love you so and love to shower concern and compassion. For now, dear child, just pray for healing every day and it will be granted. You sometimes forget the simple act of asking — notice that your tough, independent side steps up and shushes you, says "just endure it, this is nothing, you can handle it, it will go away eventually." We ask you to care about your pain and suffering. This is hard for you, because you are not in the habit of doing so. Being always healthy is a point of pride with you, so any deviation must be an abnormality, a flaw, something to dismiss. Please, take yourself seriously, take your self-care seriously. Please keep meditating so that your awareness of the trance of self-loathing will be dissolved. So much in you will be healed when this is healed!

Thank you…I think what will be hardest for me is abandoning my sardonic, dismissive inner voice that makes light of these things. To use Tara Brach's phrase, I see how the trance of unworthiness loops on itself. And it never loops more so than when it demands to know "*Why?* Why *should* I care for myself, because I'm *not* really that important, am I?" This is a pretty strong belief: "I-don't-get-it-why-can't-I-just-continue-the-way-I-am?"

So how, Michael, can you possibly overcome this kind of conditioning?

Of course I am tough and stoic – I've had to be. My experience of life has proved to me conclusively that I am unworthy. So I don't see anything wrong with the trance of unworthiness. I am asking you to convince me otherwise.

Archangel Michael: Yes, dear one, please write. If you came upon a beautiful, sad, lonely stray dog, who was suspicious, snarling and cringing, would you rush to fling your arms around it, even though you longed desperately to comfort it and shower it with love? No, you would not, as you might just frighten it even more, although your heart might bleed for it. All you could do would be to patiently, consistently keep it company, win its trust, speak to it kindly, shower it with affection from afar, and wait for the one sign that it would be willing to accept love and affection. So it is with us and you. We can only work with your willingness, your beliefs, your healing time-frame. The trance of unworthiness affects all areas of your life, some more so than others, and is woven in a complex knot of emotions in and around the issue of your health. Remember, focus on what you desire, not on what you don't — try to notice when you focus on un-health, and see if you can shift your thought, repeat a mantra, or replace it with positive energy — you could even list some affirmations. Sometimes the simplest things are enough to work — this is a great blessing!

Hold on…let me see if I understand this. Over the five decades of my lifetime, my experiences, culture, personality, choices, etc. have formed me into what I am today, and that includes this trance of unworthiness. Does that mean, that once I am aware of this trance, that I am responsible for dispelling it, that it is my choice to be less stoic, more self-nurturing, less dismissive, more loving, etc.? But…how do I prime the pump, if I don't get l-o-v-e? The well's pretty dry, Michael.

Archangel Michael: We feel your deep sadness and bleed for you, our darling Barbara. Work with us. Trust that this will happen. You love metaphors — let's think about priming that pump. How would it happen? Many, many, many pumping attempts, dozens, even, which just produce a dry, sucking sound. Then what — perhaps a little gurgle, a slurp, a cough of some water…and then the full flood. You will read back over these writings and marvel that you ever felt so desolate. You know what to do, and you have been doing it. Increase your consistency, and it will act like the pump action. A deep part of you knows this. Ask us for help with consistency! Yes yes yes yes, excellent idea, dear Barbara — write up your game plan the night before, think of all your tools: prayer, meditation, mantra, affirmations, breathing techniques, EFT, radical acceptance practices — yes yes yes! Let's start tomorrow morning and explore this. We're here, we love you, and you are so close, you have no idea. The Sahara of your soul is almost over. Let us rejoice. We will teach you the meaning of that word, too — oh yes. And because we love you, we think it is time for you to sleep. We want you beautiful, fresh, rested and happy so you can feel our angel hugs, touches and whispers. So precious are you!

Dear Michael and Angels and John, you overwhelm, as always, and you provide a plan, as always. There is nothing left to do *but* sleep. Thank you.

Wednesday, December 7, 2011, 10:20 pm
Pearl Harbor Day
Dear John and the Angels,
Every day now is so laden, so intense, so full, that each one is a world unto itself. Yesterday was the crisis of getting the park plans printed affordably. Eighteen copies in 24 x 36 format ran to about $500 – crazy. My colleagues were ping-ponging all over the map. I could have set up a table with paddles and a net in my office. Today was the City Council workshop – a day of quasi-mayhem, technical glitches and last-minute dashes for batteries. Now that our calm, unflappable former colleague is gone, that role is falling to me and I am filling it. Bizarre! Her replacement is a hyped-up New Yorker who lives on caffeine, sugar, cigarettes and alcohol, and feeds on office melodramas. I just watch her in amazement, and pray that our company culture will calm her fears so she can grow contented and placid like the rest of us. But the workshop tonight – what a zoo! The park project opposition were out in force, rallying with placards and postcards and petitions. All fascinating – especially when one of the wealthy home owners pompously held forth, the mayor tried to cut him off, and they shouted each other down. But many good things were said, and although the opposition were earnest, I think that ultimately their campaign has no center and will not hold. They don't see the larger picture, which is unfortunate.

The good news is that my back spasm is gone, as is my right thigh pain, mostly, which is miraculous. Did you do that? If so, thank you.

Anyway, it's past my bedtime, but you know how much I love writing to you, so please tell me what you think of tonight's City Council meeting.

John and the Angels: With pleasure, darling child. You are feeling our guidance and our power when you move calmly through the day — that sense that nothing ruffles you. And, you were aware of it and enjoyed it! That is fearlessness. All of your skills and powers are starting to rise, mix, blend, become natural responses. And yes, there were some fine moments when you looked at your colleagues and felt connected to them, saw how charming and fine they were in their humanness. Just a fleeting glimpse, but it was there. Then too, the dramas of the council chamber did not faze you — you were confident and calm. So different from other events leading up to this point — do you see how you have grown? We are very proud of you, beautiful one.

*You are desperate for rest and weary of the demands of the next four days — but you know we will float you right through it. Let us help you with all challenges on Friday, right into the heavy travel and socializing of Saturday and Sunday — and come home again to safe harbor and your much loved sanctuary of **bed**. Yes?*

Yes, please! Good night Angels, good night, John!

Wednesday, December 14, 2011, 11:30 pm
Dear John and the Angels,
Victory. The City Council final vote to accept the contract, to move ahead with plans for the park, was approved, 5 to 1. It was, as the mayor prophesied, an excruciating meeting. Then afterwards heading back to our office to celebrate, have a little wine, cheese, and champagne. Thank you for guiding me to buy that Veuve Clicquot – that set the tone, and no one seemed the slightest bit surprised when I pulled it out. Very nice reception with friends, supporters and staff.

So, I am here now, at home, after the cheering and the shouting have died away.

To be honest, last night's medieval Christmas pageant at St. James's seemed more real and to the point to me than the city council meeting.

Oh, those high soprano voices soaring straight into heaven, on those high notes of "Hark the Herald Angels Sing"...Oh, my. But you *know* this – I could not sing along, I was so choked up.

And it is late and I don't really have any questions, but just wanted to share and thank you for it all. We're soaring, aren't we, angels? Is there anything you'd like to tell me?

*Angels: Blessings, blessings and more blessings upon you, child of light and child of our heart. We are out in force, we are strong in and around and with you. You are quite right, there is strong "mojo" at work here, and you are an agent. You are wise to see that you are one agent of many. Just as you heard us tell you last night, that the cathedral was flocked with angels, that **every person there** had an angel for him or her, just as you did, and that learning to see this angelic field in every human was possible. This is divinity, it is there if you learn to see it. Carry this knowledge with you — but the tangible experience of it too, this is far more important, because you can transfer it to every situation. Tonight in the city council meeting was no different — every human being there had divinity shining out of him or her, some more than others. It is building! And we love sharing the joy of it with you! The powerful experience of St. James's is one you may want to repeat more frequently to build your strength, your ability to absorb divine love. Yes, the voltage is quite high! This is so good for you. We will help you to go to many churches from now on, no fears — they will attract you.*

As for the park project detractors, about whom you and your colleagues have sometimes unkind things to say, they have their role too. You know this. Use these encounters as an opportunity to become more compassionate. Yes, they are, some of them, confused, lonely, angry, or psychologically astray — at least, they are not in the flow of ordinary societal norms. And this is good, and fine, and as it should be. Practice acceptance — what opportunities for you! Ask us to remind you, and we will be there. Your eyes are being opened to the richness of community, and the need to practice kindness at all times in all ways with all people. You cannot go wrong this way.

I have just one more question. One especially vocal opponent of the park is an articulate, but delusional woman. Tonight immediately after the council vote, she spoke angrily to the female rector at the local church who was there to support us. Within moments the rector was in tears, and left the building, incapable of speaking to anyone. This incident is terrible – or is it? I only have my limited human point of view. After all, she is Your representative, how could she be so hurt?

Angels: You have used the term "lightning rod" in some of your communications. This is exactly what occurred, insofar as an extreme polarity of light and positive energy attracted her opposite extreme of dark, or negative energy, and a charge was released. She absorbed the charge, as a protective element — literally at your side — and it overwhelmed her a little. We are comforting her now, she has prayed and is seeking peace. Please also pray for both the rector and your vocal opponent, and you will learn more about the human story tomorrow.

When you explain it like that, it makes so much sense – that there is an underlying physics to metaphysics. Thank you very much, Angels – I will pray for both of them. Angels, I am so sorry, I would love to continue this, but it is 12:35 am and I'm yawning. Thank you angels, and good night!

Tuesday, December 21, 2011
Dear Angels and John,
Tomorrow night there is a big kundalini/solstice celebration at a local yoga center. Ordinarily, this would be the kind of thing I would rush to sign up for in in a trice, to be a part of the great, big, positive energy it will surely generate. Yet, I read the description of the event, and I am not interested, I am feeling a bit flat these days. Where is my old passion for every class that promised healing, change, enlightenment?

Angels: What would you rather do, than attend this event? You could spend the evening with us — we'd love that! Could this be more powerful and organic, to practice kundalini at home, light candles, meditate, go for a walk, play music, listen to us? What moves you? Yes, outside masters are powerful, but it is time for you to start trusting your own ability to generate peace, well-being, healing, and divinity. How else does the student become the teacher, then become the master? Ultimately, all classes and teachers are outside events designed to drive you inwards. Can you find this inner core of teaching within yourself, as you call upon it in your practice? Now is the time. Ask us to transmute your fears and insecurity. You are stronger now than ever before, it is time to transform. Yes, you are emerging — this is an excellent card to draw. See it all around you. Test your power — all things reflect this back to you. Feeling "flat" is merely the stillness preceding change. You can shift this at will now, you have the skills.

Oh. I see. It only *seemed* like a less important question, but in fact was not. I like your suggestion of tomorrow night's solstice much better – we can celebrate peacefully together.

As far as the student-to-teacher-to-master transition, well, of course you are right, but I am not sure I feel it for myself yet. Please guide me – I'm shooting the rapids with you, so please help me paddle true and straight. Time for bed, it's exactly midnight. Thank you angels, and good night!

Angels: Beloved child, see if you can remember your dreams tonight. We are always with you. Blessings upon your night of rest!

It Is in the Overcoming That You Are Healed

Tuesday, December 27, 2011, 6:30 pm
Dear Angels,
A lazy three-day Christmas weekend is just past. But Sunday afternoon the blues hit again, *hard*. Maybe not so much the blues, as that dear old friend of mine, An-Overwhelming-Feeling-of-Pointlessness, coupled with the realization that, unknowingly, I have slowly been building up expectations about what is supposed to happen between you and me. This *is* a relationship, after all. But I keep coming back to the same deep funk. I then go into a state of angel-avoidance, of non-communication, like a sulky teenager, because my understanding is so limited, and it hurts. I feel like a rat in a maze of dead ends. What is this sadness and pain?

Angels: Please write, we miss you so much and have been reaching out to you this whole time. What a blessing to get through to you.

This may not be a dark night of the soul, but it is certainly a dark moment of the soul. The trouble is, it is so very deep and dark, it feels almost external to me, like a separate agency. Pulling out of it is extremely difficult. And you see, even right here, right now, I have an expectation that you will explain this to me and help me feel better about it. But that may not happen at all. Nothing is coming through but flat, bleak helplessness.

*Angels: You must plumb the darkness before you can soar into the light. Each time, you will go deeper into the darkness and soar higher into the light. Expectation is a psychological state we can help you manage. You **will** find balance — it is in your nature. In the depths of your bleak sorrow, can you turn to us, pray, ask, and write? This is faith. Those very acts are utterly contradictory to the spiritual sadness you are feeling, which paralyzes you with fear. It is in the overcoming that you are healed. When this state hits again, as it may — recognize it, name it, find the place beyond it. This state is not real, even though it possesses you in such a deadly way. It is a somewhat dangerous place to remain, so it is important for you to find the willpower to get through to the other side. Your hurt, anger and fear are very big emotions, and though they cannot block us, they distort your receptivity. Sitting in a church is an excellent idea, and we would love it if you would do that, any time at all. You may grow to like it!*

If you are surrounding me all the time, and so constantly with your love and light, why don't I feel it as clearly as I feel the fear, sadness and pain? These negative emotions are quite tangible to me. If your presence is so true and right, why do I still *feel* nothing? This is all merely a mental exercise for me. That's the deadly part – that when I compare and balance what I actually feel with what I am told I should be feeling, it does not compute. There is a huge discrepancy between what you tell me and what I experience. No wonder I am sad and baffled – I cannot reconcile the messages I am receiving.

Angels: How well you put it, and how true. What would you do if you were us? How would you get through to sweet blessed Barbara, light of our hearts, who is so sad and lonely?

Hmph. I probably wouldn't – I'd give up on me. Therein lies
the problem.

*Please don't be flippant – it hurts you too. Acting tough is one of those ego strategies Tara
Brach talks about.*

Angels, I can't do this! I don't know how! Not my job. Clueless. Sorry to
disappoint, but I do need my protective strategies for a little while longer.
Oh, this isn't going anywhere. Back to "I-don't-get-it, -it-hurts."

You could lay out the oracle cards, would that help?

The cards are: *Friendship, Signs, Celebration.*

But the question I asked is: "Why don't I feel love? What is **wrong** with me?"

I think, angels, I had better just go to bed, even though it is only 7:30.
I am just too sad to figure it all out.

*We send you blessings of peaceful sleep. Tomorrow will be a beautiful new day, and good
things will happen for you. We love you, please carry this thought, **even** if it is not an
emotion yet!*

December 30, 2011
Dear Angels,
What an outlandish, extraordinary finish to the week, as though
exactly what you said about soaring into the light from deep, dark
depths, came true. On Tuesday, my sister called me at work to tell me
that we had had a clean, solid cash offer on the Florida property for
$300,000 – no contingencies, no financing, no developers. Wow.
Then came the flurry of emails with the contract. Right – fine – signed
it, scanned it, sent it back. Pinch me, is this happening? This is a
miracle, pure and simple. The contract was due to expire yesterday,
12/29. Yesterday came and went, the deadline expired, and I came in
this morning expecting the deal to have folded. I called the Florida
realtor – and miracle of miracles – both siblings signed and returned

the contract. So, all of the pieces are in motion, the closing is set for next Wednesday. I hardly dare hope – I am going to try to keep my expectations low – but it is hard not to dream about the extra $47,000 that will help break the back of my debt, help me buy a new car and new mattress, and *everything good*! But I must be patient and see. We've been disappointed so many times before. More than anything else, the sale of this property will cut the painful bonds between my cousins and me. Above all, I am thrilled that that the native Florida mangrove will be protected, as this couple is buying the lot as a buffer zone to protect their back yard. Oh, **joy**.

It does look like celebration is coming home to roost. You know, even if this deal does fold, it will have shown everyone that there is a way to sell it which does not involve property developers. And, it gives us hope. Hope hope hope! *Wow.*

I am post my spiritual-crisis slump, but I am not sure why – I would love to figure out what it took to lick that. Was it just abundant sleep? I have been going to bed at 7:30 pm every night, and I feel fantastic because of it. What a revolutionary difference it has made in my life. Right – over to you now, really.

Angels: Our sleepy girl, you were deeply exhausted and didn't know it. Now that you have the proof of a whole new energy level and clarity level, it will be easy for you to keep up the discipline.

As far as the Florida property goes, thank you for appreciating our work. We took your blessings and magnified them — so you see, we needed your help on earth to work the miracle. Do please keep praying and blessing. You have these proofs of how effective we can be when you have the courage to practice all the spiritual disciplines consistently. Yes, it is miraculous! You are our agent of miracles. What else can we accomplish with you, sweet friend, beloved child, our searching sister?

Ah – I think I am starting to see how this works – this understanding is a big help. I will indeed keep blessing and praying. I welcome suggestions, if you want to pop some ideas into my head (is it okay to ask for this?). For example, angels, oh I would be so thrilled if you could help me pray and bless and take action to banish all duck hunting from my town. It upsets me terribly to hear the guns booming, *blam! blam! blam!* early on these winter mornings. Horrible. But I have been praying and blessing, even blessing the hunters. So this would be a great arena in which to practice our partnership.

Angels: You've got it — you know what to do and how to do it. We would love to help you save the ducks, and we're already at work with the energy you're sending. Good job! Reverence for life and diminishment of human violence, protection of habitat and all natural creatures — this is peace-building, and we love you for thinking of it, and bringing this to us to solve.

Blessed girl, an early morning kriya beckons to you! Rise with the sun, learn what real joy is. Write to us in the morning when you're clear, and see what the difference is! Goodnight, our agent of miracles!

Good night angels, and thank you a thousand thousand times!

Our First Smile in a Long Time

Wednesday, January 4, 2012, 6:35 pm
Dear Angels,
Things at work are quiet and ticking over nicely, which helps me to address other things, like the Florida closing. Express package was delivered bright and early this morning. Had it signed, notarized, scanned and sent back to the title company by 11:30. But then...the uncertainty...tick tock, tick tock. Everyone has been communicating badly, and all is chaos. No one called or emailed me to say "IT'S DONE." So I sit here, slightly blue, wondering. Do I have permission to rejoice yet? I am so tired of being disappointed. So, please angels, I know you hate to spoil the ending for me but can you tell me something happy and hopeful? I hate uncertainty!

Angels: Write to us a little more about this — you have some thoughts to express.

I could take myself in hand and manage my mood using my spiritual skills. Yes, I could do that. But sometimes, I just want comforting. At what point do I draw the line between being independent: "I can manage that myself! I'm a big girl!" and turning to you for a hug? I can see that I may grow out of some needs as I grow stronger.

Angels: You're happier already just writing to us, thinking it through and making it concrete by putting it in writing. That's half the battle. As for managing your moods yourself, versus coming to us for comfort, that is up to you! We love to help, love to comfort, love to love. You're still struggling with human beliefs of limitation in love, and that colors your expectation. We are infinite, dear, and our love is infinite. You will not grasp this in your lifetime; it is beyond you. In the meantime a good guideline is just always be gentle; no matter what the circumstances. What can you do to be gentle to yourself right now?

Give myself permission to cry. But…the Internal Editor is too strong, so I'll bottle it up. But – how can I be gentle with myself, if I don't really know what that means?

Angels: We're here to teach and remind you! Tiny steps, small victories.

You know, I'm not completely dippy – I have been trying to pay attention to the signs, and friends.

It seems the last oracle card reading is truer and truer: *Sign*, *Friends*, and *Celebration*! Celebration for the Florida property, friends in these kind people I just met – as well as dear Margaret – and signs.

I've just received an email from Margaret in Florida, describing a bald eagle sighting right over her car!

I looked up the power animal meaning: "…The universe is presenting you with an opportunity to soar above the mundane levels of your life…feed your soul… you are put on notice to reconnect with the element of Air."

I love Margaret's excited comment: "CAN YOU STAND IT!!"

Angels, please tell me more about these powerful friends and signs that have landed in my lap saying *"look at me."*

Angels: Ah, our first smile in a long time — bravo, darling girl. Yes, you want to celebrate, and the messages say go, but the human details haven't quite clicked into place yet. This is not important. We have much bigger plans for you, ways of soaring and flying and celebrating which have only begun to begin. You feel confused because your feet are still on the ground, your horizon is low and level, and so you don't understand all this talk of Soaring and Creative Forces of the Great Spirit. Nor do you understand Margaret's giddiness — you wish you could feel her joy, but you don't. You have a mortgage to pay, a job to go to, body and soul to keep together — mundanity, in short. Stay the course, darling child. Get yourself back to kundalini yoga and start refining your whole being again. We'll help you get there — your schedule and life logistics baffle you sometimes. Please do sit in places of worship, and see what rises. Resolving your major debts will clear out old energy and create room for all kinds of good things. You will feel so much lighter! Everything is in place, all is on track, everything is good and right and becoming more miraculous by the day. Bear with these little ups and downs a little while longer — healing is here and all around you — meet us halfway by continuing to practice all your skills.

Thank you so much for these true words. It's just…many times I pretend to be cheerful or happy, because it is expected of me. But I know that if I had that clear wellspring of true joy back, everything else would be immaterial. So please, Angels, please just heal me and bring my joy back, the fizzing, spontaneous joy I had so many years ago, while I was still single. Please?

Angels: Dear child, it is I, Michael. We will restore your joy. You are a child of light, returning to the light. There is no doubt this will happen. There is a reason things happen in the sequence they do, which we cannot explain to you. This is why we ask you to manage your states and emotions, as a way of helping you until the deep clear true joy comes back. Can you trust us, and keep working with us? We are smiling at you, brave girl and precious child of light. You are very close to feeling us. That will make all the difference! Come, take our hands! We will lead you into sweet sleep.

Yes, I will. I get caught between trying too hard, not trying at all, being confused, being too hard on myself, and a whole bunch of other states which you know about. Which also has the effect of driving me into the refuge of meditation, which may be the goal in the first place. Thank you, Michael. I am back to my state of fatigue, which I recognize by now is not a good place from which to communicate.

Good night, Angels...

Taking Charge of Your Own Story Line

Sunday, January 8, 2012
Dear Angels
A sleepy, quiet Sunday morning, sitting propped up in my bed in the weak sunshine. All is silent, as I sit here reviewing possibilities for the day.

Yesterday, listening to the car radio on my driving errands to the transfer station and the library, I heard a woman narrating her story on NPR. She was Southern and sassy – the storyline was about how she had observed other people's experiences, and decided for herself exactly what her experience (in this case, losing her virginity) would be. She said she wanted her story to be *juicy*, real, not some flimsy, inadequate, awkward event. So, she took charge. At the age of 22, she had a very clear idea of the kind of man she wanted, and she held that idea in her head. Circumstances fed just the right man into her life, but it wasn't until he showed up at work wearing a trench coat (one of her conditions for sexiness) that she perked up and took notice. Then, she methodically set her plan into motion – slowly, carefully, she would edge closer to him, touch him lightly, or kiss him goodnight in a friendly way. Then, she plotted the date – it turned out he was being transferred out of town in a few weeks, which would solve the question of awkwardness afterwards. And then, she invited him in for coffee one night, and made her move. He was shocked, but did he ever respond – he figured it out fast. And that was it – she lost her virginity in the best way possible, on her terms, and with a juicy story as a result – which was exactly what she wanted in the first place – to take control of her destiny. It seems that the main thing in the entire process was that she got *clear*. She made a crystal-clear decision, with an inner knowing, about what she wanted. Everything proceeded from there.

I am intrigued by this story. What a message! It makes me realize how rarely in my life I have been crystal clear about anything, and how lucky I am that I haven't drifted into worse things, because I have drifted, a lot. I'm drifting now, the externals of my life in place, but with no real inside passion to help me create my own story.

It was clear that the narrator above was also working in perfect partnership with guidance, though she did not realize it. Angels, what do I need to do to jumpstart my passion and take charge of my own juicy story?

Angels: We're working on it! Now the idea is planted, and you're going to start thinking about this concept of taking charge of your own story line, with us to help you. Isn't that what has been happening all along? You're simply becoming more aware and conscious of it. The one area you need help in most is your physical health—your energy levels are low at the moment, and we just need to find ways to raise them. You know what to do, and you're doing it. You are a little discouraged because at 51, you are starting to encounter signs of aging, which frustrates your expectations of your abilities, as well as your real need to accomplish daily tasks. You may have to step up the vitamin supplements, and yes, stop caffeine and sugar altogether. Try it for a week and see if it makes a difference. We are sorry if it means losing your treasured ritual of coffee and tea—this is a serious blow to humans, who count on their ritual comforts. But we will help you to find something better to replace it.

As for the juicy story, it is all unfolding. Selecting and purchasing a new car was a practice run, which will give you confidence. You're already in active partnership with us—you're gold!

Thank you for working with me and reminding me. All I can do is wait, practice my disciplines, and see what each day brings. Thank you, angels.

Friday, January 13, 2012, at the office
Dear John and the Angels,
Please note the above date. It is very much Friday the 13th. Today was going just fine, until this afternoon...and...oh, help.

One of the clients (whom I shall call Sue) is an angry, bullying woman who enjoys manipulating people. She is emotionally unstable, and has harassed numerous employees over the years. I had to meet her at the apartment today, and all the way there I was asking for protection, chanting *sat-siri, siri-akal*, etc. I showered blessings on her. Once at the house I tried to breathe deeply and keep blessing her. When we finished the tour of the house she verbally attacked me and aggressively demanded to know why this, why that. I felt cornered; I lost my temper and raised my voice. She immediately gloated: "You raised your voice to me!" she accused with an evil smirk. I apologized, but it was too late. She provoked me into saying unwise things. I came back to the office shaking with anger. This is horrible. Help.

Angels: First, let's calm you down a little so you can hear us better. We are all around you, soothing you and blessing you, and comforting you right now. Our poor child, this is very distressing. Help us by breathing deeply, that's it. This was not your fault. You know she is full of negative energy and everyone she encounters struggles to overcome revulsion. Use this incident as a chance to keep working on everything you know that needs healing. What are these feelings of revulsion, what do they mirror inside yourself? Let's go home and pour a wonderful glass of red wine, curl up with a book (maybe Radical Acceptance?) and move forward. There is deep fear in you still, and you noticed how quickly she triggered you. Can you possibly entertain the idea that this woman was sent to you, so that you could learn from her? This is a big point to understand, unpleasant as it is.

Sigh, *aaah*, this is work! It would be so easy just to keep calling her names, a mean, squint-eyed pig of a cow, that would feel so good. But that is not the way it works with you, is it? And I am so tired, too. This is tough, to the degree that this woman has a truly awful personality. Ick. Ick. Ick! I don't see where I am going to find the courage to figure this out. But you are right, let me get out of here and go home to refuge, and we can take this up again. Is that why you wouldn't/couldn't protect me against her — because I needed this encounter, this contrasting situation? *Ewww.*

Angels: You are so funny with your expressions of disgust! We are laughing at you. Yes, child, some things we stand by and watch over — actually, we stand by and watch over ALL

things — but must let you have the full experience for yourself, for the growth of your soul.
Trust the pain, it will bring good things to you, and we will help you to understand as you
go. Now, homeward?

Yes please, help me close up quickly and get out of here. There
have been howling, buffeting, ferocious winds all day, and it is an
unfriendly, cold and dark night. I need to be home...thank you so
much angels, you have calmed me down a lot.

January 12, 2012, 8:00 pm
Dear Angels,
Some dinner, a glass of wine later...I am curled up in front of the fire
re-reading *Radical Acceptance*, and thinking through this anger-fear-
triggering incident.

I need to go to bed immediately, but there was one more thing I
wanted to write to you about. Last night I stayed up reading a
mediocre murder mystery – stayed up way too late, finished it at
3:00 am. Not good.

But this morning, just as I was surfacing from sleep, I had an image
from a dream come to me vividly:

I was with several English police detectives, and we were standing
around a small pond, which had been completely drained of water.
We were staring down at the revealed muddy bottom. All was empty,
except for one thing. The drained pond revealed, stuck squishily in
the center, a large, heavy, rounded metal weight, embedded in the
mud, perhaps 3' in diameter or smaller. It was solid iron or lead, and
could have been used as a mooring weight, or some such thing. But
what popped into my mind immediately, was that this was precisely
the metaphor describing me: sleuthing and detective work to uncover
my inner being, my soul, slowly draining away the detritus and muck
to see what was at the bottom, only to have my hard detective work
rewarded by finding the last, single, giant condition or solid issue in

my body of water. This, then, was what I needed to solve, finally – this was the heart and soul of the problem, the giant brown iron weight in the muck.

So as the detectives in the dream stood looking at it, wondering what to do to levitate it, so do I stare at this scary, muddy brown mess and wonder how to levitate it.

What a brilliant dream image, so literal. It suddenly made me realize why I've loved detective stories all these years: it mirrors my own inner sleuthing, literally and figuratively. And here is my horoscope for the day – word for word. I rest my case:

> January 13, 2012. Have you been reading a lot of Agatha Christie or PD James novels lately? Because when a doozy of a mystery has everyone scratching their heads today, you'll be able to see right past the red herrings, make sense of obscure clues, and discover the truth. You're especially perceptive and meticulous today, so consider applying these skills to a personal mystery that has been vexing you lately. A face-to-face conversation is the only suitable way to gather more evidence.

Well, Angels, I guess the face-to-face conversation was my encounter with the client. Yuck, gathering more evidence. And I have come such a long way in accepting these things – these energies – that it doesn't even strike me as strange that the horoscope should be so precise, to the day.

*Angels: You are the heroine of your own story, and you are winning through. You have put all the clues together and you are solving the mystery of your life, moment by moment, encounter by encounter. You have no idea of how brave and true and heroic you are. We are **so** proud of you, we love you dearly and cherish the direct way you work with us. This is rare and special. Stay the course, ask us to help every day, and magic will continue to flow into your life, we promise. Now please turn in so that we can rise to a beautiful new day, for more adventures! **We love you!***
The Angels and your beloved John

Monday, January 16, 2012, 1:05 pm
Dear Angels,
Last night's kundalini class was powerful – gentle, subtle, moving.
I am sure something shifted.

Where were we? Oh, the question at hand – first the car purchase,
then the client Sue.

Angels, I am doing my best to continue the trajectory of purchasing
a 2012 VW Golf TDI, manual transmission, in graphite blue, for as
low a price as possible, and with few or no attached fees. I'm slowly
chugging away – I am at the stage of talking to friends, estimating the
calendar time, and figuring out final negotiating point and logistics.
I have come light years from one year ago, when I was petrified by the
prospect. Please take over from here, grease the wheels of the process,
and get me behind the steering wheel of that car as quickly as possible,
and tell me anything I should know about this final stretch.

*Angels: Barbara dear, all is well. You know this, of course, and your confidence in the
process, and in yourself, shows how much you have grown. We are **very** proud of you.
Thank you for coming to us with this list of your completion details. This is play for us, and off
we go to arrange matters to your best interest. Yes, you have just a touch of resistance left,
and the final jump puts you into new territory. If you feel that come up, just ask us to
transmute it or help you release it. Otherwise, just be ready! We'll make things happen
beautifully, and we cannot wait to take your first drive in your very own, brand new car.
You will appreciate this car until the end of your ownership, since you put so much hard
work into it. And, you are now in an excellent position to help and advise other people.
Isn't that a good feeling?*

Yes, it is a good feeling; and also knowing that I can sell my current
car with peace of mind because I've had so many repairs done.

I see that the process of researching a new car has very little to do with
the car itself. It became a matrix, a template, for me to work with you
angels, work through doubts and fears, and start relearning tiny steps
of faith. It was all about the process, not about the car...once again

you've shown me the metaphysical behind the physical, and my role in things, by way of using willpower in conjunction with turning things over to you, to affect the outcome. How am I doing?

*Angels: Spot on, as the English say. Additionally, you have a **record** of every stage, which, when you look back at it, will constitute proof, and provide evidence of your spiritual growth.* **We love you!**

I must come up with a better adjective than "wow." But this partnership structure is just so… extraordinary, I may never get used to it, and I hope it always awes me. Thank you.

January 18, 2012
Dear Angels,
Things are heating up. I don't know if I'll even be able to write to you much in coming days. Angels, I am tired just looking at my to-do list. Please take over and give me wings to fly through this complicated time.

Angels: Darling girl, we are always here for you and we love love love it when you ask. We know how busy and distracted you are, and what we would remind you is that in the middle of your busyness the best possible thing to do is to stop and ask for help. We wish for nothing better! We are working on your list and will absolutely wing you through your exciting days to come. You are performing like a star and you need do nothing more. Let's start right in with getting back to marketing those properties — we can do a little more before the end of the day. If it's nice enough, you could go for a walk when you get home. This is medicine for your soul, sunsets and winter breezes. One more hour, and we're away!

Love,
The Angels

PS We are very proud of you for making the appointment with Carrie at the auto dealership. It is indeed time for action, and the time is ripe. Excitement!

January 25, 2012
Entries from an Angelspeake class with Stephanie:

"Angels bring a special feeling or knowing that everything is going to
be okay. This feeling takes away our immediate fear and worry and
puts us into a state of hope. This positive feeling also helps us send
comforting thoughts to those around us who are afraid."
Barbara Mark and Trudy Griswold

*Angels: We love you and we want you to know that...you are a child of God, and we love
you. We are so happy that you are here in Stephanie's Angelspeake class. Thank you for
blessing your classmates. We are here with you now, as always. The Angels*

"Working with your angel is easy. Just ask them for what you need help
with. Believe they are going to do it. Allow them to do what angels do
and then say thank you for the results."
Barbara Mark and Trudy Griswold, The Angelspeake Storybook

Dear Angels,
How I can access higher states of consciousness to do greater good?

*You are well on the path. Trust and keep having patience and asking us questions as
you go. You are a true friend to those you love and you will use your influence to guide
and teach them. This is how we will use you. You will have much joy in sharing your
knowledge. The path can be fun, too, it is important to mix it up with joy as you spread
light. Being here in this class is an important step — continue! We will place the stepping
stones in front of you every day. Lovely Barbara, keep smiling for us and thank you for
writing to us! Love, The Angels*

(same evening)
Wednesday, January 25, 2012, 11:05 pm
Dear Angels,
It is way past my bedtime and I have to be up at 6:00 tomorrow, ready
for my big day with the architect and her entourage.

Just back from the Angelspeake class. So helpful, fascinating, cool.
Stephanie is extraordinary the way she downloads your guidance.

My reading was interesting, so I wanted to find out a little more, please. The teacher was getting something about Earth stewardship and the larger planetary picture. Another student was getting a strong message that he had to talk to me about the unseen, subtle beings in nature, what we call elementals, devas, the fairy realm, and shamanism.* This is surprising...I mean, it interests me, but I don't necessarily have a strong tug towards it. Please tell me more about these spiritual beings and how I can start to sense them or work with them.

Angels: Hooray! We're here and we love you! This is very exciting. The devas and elementals want very much to talk to you. You have a precious skill of communicating which we wish to use for the higher good. We will tell you what to write when the time comes. Please bring your paper and pen outdoors and write to us there, as often as you can. This is just an aspect of your life that is developing — much more is underway.

Why do I have no success hearing or connecting with the devas and elementals? I mean, I can hear you angels just fine. Or is my expectation of instant communication too high, like it was in the book *The Elves of Lily Hill Farm*?

Angels: You must make time to sit quietly. They are there, they know you are trying. Sometimes just the willingness doesn't guarantee a clear signal. And yes, your old habits and thought patterns relative to your garden are very task-oriented, very do-do-do. Not much simple appreciation. This is what we mean by going back to basics — you have to unlearn your horticultural training — perhaps just a little.

Angels, you know quite well that one of the greatest sadnesses of my life happened the day when I woke up one morning at age 44 and my fierce gardening passion and fizz and joy was *gone*. Poof. Like that. The daily joy and thrill of all things botanical, horticultural and plant-related just disappeared – the green magic disappeared from my fingers and my heart. I can garden now, yes, but it is very flat for me. The living connection is gone. I have never understood why this major life force disappeared overnight. I am just puzzled by all of this, as well as deeply sad, which I try to be brave about.

*Shamans and shamanism: A shamanic practioner uses traditional healing energies to access the spirits of the natural world, and often works with totems or power animals.

Angels: Our dear child, trust us! Life, joy and love of green and growing things is only dormant, not gone. We are wakening you. Human "trying" is important and valuable but sometimes misapplied. Sleep now — we will come to you in your dreams — thank you for asking us. Big day tomorrow — we wish to help, so ask ask ask and we are there! We love you, our greenfingered goddess!
The Angels

Know Your Value

Thursday, January 26, 2012, 5:10 pm
Dear Angels,
The strangest thing happened today: *everything went well.* Today was supposed to be the crazy, circus-act day when the visiting professionals came to meet with the construction contractor and city arborist, but it multiplied and expanded and grew until we (we, meaning *me*) were planning for eight people for coffee and twelve for lunch, including the mayor, two city councilors, and two directors, but whoosh! It all worked like a charm. The energy was productive and cheerful, and it didn't have that fraught quality that board meetings usually do.

I could tell you were in charge of the day, because 1) I was calm, happy, and centered throughout; 2) even though the agenda for the day was tossed out and I had to guess about everything; 3) it all just *flowed*; 4) the irritating logistical details didn't bother me a bit; and 5) I was actually quite productive in my own right – got a lot accomplished.

I am witness to this day, and angels, I have to hand it to you. When you take charge, it is a beautiful sight to see. Even the director grudgingly admitted that the day went well. Not only that, but there were zero mentions of our company or the park project in the paper or in social media – not even a tweet. This is unheard of, as the protesters have been active in their attacks lately. So I just wanted to say, thank you for this excellent day. I've been talking to you all day, and you've answered all my prayers. You know, a girl could get used to this. I feel almost as though last night's energy is carrying over into today - please tell me more.

Angels: Dear child, we are so happy to be of service, it was a joy to be included in the creation of this day's work. You may think it ordinary, but magic is happening right under your nose. You sense the creativity and increasing excitement of the team, and you sensed the consensus building and agreement making that also occurred. This is what human beings do at some of their highest levels, and yes, you were witness to it. We could not have stepped in had you not invited us to, so we would like to thank you! Your role in this is pivotal, more so than you will ever know. Do not be modest about accepting credit for your ideas or participation — know your value. You have tasted the success of co-creation with us and found it sweet — let us do this every day! We can make your life this beautiful every day, and more so. You now also know what skills and practices bring you to a state of openness, invitation, clear knowing, and peaceful acceptance, that transmutes energy continually. Flex these new muscles and magic is yours to have every day. You know you know you know you know! Is it not a luscious feeling? It is hard earned, sweet one, and we love you more than ever. Bless you for writing to us. Shall we go home and celebrate with a glass of wine in front of the fire? You deserve this comforting rest!

You put things so beautifully. How far I have come from the frightened girl I was a year ago – not that it doesn't still happen – but my foundation of love and understanding is growing stronger. Thank you for this day of excellence.

February 2, 2012, 1:50 pm at work
Dear Angels,
The changes are all happening fast, and I am fielding them (I think). Ever since reading *Conversations with God* by Neal Donald Walsch [Ed: commonly abbreviated as CWG], there has been a new voice in my awareness. Tends to be on the left side, and it comes through pretty clearly. Now there are three energies to communicate with, all at different levels, so between you, John, and God, so I feel like I'm at a cocktail party. I am trying to get used to all of this, and it helps to

ground me just to talk to you on paper, because you are a known and comforting presence. Not that God isn't but it's just new territory and I am peeking out from behind your skirts, if you know what I mean.

Between my fuzzy fatigue and all the things zooming at me today, I just needed some reassurance from you. Can you just say hi and tell me how I'm doing?

Angels: Blessed child, it is our delight and privilege to come say hello, and lift your spirits with love and encouragement. Yes! We are sending you client prospects, just as you requested! Don't be surprised when you succeed, this is how it works, quite directly. Taking time out to write to us is the best thing you could have done for yourself today. You get so busy...we miss our chats and your searches for answers to your questions. You are building strength upon strength, and one day soon you will be comfortable enough to talk to God directly without "peeking out from behind our skirts" — but we love the image, and we LOVE you, and please always always always write to us if there is ever any doubt. Yes, you are having amazing days now, they will increase and become more consistent as you leave your fears behind. Experiencing true confidence is a blast! We enjoy your enjoyment of it. Are you feeling better now, dear child?

Ahh. Yes, *much* better, thank you so much. This life I lead is my own personal jigsaw puzzle, and every day it is a challenge to fit the pieces in. I see now that if I want to do it all, then I have to really participate in this partnership and increase the frequency of high-energy-high-clarity days. What a difference in the quality of my life. So, Angels, thank you again for winging me along on this breathless path.

Tomorrow is a very big day, starting with a breakfast meeting at 8:30, and finishing with a Beppe Gambetta concert at 8 pm. Lots of blessings! And hopefully, a slightly lazy weekend. And one of these days, my new car should be coming in – this must happen soon!

Angels: As you say, lots and lots of blessings! Don't forget to think about making an appointment with Stephanie. And we would definitely encourage you to sign up for the Guru Singh weekend at Kripalu. Oh, the flying has not begun to begin. Come soar with us, we will show you how!
Love,
The Angels, God, and your beloved John

I Bought the Car!

February 5, 2012

Dear Angels, I just wrote down a wonderful dream I had about driving my grandmother's big blue bouncy 1950's Plymouth, which I remember so vividly from my childhood. I think I got all of the metaphors right, but could you please give me more interpretation if there is something more I should know?

Angels: Happy Sunday! The sun is up and it is a beautiful day to be outside. We were so happy outdoors with you yesterday in the garden. We love to help and guide you with this so please ask us to do anything!

About the dream, blue is an important color for you. This is our happy dream to send you, telling you that everything is going well and will continue to go well, that you can take your foot off the brake a little, that ancestors are indeed smiling down on you, that cars have a more significant role in your life than you know. This is also a good metaphor for your upcoming purchase, to let you know that your new VW Golf is so right for you, also blue! And you are carrying on a tradition of good cars in your family. There is nothing to fear! Proceed bravely and with confidence! Ignore all that does not serve you! Enjoy the delicious sensation of being in control of your little craft! Be grateful for safety and the open road! And above all, know that we are flying with you, enjoying your enjoyment of the journey — so enjoy. Blessings of a safe and fantastic journey upon you, dear child. Let us go play in the garden on this wonderful new day!
Love, The Angels

Tuesday, February 7, 2012, 8:45 pm
It's a miracle. It is achieved, completed, executed, acquired, transacted.

I BOUGHT THE CAR!

There is now this miraculous, gorgeous, adorable, high-tech miracle of German engineering sitting in MY driveway. Yes, Angels:

a 2012 VW Golf TDI in graphite blue with manual transmission and HEATED SEATS.

My perfect, ideal, dream car!

I am in awe, dumbstruck (not really), pinching myself, tickled, appalled, afraid, astonished, delighted, and at the same time, nothing has ever felt so right or perfect for me. And what is more outrageous, is the feeling that rings through me over and over again: *I deserve this. I am ready for this. This is right and true and excellent, exactly as it should be.*

And so much goodness and abundance is a little terrifying when one is used to lack and self-limiting thoughts.

It's a miracle, a graphite-blue miracle, and I am dancing inside.

So thank you, everyone. Thank you for walking me through this last year, thank you for accompanying me on my rollercoaster ride of shrieking highs and cursing lows. Thank you for everything you have done to lead me to this point of new-car-acquisition.

This is all so wild, this day, this night, this point in time. Tonight there was a luminous full moon rising over the bay, as I drove across the bridge at 5:30, full of gratitude, astonishment, and a tickly sense of terror of *oh-shit-what-have-I-done?*

The contrast, you see, is so extreme, between my former car and this gleaming, automotive minx that I find am straddling two identities. But not for long, oh NO. No, I am taking to this little minx like a duck to water. There is something bold about claiming the right to luxury – it is a mental shift.

So, God, please tell me: is this your idea of magnificence? It's pretty magnificent for me. I am trying not to use the w-word (wow). Okay, I'll let you answer now. Oh, Angels, I am so happy. Thank you. You knew this was going to be good, didn't you? So let's do it again. Keep the miracles coming — we're having fun! Blessings upon me and everyone. Joy joy joy joy. Angels rock!

*Angels: Please keep writing, keep going, keep celebrating in your heart. This is our loving partnership, our gift to you, proof that together you will work miracles with us that manifest on earth. Now you know how it is done, now you will do it faster and faster, will have fewer doubts and fears, will come to us continually with joy in your heart and a song of gratitude for this precious life. Blessed child, do indeed count the days from that very first evening, less than one year ago, that you first wrote to us. If such transformation is possible in one year, what can we accomplish in the next 12 months or less? You are the miracle, and you know it not. Celebrate yourself, your strength, beauty, courage, intelligence, commitment, openness, honesty, passion! Celebrate your human ups and downs — do you not laugh at your past extremes of emotions, and do you see now how precious they are? You can only go from strength to strength from now on. How we appreciate your jumble of feelings, and we **love you more than ever**. It is such a privilege for us to guide you and participate in your triumph.*

Bad pun, it's not a Triumph, it's a VW...

*Angels: ...and even more your silly plays on words. Miracles abound, oh how we love granting them and **feeling** your appreciation. Let us go forward and find new horizons together. What next, precious oh precious Barbara of ours?*

Well! If it is going to be like this, then bring on the marching band! Let's see, next, please help me think of a very beeyootiful gift for my friends Prim and Jerry, to thank them for their help. Then, please help me focus on selling my old car immediately, for the highest possible price. Please move the dear old car along to its next grateful owner.

Right now, my blessed friends, there is nothing I wish for. All is perfect and sublime. Full February moon smiling down on a minxy little VW Golf in my driveway. Sweet cosmic perfection. I love you, Angels, and God, and John! I love the world at this moment.

Tomorrow I will ask you to help me become familiar with this high-tech stranger, and learn my way around all the controls. Then... just enjoying the bliss bliss bliss!

Angels: pen down, sweet dreams, let us plot and scheme merriment tomorrow! Your beloved friends, John and the Angels. Oh, and God, too.

February 9, 2012, 4:50 pm
Dear Angels,
So, my wishes have come true. I did actually experience an entire day
at work, which was peaceful, with zero interruptions, not much work
on my plate, few emails, no demands, and just one or two phone calls.
I am scratching my head – this is downright peculiar. Other staff are
having the same experience. And I LOVE it.

The weather is mild, the sun is out, so I took a drive down Grande
Avenue to show a friend my new car, and we strolled around the
grounds of the estate, and looked at the nubs of green coming up in the
early-spring garden. It was good to catch up with her. Then back to the
office, tootling down the avenue with no traffic and the late winter sun
gleaming off everything. These days are all about my new car, however.
I adore but *adore* my sound system (blasting Buena Vista Social Club
while flying over the bridge!), I am enchanted by the color, its lines,
its muscular, high tech driving style and transmission, its interior –
everything. I hope this wonder and appreciation never fade.

This was an enormous hurdle, and I am now somewhat breathlessly on
the other side. What I realized today, Angels, is that we're at the point
of "Next!" so that I can keep expanding my horizon with your help and
partnership. Quite miraculous, this system. Therefore, please help me
sell the dear old car quickly, easily, and for the highest price possible;
and THEN…let's talk about what's next. Right?

Angels: Didn't we tell you, you would fly and soar with us? So we build your trust and
fearlessness, little by little. We are so delighted at your delight, this is all we ask. We are
excited at your excitement, and are always ready to help you move into the next state of
magnificence. You're starting to get it! Blessed child, let us wing home with you and finish
the week with a flourish. Take your dear friend Anne for a ride and perhaps we can walk by
moonlight later? You can never have too much fresh air. Oh, how we love love love you,
precious child of light. Off we go! Love, The Angels

Chapter V: Stretching for the Light

We bring you the power to understand your power.
– THE ANGELS

This Is Creation!

Wednesday, February 15, 2012, 8:00 pm
Dear Angels,
I have had my beautiful, excellent new car for just over one week
now, and I still actively enjoy it, and marvel at this new level of
luxury in my life. It seems so adult to treat myself *very* well. It is a
tangible manifestation of my own inner attitude shift. I feel like
I've finally joined The Grownups.

As mentioned before, now that the car is achieved, I also have a
sudden sense of a new, clear horizon before me, beckoning with its
next-ness. And what is rising up, rather terrifyingly, is the vision of
a bookstore of my own with an attached conservatory. Last night I sat
here in bed surrounded by magazines and scribble pads; I chewed
on a pencil, and dreamt of names for my bookstore. I cut out pretty
photos and brainstormed the emotional quality it should have, drew
diagrams and bubble-idea-flow-charts.

This was all just play, but then I made a list of tangible things I could
do today, like looking up and printing out info on a property on
Maple Avenue which has been on the market for 2 years – which I did.
Ping, click, pop, print – ooops, there it is. I looked at that printout
and realized, *this isn't play*. This could be real.

This is just how my new car started. *Gulp.*

Then today, I called my friend Annie, who knows about my shy dream of a bookstore, and asked her if I could look at a property on Greene Street without wasting a broker's time. We both understood that this is just brainstorming, and so we let the idea sit, simmer, and...er...germinate.

Here we are again, angels! Back at the creative cauldron, peering inside and facing down fears, doubts and uncertainties. If I may?...Eeeeek!

Ah, that feels better. Please tell me everything is fine and wonderful, that you're going to guide the heaven out of me, and oh, what NEXT?

Angels: Which question shall we answer first?

Well, the surface issues are always roiling around fears. A big part of me knows that I just need to proceed as-if, and each step will be placed before me as I go. Like the magical stairs at Hogwarts Castle. So, my first question to you would be, please transmute my fears so I can proceed with confidence. Taking true charge of one's dreams is alarming. No wonder so many people choose to play it safe. Please tell me what some next steps might be.

Angels: We're so excited with you and for you. Trust us, this will be wonderful fun. You have a very special role to play, and you are the heroine of your own story. You can even track the development of your own courage when you go back and re-read your entries. What a miracle, what a blessing! We laugh and laugh, because we use phrases like "all good things are coming to you now" or "blessings are raining down upon you," but you are only just barely beginning to understand the literal sense of these. You are an expanding sun, and ever-cresting wave — there is no end. So yes, back to play and creation and that glorious beckoning horizon.

You feel yourself in a little bit of muddy-mindedness, like choppy seas with too many currents. Yes, much is converging, so you will continue to manage many, many things. Take this process slowly, and trust your impulses. Especially focus on the part you love, like researching new books. Get the database started, that is a very good exercise which will always feel like play to you. Do what you know best: make lists, break them into components just as you did today, and enjoy the process of shopping, researching, creation. Surrender all your fears to us, get lots and lots of sleep (please!), and sit up and take notice when an angel-sent event or person comes your way with exactly the right message. You are already seeing synchronicity all around you, so our play-partnership is well assured.

What I come up against are these two separate ways of viewing it: 1) it's pretend, not real, will never happen, and therefore SAFE; 2) this is real, will really happen, and is therefore SCARY.

Attitude one denies that it will happen, but keeps me in a play-pretend zone, where I'm free to dream.

Attitude two, recognition of this as a real-life possible event, hamstrings me with concerns about money, resources, income, livelihood, survival, success – and hampers the creative side.

So...I guess I will just notice when these two sides are operating – or which side is operating – and call you in as soon as I notice fear creeping in. Is that right? I mean, that's about all I can do.

Angels: Now we're talking! How we love love love you. Excellence is only more excellent as we go, yes indeed, and there she goes, transcribing like a dream. Dear Barbara, joy of our hearts, there is a troop at your beck and call, no fear at all, wonders will rain down. If it helps you to get clear, meet with Stephanie and see what she can share.

Yes, there is an angel for everything, including bookstores and conservatories. You do not need to know the name yet — we are taking this in tiny steps, right? Your anxiety creeps in when you think you must do something the "right" way and give it names.

For now, sleep,
For now, dream,
For now, smile for us and pick up the pen again and again and again!

Yes, we like the name "Jungle Books" as a name for the store. Tee hee!
Goodnight, our little Mowgli –
Love,
The Angels

February 16, 2012, 3:50 pm
Dear Angels,
Here I am, showing up, on a drab, flat overcast February day. My best
bet is to turn to you, listen and listen again, ask and ask again. Angels,
let us continue the conversation about this pipedream of mine, the
bookstore-conservatory. What other steps would you suggest that I take?

*Angels: Shift your focus, find things to be grateful about. Choose different thoughts;
transform the day into one of energy, light and joy. You can indeed do it! Remember your
clarity and happiness this morning. All changes in the blink of an eye — you merely have the
illusion of pinning it down because you happen to be writing at this moment. But you are
our wise child, and we so appreciate the chance to communicate with you! You are doing
just fine in pursuing small items on your list, and above all, in beginning to carry the IDEA
about with you at all times. It is starting to color your choices and your outlook. **This is
creation!** You are a star! The rest is coloring in the outlines. Let this gently evolve so that
it always gives you pleasure in the dreaming of it. Nothing more is necessary (you have to
leave a few things for us to do!).*

Tell me, angels, will realizing this dream feel as good as the heated
seats in my VW Golf?

Angels: Better!

Saturday, February 18, 2012, 8:10 pm
Dear Angels,
Thank you so much for helping me check off all of the items on my
to-do list today.
Today at the library I picked up *The Art of Dreaming* by Carlos Casteneda,
and have read a little bit of it this evening. It is hopelessly esoteric,
over my head but I have to try it, at least.

*Angels: That is what we love about you (among other things) — how hard you try in spite of
knowing you'll only ever have a dim grasp of the enormities that Our Energies represent, in
your lifetime. Yes, we reach you through many mediums, which you know, and books work
beautifully, so we do indeed guide you to them. What would you like to know about this title?*

I am fascinated by the Casteneda. Angels, is there information in this book that you think it would be helpful for me to apply?

Angels: **It is I, Uriel.** *Blessed child, glory of our hearts, how magnificent it is to communicate with thee. May your pen flee across the paper like lightning. We are guiding you slowly, gently, carefully. The Casteneda is not meant to be digested in the space of one evening. Already you discern that this realm of energy bodies, shifts, second attention, and dreaming awareness can open portals which let other energies through, and this is not to be trifled with by the uninitiated. Yet you are curious, and wonder if you could attempt any of these practices. We say to you, sound your motives first. Curiosity is not enough. Commitment to the process is better. If you* **do** *practice any of the dream awareness techniques, please always ask for our guidance and protection before you go to sleep. Make a deliberate practice of it, and do it on a day when you have purified yourself with yoga, kriya, chanting, and meditation. If your mind is not pure the energies you attract may not be beneficent. We wouldn't send you this book if you were not ready for it, so have confidence and faith, both in yourself and in US. Make the angels your partners in dreaming as well as in waking. Actively invite us in.*

Above all, be gentle with yourself and do this only as it feels natural, not as a "must-get-to-next-level-of-enlightenment" practice.

You know not how many threads you already hold in your hand, and have but to weave them together to see the pattern. Trust trust trust! The fog is lifting, the sun is starting to peek out — can you stand the full blaze of glory intended for you? Beloved child, does this answer your question?

Uriel, thank you so much. Sometimes – to use the fog metaphor – I feel as though it is starting to burn off, whether I want it to or not. Just do hand me some of that Celestial Bain de Soleil, won't you? I'd hate to be enlightened with a peeling nose.

Uriel: Ho ho ho! This is excellently funny, adored girl! We will shade you with our wings, they are **very** *large! End of page, end of question, for now — end of evening — we must tuck you up now, you resist sensible bedtimes and this can be continued tomorrow. Good night and sweet, sacred dreams!*

February 22, 2012, 4:55 pm
Dear Angels,
Ah, I knew the peace and quiet was too good to last. The director
went to an environmental meeting with the DEM today. He came back
spitting nails, disgusted and discouraged. Apparently the protesters have
been harassing the environmental consultants, so they are interpreting
their soil test findings as conservatively as possible, fearful of a lawsuit
or public outcry, despite our assurances that the protesters are a total
of only two very confused people. Thus, it appears that our company
may be in for an expensive site remediation of $100,000 or more.
The director stormed out of my office saying "I rue the day I ever heard
of this project!" Ow. Then Mindy leapt to his defense, angrily calling
the project a fiasco. We're back to battling serious negativity and poor
attitudes. Please help me – what can I do?

*Angels: You've been so far away all day, we cherish it when you lend your attention to us again!
This is not as dire as it seems; it is more of an emotional setback for your colleague than a true
setback in reality. You went straight to work on another grant proposal — excellent! Your own
attitude is calm and sensible; you can see clearly where others cannot. As you did before, rain
blessing upon this, and especially upon your opponents. Just as with the situation in Florida,
be prepared for a surprise when the energy starts loosening up around this. Stay the course,
you're almost there. Whether or not this project succeeds has little to do with what you
experience through it. So, remain calm, centered, happy, and do your deskwork. Ask ask ask,
and we will flock around you every minute to wing this through to its destined end.*

Thank you SO much! I know these things, but I need to hear them every
day. How short and impermanent human memory is. And now, Angels,
I am going to head home so I can go for a lovely long walk. Thank you.

February 23, 2012, 12:20 pm
Dear Angels,
I am beginning to hope that one day someone reads this narrative,
and finds it interesting. It will never match *The Berlin Diaries,** but I do

*An autobiography by Marie Vassiltchikov, based on her diaries, and detailing the final days of the German Third Reich
in Berlin.

see that having the urge to record events, and being the chosen one who sets them down, is a privilege.

The whole day dissolved into managing calls and emails from everywhere, as though everything had decided to spew. Oddly enough, I felt calm throughout it all, rather non-reactive for most of the day. I did start to feel like my old octopus-self for a couple of hours when I was just spinning from one phone call to the next and from one email to the next. Appliances, appointments, group tours, police officers, carpenters, gardeners, colleagues, real estate agents, smoke alarm people, the director about five times, reporters…paperwork mounting on my desk, all just *spewing*. And that doesn't even include all the personal calls, emails, and follow-ups I did today.

5:10 pm – It's all I can do to find a moment to continue writing this. It's *really* time to go home. Oh, Angels, I know I am on a special path here, but some days I have to scratch my head and say, why me?

Angels: You are our own darling girl, and we continue to be so proud of you. You had a strong, clear day today with more accomplished than you know. Being centered and calm in the middle of the storm is a powerful feeling. You are starting to pull your strengths together. Always recognize that there is a bigger picture, and yes, you are a very important cog in the wheel. Keep blessing, trusting, breathing, and maybe even smiling for us, beloved Barbara. Let us go home and enjoy this gorgeous spring-like evening.
Love,
The Angels

The Soul Always Comprehends: One Year Anniversary

Saturday, February 25, 2012, 6:30 pm
Dear God,
Well, I said I would write to you directly and I must be ready for it, because here I am, keeping our paper date. I am choosing tonight to celebrate – OH ANGELS – the one year anniversary of when I

first picked up pen, put it to paper, asked you a question, and my life changed *forever*. What a year. Am I different, have I changed? Definitely. I am calmer, happier, have more self-confidence, have lost some weight, and am getting better and better at choosing my emotions, words and deeds more carefully, *with your help*. I am awed by this partnership and this process, and am only just starting to see how much I still have to learn about trust, asking, making clear decisions, surrender, and the hardest part of all: letting Good flow into my life.

Dear God, happy anniversary. Let me write just a little more, and then I'll open the floor to you. I have two very sticky questions to ask.

I lied to my dear friend about my plans to go to a movie. Fortunately, another friend called me, and I was able to back-pedal and accept her earlier invitation to the movies – so I quasi-justified it to myself, or at least can say that I did see the movie. But as to 1) my guilt at having lied to a dear friend; and 2) the lie itself, I am in over my head. This was a lesson about how guilt compounds on itself. These items are so out of character for me (how lucky I am, I see that), and I am puzzled that I allowed such a situation to develop. What can you tell me about this mess?

God: Let's talk about this as if we're old and dear friends. There is much to address here: the initial incident, your reaction, your coping (or non-coping) with your aversion, the guilt that bred more guilt, and the consequence it had on your conversation today. Thank you for bringing this to me, it is the best thing you could have done. I do know you've wanted to unburden yourself of this for over a month. So let's take it piece by piece. I see into your heart, and I know you cherish your friendship with her, and preserving that friendship is a priority.

Please release your guilt, and I and the angels will transmute it for you. The best solution here is for you to have a very private, kind, caring, honest conversation. Ask us to help you schedule it, and we will be happy to make it happen, and see that it goes well. We will help her reach out to her angels, too. And do bless her in the days to come. You know this works! As for the lie, confess it to her. She will understand. She may be hurt, but you are too good a friend and too valuable to her on her path, for it not to be resolved and released.

I guess the chain of events, its confluence, and my (so I think) atypical reaction brings me up short, and forces me to examine my attitude and behavior. An ugly side of myself popped up and I couldn't shush it. What is this about?

God: How I love writing to you — this privilege is altogether mine, and I thank you for this opportunity! What this is about, is growth of the soul. You are infinite, dear child, but you don't know it. Every challenge will be presented to you as you have the strength to handle it. Your choices in the face of these opportunities determines your soul's growth. Nothing is typical, and every human, including you, is capable of the extreme opposite of love — which you know, is fear. Find the fear in the equation, and you have your answer. Find yourself in the person you despise, and face it.

But all of the spiritual literature carries on (and ON) about loving the self – which I have had a hard enough time doing to begin with. How can I face an ugly facet of myself, or my dark side, if I don't even care for myself that much to begin with? I could easily spiral into despair – as many people do. There is a point of no return, a point where I cannot hear you or the angels. You know this.

*God: You are desperate for comprehension, and I know that finding, achieving, having comprehension makes your human experience more bearable. Sometimes the comprehension will be possible, sometimes not. The soul, however, **always** comprehends. Join forces with your soul. Where there is no comprehension, ask for the strength to trust. Even despair has its time and place in the growth of the soul. Now that you have found Us — Me, and the angels — you have many more options than most people. Rather, you know about your options; many other people choose to ignore them.*

There is no need to talk to your soul, it is at one with you, and guides all that you do. Think of the moments in your life when you know the purest, clearest, deepest happiness, and that is your soul welling up. What you call your "joy."

I'm beginning to think this is one of those cases where there will be an absence of comprehension – oops, too bad! – my "joy" as you know, *fled* from me on that evil night years ago when a deep essence within me **died.** It was a physical sensation; something LEFT out of the top of my head, it flew right out, and in that split second, I became a shell of myself, a curl of ash left in an ashtray. We've been here before: you know I've been seeking reunification ever since. So you're telling me to be at one with something I don't even feel any more, haven't felt for decades. Oh, thank you so much. No comprende, and it's just tough luck for Barbara. Is that right? I keep hitting this brick wall, no answers, no solutions, just soldier on.

God: Ask me to heal you.

Dear God, please heal me. Please return my soul, my joy, my fizz, my deep inner cosmic happiness. Please make my life worth living. Please heal me so that I can stop replacing inner love with things like sugary foods. Please heal me so that I can stop feeling so isolated, faking it in a cold and uncaring society. Please heal me so that deep comprehension runs in my veins. Please heal me so that I can understand what the word "love" means. Please heal me so that I can stop having these hurtful dialogues. Please heal me so that I can have a rich and meaningful life. There, will that do?

God: Perfectly. You have just answered your own questions and saved your own soul. You do not need to ask again, ever — but it may make you feel better in times of doubt. How do you feel?

Better...baffled, maybe at my limit for what I can take in. I need to let this percolate a bit.

Tuesday, February 28, 2012, 10:25 pm
Dear Angels,
...and that's it. I'll stop chasing my tail now and go to bed – but not quite yet. Having gotten this far, I really must give you time and space to write back to me. It would be too lonely otherwise.

When I ask you questions, is there such a thing as standing orders, or do I have to ask repeatedly for every fresh instance? For example, can I say, "Angels, please help me to find the energy and focus to clean my bathroom thoroughly and spotlessly every week for the rest of my life"? Or, do I have to ask you afresh every single time, or 52 times a year for weekly chores? I am so relieved to open it up to you.

Angels: Dear Barbara, we are here, we never left, we are singing and dancing merrily around you. Thank you for staying up late to talk to us, which we love love love. No question of yours is ever too mundane or silly, sweet child of our hearts. Housekeeping is serious and important! We want to help you with it, and with everything that you feel is serious and important, or fun and celebratory, whatever it may be. Joy in all facets of life! As to the asking, both ways work, either moment by moment, or by large brushstrokes, entire months in advance. What you are really asking for is focus, energy and consistency — this is easy! Yes, by all means draw up your domestic battle plan, get more organized, be methodical, and give it all to us. We'll have your house spotless before you know it is happening. As with everything, merely set your goals and intentions, get clear, make clear decisions, and ask. Then, it is done. You can even ask for help in being clear about getting clear — however you wish to phrase it!

Angels, this is wonderful – I can't wait to try it. Thank you, angels. And thank you for this excellent, oddly serene and magical day... Something is in the air. Good night, angels.

This Is the Paradox

Wednesday, February 29, 2012
Dear Angels,
HELP! I just had the most horrible experience, am still shaking, trying to calm down and breathe slowly, do some EFT, get back on an even keel. How bizarre to have my emotions so completely hijacked. What happened was that I went to tai chi tonight, which is at a new time and in a new place: it was at the new arts center. Huge studio in a converted commercial garage, with 20' high ceilings and polished concrete floors, with beautifully unusual works of art from local artists covering the walls. We stood around for a bit – the tai chi teacher and the four of us

students, admiring the space, everyone feeling "Wow! Finally! A great place to practice tai chi in!" We've been in a few run-down buildings, and this seemed like the Ritz. The only disconcerting thing was, the overhead studio lights were dimly lit, and the cavernous space was dark. It made me uncomfortable, but no one else seemed to mind, so we began our practice of the form, a 45-minute tai chi choreography done in total silence. Immediately, my discomfort increased – I was disoriented, could not sense my body relative to the walls or floors, and had a swimmy, almost dizzy feeling of spatial relationships. Whether it was a problem with depth of field, peripheral vision, or what, I don't know. All I know is that suddenly I was fighting down a panic attack, I kept forgetting parts of the form, and my frustration and anxiety built. Finally, I couldn't stand it, and I simply bolted from the room, utterly possessed by panic, shaking, hyperventilating, wild-eyed. I could not wait to get out of the building. Judy came after me, to check on me, I could hardly speak, I just kept saying *"I'm fine, I'm fine, I'll be okay."* I walked home, shaking. I burst into tears en route, overcome with emotional flooding.

I am starting to calm down now. I will call the teacher as soon as class is over to apologize profusely, as I am stumped by this outlandish incident. Oh, Angels, how could it be? Everything was going so well and we were in our beautiful new space and I was trying so hard to get it all right and – *what happened? WAAAAH.* I feel like a little birthday girl in a perfect pink dress who has just gotten chocolate cake all over it, who has pitched a fit and ruined her own party. I have **never** had a panic attack before in my life, ever (though severe lightning freaks me out a little). Angels, please write to me and help me through this pathetic, unnecessary trauma.

Angels: Breathe, breathe, breathe, child. We are here. You've just been through a very frightening experience, and you're trying too hard to be brave, figure it out, solve the problem, release the symptoms, write to us, and tie it up in a package you can understand.

Yes! That's exactly what I am trying to do. Thank you for recognizing it. How else would I handle it?

*Angels: First of all, please don't be so hard on yourself. Please be very kind and gentle, even if you're not sure how to be so. Your system has just gone on overload and something in your judging mind has labelled it "**WRONG**" so you're trying every remedy to make it go away. You're struggling doubly with this because you have no one to hug you, comfort you, tell you that it's okay and normal, and yes, that it's **okay** to cry! So please, dear dear Barbara, look at this pile-up of pressure you put on yourself, which is what makes your heart hurt so much. Give yourself permission to be frightened, to need to cry.*

...but, but, *but* – I thought that's why I learned all these different spiritual skills, like breathing, meditation, prayer, stillness – precisely to manage these emotional states! Now I'm confused. And sad. Am I supposed to allow these things or manage them? Do I wallow, or not wallow; try, or not try? This **is** the whole point of free will and awareness, *right*? That I am supposed to hold these things at arm's length, take a look at them, and then make an active choice regarding them, right? But how can you make a decision if you're so hurt and confused that no option seems to matter? That's what I don't understand – and what appears to me to be a pretty big flaw in the free-will system. Okay, over to you, angels.

Angels: What do you think would make you feel better right now?

Ha. Trick question. I would feel better right now if you could answer all my questions completely, in a way that explained away ALL my confusion and hurt. There are so many times when I feel as though my itty-bitty human understanding will just never stretch to accept all of the metaphysics involved with this soul-growth process, and re-membering who I really Am. How does having a fucked-up panic attack for no good reason at all, help me re-member who I really Am? What good did that episode just do me?

Angels: You're writing to us, aren't you? The most uncomfortable episodes in your life are the ones which provide the greatest opportunity for soul growth. You are having trouble reconciling this periodic discomfort with the expectation that your life will become happier and more serene as you become wiser on the path. This is the paradox humans must come to terms with. It is why it is important for you to remember your radical acceptance practices, which are applicable in every single human situation. How, for example, would your panic attack appear in the framework of radical acceptance?

Hmmm...ah, so. Yes. Something relaxes in me when I stop creating "wrongness" and projecting it.

Angels: **Very good!!**

Which then leads to the realization that (sigh, this is a very complicated formula): Episode + expectation + judgment + emotion + forgetfulness of practicing acceptance = compounded human cocktail of real, wallowing unhappiness, compounded by possibility of not even being able to hear/reach YOU.
Howzat?

Angels: Excellent!

So the first thing I should reach for when hit, sideswiped, poleaxed by emotion, is – **acceptance**, which will calm me down. BUT ANGELS – here we go again – the whole problem is that extreme emotional states block the very rational thought which might jog one's memory to say, "Oh, yes, that's right, I can practice X right here and now." And thus it goes, round and round.

Angels: You know the answer to this one, too.

You mean, after experiencing sufficient amounts of pain and being sick of it, reaching a breaking point, one eventually says, "That's IT. I've HAD IT. Something has GOT to change." And one makes an effort of will to REMEMBER in spite of the trauma/emotional flooding. Is that it?

Angels: You can make that choice anywhere along the line.

I know you are trying to help me here, angels, but my experience is that deep despair obliterates free will. I have not found a solution to this. Really, I'm sure you'd jump at the chance, but I'd like to see *you* make a fabulous free will choice when your heart and soul are desolation and ashes.

Angels: Humor in the face of even the most serious discussions — you are a treasure. Yes, we'd jump at the chance, but it's not our role. We can help you better from here.

To get back to my very first question, what was this panic-attack incident about? It was extreme, bizarre, out of the blue, and yes, okay – my sorting human mind needs to make sense of it, please. Though I must say, I am so grateful to be a) writing to **you** and able to hear you (PHEW); and b) so grateful to have calmed down and have gotten back to – er – normal, whatever that is these days.

Angels: Look what happens every time you have a crisis. One, you run to us (which we love). You open up, you write, you communicate, you ask for and receive answers, you practice trust, faith, willingness, and surrender. You learn a little more each time, you release a little more each time, you go deeper a little more each time, you learn faster each time.

*So, does the actual incident matter? No. As you yourself pointed out before we could even explain it to you, the incident is merely a template, a medium, through which you experience more-of-who-you-are. You are million-faceted, therefore you might do well to practice million-acceptances. You are an unbelievably shining star, and it gives us such joy to guide you, heal you, hear you, surround you, help you. Your turning to us is our reason for existence. Through you we manifest our completion and glory. Through us you manifest **your** completion and glory. Do you see?*

I'm trying to see...from where I stand a panic attack due to spatial disorientation in a tai chi class is an odd way to achieve completion and glory – but if you say so. I'm sorry, I must be feeling better because I am making bad jokes at your expense, when you have been so patient and loving with me. And yes, this is earnest, and I do treat it as such. Flippancy is a way of warding off intimacy, isn't it? We'll have to work on that, too.

Angels, back to being serious – yes, actually, I do see. That was an excellent and complete answer and I am so glad to be here with you now, I just can't tell you (oh, the inadequacy of words). Drippy, cool February night, foghorn lowing, gas fireplace burning, all peaceful and cozy and safe. Angels, please PLEASE – next week could you prevent stop transmute intervene protect guide me from having another panic attack? Million-faceted, eh? Gee, thanks. Being one-dimensional is starting to look very attractive.

This has been an exceptionally illuminating exchange tonight, and I feel particularly connected to you, in spite of everything. Thank you very, very much.

Angels: We love it, you know that, and the feeling is more than mutual. One day soon you will sense us more strongly, and everything around you will just hum!

Goodnight, dear angels, and thank you!

While editing this this book in late 2018, I felt the concept of paradox mentioned above needed more explanation. This was the angel's answer:

Beloved, we are ready if you are. What you call a paradox is something which only appears to the rational, logical, linear mind, because of the way it — the mind — is wired or constructed. The re-education of humans will involve teaching them to resolve paradoxes by learning to switch with facility from the head brain to the heart brain, on command, on preference, on invitation, situationally and fluidly, as instances and needs dictate. What appears to be two mutually opposing conditions, irreconcilable from a logical point of view, is simply that: appearance. The human species is in crisis now because of the widespread refusal to incorporate wisdom practices — all of which have been mentioned many times in this book — of love, faith, trust, hope, acceptance, patience, tolerance, and self-restraint, to name a few. Therefore, many humans will encounter teaching situations, and some will learn, and some will not. A paradox is only a challenge; it is only a word which names a condition which humans have dealt with for time immemorial. The solutions are within you, as they always have been. We stand by to encourage the learning, to ease you through the teaching, to bless your every effort towards making simple, better choices. Having

experienced this first-hand, darling child of light, you know these things in your bones. Can you help us spread the message?
Love,
The Angels

Thank you, angels!

And Sing You Songs of Courage

Friday, March 2, 2012, 5:10 pm
Dear Angels,
I am showing up. I really want to write to you about next steps on a path of life and career transition. I am trying think bigger, along more magnificent lines. As you have said before, I hold all the threads in my hand already, it's just a question of weaving them.
So please tell me where to start.

Angels: First of all, congratulations on making the appointment with Stephanie. Beautiful — well-done — count that as a turbo lift. Secondly, thank you for writing to us with this excellent and exciting proposition. Now we're talking. We feel how thrilled you are to contemplate the majesty of creation. It only gets better, and we LOVE you for it. Nothing is more important than being here right now and connecting with us. This is a fantastic start, and we will indeed get to work to help you make these transformations. As you know, all manifestations begin as thought. You know what needs to happen next. Keep doing your homework, and work on an overview of your major life brushstrokes. Write them down, draft a plan. Ask us every day for ways to take steps forward, and we will guide you. Refine the picture as you go. Perhaps create a reminder list of all the spiritual skills which you can draw on, on a daily basis, especially ferreting out and releasing those last, tiny fears which block you. You are doing beautifully. Bring all these thoughts and dreams and creative hopes together in a cohesive list, so you can see how to weave the pattern of your life anew. Then just give it all to us, and yes! The partnership is underway! Beloved child, will that do for a start?

Yes! As you know, I am also going to start reading more seriously, *The Amazing Power of Deliberate Intent* by Esther and Jerry Hicks, and use it as a guide. I need reminding about the phenomenon of contrast, I see that. Is that what that odd episode of panic was last Wednesday, or was it something I attracted to me?

Angels: Let us go home and read through the book again. It was a combination of both. You struggle most in finding perspective on these uncomfortable incidents in your life. We can help you with that. The Abraham–Hicks book explains it wonderfully. Long day, long week, it's after hours — home?
We will meet you again on the written page anon, our beloved Barbara!
Love,
The Angels

Sunday, March 4, 2012, 8:35 pm
Dear Angels,
Today I stopped at the yoga studio gift shop and purchased a small, round, stamped silver token, about 1½", with the image of an ANGEL on it. Angels, I am possessed by this little token, I am bringing it everywhere with me, and hate to be parted from it. I carried it outside when I gardened, it was such a help. This is exactly what I needed, a little touchstone reminder to keep me connected with you and **asking, asking, asking**. I love this little coin, because it works.

Angels, thank you for guiding and helping me this weekend. Today I am monitoring an emotional weather-system that made me edgy. Low level anxiety has moved in like a storm front, and is sitting on my chest. This is a familiar feeling – I suspect it's the backlash from my high of Friday, with the cold, chill realization that, yes, it's time to change, and that boy, am I ever in for it now. I could use some reassurance and wisdom. Please write and tell me anything I need to know to help cope with these blues and uncertain days ahead. Thank you.

Angels: You can't keep us out, you can't keep us out, you can't keep us out, oh joy! We are dancing all around you, because extraordinary days are ahead. Your path is taking hairpin turns and mounting steeper and steeper — but wait until you see the view! Our job is to lead you by the hand, push from behind, loft you up from underneath, and sing you songs of courage. We are singing to you now and promise you — we PROMISE — that it is going to become amazing quite soon. Such a brave, adorable child. It does you no good when you are sad and cannot feel our hugs and angel touches.

Now, about these "blues" of yours. You have diagnosed them quite correctly, but they are also mixed up a little bit with your deep weariness with your present job. See if you can keep the two separate, because you don't need a double effect right now. Definitely use the practices in APDI to re-align your thoughts about work. Remember, this is one final sprint, and you have started to delineate the finish line. Ambiguity also opens you up to depression, remember that. Once you define your new life, and define the end of the old one, you will feel much better — all the more reason to start getting clear about it soon. We will help you! Yes, there are many firsts happening along in your life now. White Tantric Yoga is a huge step, and we are so proud of you! You will need all of your disciplines as we go forward, especially self-care and lots of sleep. Yes! We are louder and clearer to you now, you can feel it. So take heart, Barbara darling, the summit is within reach. Our eagle chicklet is hatching. To bed now, sweet girl, to enjoy those lovely dreams you were told would result from the kriya. And yes, thank you for releasing your old car to us — all is well, and it shall be sold. Thank you for blessing the process! Good night, wise child.
Love, the Angels.

Thursday, March 8, 2012, 6:45 pm
Dear Angels,
I have been trying to catch myself every time I dwell on or think obsessively about anything relating to our company (for example, describing the day I just had), bearing in mind the Law of Attraction from APDI:

"The more you focus on a subject the more active the vibration is, and the more of that which is a vibrational match to it is attracted to it. Eventually you will begin to see physical evidence showing up in your experience that matches the essence of the way you have been feeling about the subject."

Therefore, my challenge is to ease myself out of the company mentally and *replace replace replace* every concocted work scenario I take home with me, every habitual mental return to the office dramas, with a thought, dream, idea or imagining of my non-office future. This is a tall order, as I am sufficiently conditioned into company culture that I say "we" unthinkingly, many times a day. However, I have pried a mental crowbar in there, and just today interrupted an internal company broadcast playing in my brain and replaced with some open-ended questions to myself:

"What does my future hold? What can I do with my life which will fulfill my need for peace, calm, abundance, and control over my working environment?"

Asking these questions is soothing, and it's about all I can do right now, since the field is wide open, and I don't know what my post-company future will hold. But I know that I have to start shaping it somehow. And it feels wonderful to open myself up to possibilities.

Angels, I am trying to apply this vibrational law of attraction to my thoughts and feelings, but it's hard to get started when I am a) so brainwashed; b) genuinely need to keep thinking about things company-related to do my job. Tell me more about how to change my thoughts and feelings to a better vibrational match. How do I do this when I don't know what I want or the enormity of it is too big to grasp?

Angels: Do you remember how you felt driving over the bridge this morning, blasting the "Bell Song" from Lakmé* on the sound system? Strong, clear, happy, open, hopeful, as if you could fly. Remember this and seek this state again and again. It is very powerful and can blast away your old thoughts, to make space for new ones, more easily than your willed thoughts. So you see, you have several facets to work with: the willed, deliberate thought choices; and the sometimes spontaneous good flows of emotion. If you can pair the two, your work will be

*An opera in three acts by French composer Leo Delibes.

147

easy. You are a creature of balance, it comes naturally to you, and so you will intuitively shift the bulk of your thoughts from work-based to future-happiness-based, without difficulty and without diminishing the quality of your office work. In fact, you may find that you have more energy and clarity as your attitudes shift, precisely because you have a hopeful new horizon.

Work on your happiness first, work on feeling hopeful and inspired, and the rest will follow. It is easier than you think, do not over-process it. We are winging you along and will make sure that everything happens as and when it should.

Ah, this is what I needed to know. I can set aside my goal-driven persona, and just flow a bit. I am also using the contrast of icky office situations to fuel my desire to get the heck out of there. This is a good tool for creating perspective and reminding me that I am not trapped.

Angels, we have done a lot tonight. I am going to bed without being encouraged.

Angels: we will meet you in your dreams. Sleep sweetly and deeply, dear one.
Love, the Angels and John

You Become You!

Sunday, March 11, 2012, 12:00
Daylight savings – spring ahead!
Dear Angels,
It is very March-like today, bright, sunny, windy, cool but starting to be warm in the sun. I'd be out in my garden if I weren't so bone-achingly weary from White Tantric Yoga* yesterday.

What can I say about this experience? I suppose the most significant thing about the day was the way I felt all day long (talk about a vibrational match): calm, centered, and strong. I was **ready**. I was prepared, I handled the exercises just fine, except for the second 61-minute

---

*White Tantric Yoga: In the kundalini yoga tradition, a full-day, group meditation. All participants wear white, and sit facing each other in pairs to facilitate the flow of energy. Referred to colloquially as White Tantric.

meditation, when I had to rest my right arm a few times. What an extraordinary scene it was – everyone in clean, pristine white, with white head coverings. The room glowed with happiness and buzzed with positive energy.

And so, another first: White Tantric Yoga. My partner was someone named Ed whom I met for the first time when we left from the yoga studio bright and early. Even though I had overslept and woke up late at 6:00, and flew out the door feeling half-prepared, that flustered state of "oh-I've-forgotten-something" felt old to me, just an overlay. Underneath I was calm and sure. This is a novel feeling – I like this shift.

The second significant part of the day was the moment when Ed leaned forward (we were facing each other, seated knee-to-knee) and said, "I have a message for you. Would you like to hear it?" I had never met this man before, but I immediately knew exactly what kind of message he meant (i.e., channeled), and I said, "yes, absolutely."

He said, "The message is: *You don't have to be a good girl!*" I smiled at that, thanked him, and we talked about it for a bit.

I learned later that he is clairsentient and gets clear messages via Spirit. As White Tantric partners, we were well-paired and complementary to each other in terms of the kriyas and meditations. He had only been doing kundalini yoga for six months. I think he was in a little over his head – I felt myself supporting him throughout, and that made me smile, because it would be my first teaching opportunity, and also, the awareness of the complementary mirroring was so logical. Also, his confident attitude was amusing. He will be a good yogi.

The day was everything that I expected, and more. The seasoned hands felt that it was a difficult White Tantric session. I didn't find it that difficult, only challenging in spots, which is what we came for. It was a phenomenal feeling to realize that not only have I been well-taught, but that I can have real confidence in my practice, discipline, and the effects of the seven years or so of foundational work that I have done (thank you, Yogi Bhajan). Afterward, a hungry, spacey group of us went to dinner at a Mexican restaurant, where the food tasted delicious.

It was interesting to listen to the instructors discuss the expected effects. They said that we were still vibrating heavily with the energy of what we had been through; that we would either go home and be wide awake, or crash; that we needed to drink lots of water, meditate, and eat purely for the best effects to continue; and that we would feel the reverberation consequences for the next 40 days. They were quite serious about it.

Ed was silent throughout most of this, but on the way home we had an interesting, intense talk about past lives, channeling, spirit guides, messages, etc. He made me laugh because he was pontificating a bit, and I recognized myself in that. We all think we're the ONLY ones receiving messages, when in fact the opposite is true.

Anyway, to get down to brass tacks, I am again revolving the latest message received, in hopes of figuring out a few more things. The message was **"You don't have to be a good girl."** Oh, like an arrow, straight and true to the point! You know me intimately, angels. I see its truth and yet I also see the many benefits such conditioning brings me in my life. Is this something I need to surrender?

*Angels: Clearer and stronger, day by day, you are our precious child. If only you knew **how** precious – we hope to get that through to you one day, that is one of our aims. About his message, it has given you something to think about relative to your world view and conditioned responses. It gives you one more option in your choices as you go through your days, a recognition that things will be fine even if you miss a phone call or disappoint someone. You are not intended to be perfect, no one can be in the human plane. Yes, surrender this, and see if you can be kinder to yourself as a result. Being kinder to yourself is more important than being kinder to others — do you see the imbalance?*

I think I do...and because this good-girl persona has been a subtext all of my life, and I know it has created frustration for me spiritually, because I think that if I just do things right, it must follow that the situations will be solved, explained or healed. So who do I become, in place of this, if I am not a good girl?

Angels: You become You!

Um, er, yes. Indeed. I just burst out laughing. There is nothing more to be said, and I thank you so much for this answer. Time to get on with my day. Thank you, Angels!

Sunday March 18, 2012, 8:30 pm
Dear Angels,
Fresh entry – picking up where I left off on Wednesday. Much better tonight and continuing with my inner questions to you about these writing sessions, and my good-girl conditioning.

Have just come from Sunday evening kundalini yoga class. The set was titled "Sound Current," and it was very different. The teacher gave us one guided meditation where she said, "*Now leave your body through the top of your head,*" and pop! Suddenly I had a picture of a little Barbara in white yoga clothes climbing out through a trap door in my head, proceeding to wave to me, flying up to rest on one of the ceiling beams, and then whizzing straight into space like Superwoman, where she encountered Sacha-with-wings, Sirus-with-wings (such a joyous reunion with my passed dog companions), all of You, John, relatives, and many other divine beings. I am amused by this! Angels, please tell me more.

*Angels: Here we are, here we are, back with paper and pen, connecting again and again. As to answering questions, you are wondering why some of your answers seem a little vague, don't address the point, or steer you towards something else. We're all here, we're all clear! There are many factors here. We wish to help you and do what is best for you. If you ask us for guidance but are so tired and sleepy that you can hardly hold the pen, then we may keep the answer short and counsel you to hit your pillow. If the topic is abstract and requires a lengthy answer, we could certainly hold forth, but you may not be receiving clearly. You are just now, also starting to experience the liberation of "not having to be a good girl" one of the benefits of which is that you don't **have to complete** the question and answer period during the same session that you started it! Just as we will now do with your question about White Tantric Yoga. We always answer your question as fully as we think best for you at the time. Yes, this does leave you still* *wondering and not quite satisfied on some occasions, but does not the answer always come through other mediums, often in remarkably expanded format? If it does happen, as it will, that you are dissatisfied with the answer, bring it to us again in a different phrasing another time. We **love** working these things through with you. Does that help?*

Yes, very much, thank you. Yes, this would be a good time to have a little exchange about White Tantric. Will it heal me faster and better, bring me closer to getting back to what I consider normal? It has been such a long, hard road, angels, and I just want to FIX MY LIFE.

Angels: We hear your cry for help, dear one. How can we reassure you best? Truly, your life is not at all broken — you are doing everything "right" and the Universe has certainly responded! This you know, but the core healing still eludes you. White Tantric Yoga is powerful, yes and it did create a shift in your Being. Timing, timing, timing, this is what we would say to you. You feel your life going by and want to regain your Joy so that as much time on this earth that you have remaining can be experience with this fundamental part of you. Would more White Tantric yoga bring deeper changes, and be good for you? Absolutely. Pursue it if you can, and if you wish. We sense your rational mind balancing this against the consequences of such immersion — would you become a disciple, a teacher, a guru even? Part of you is apprehensive of this. Therefore, take your time. You have abundant opportunities before you.

We fold you around with our wings of love. Yes, yes, yes, follow your questing soul, that leads you ever deeper and inward and upward and outward. The traveling is joyful!

By the way, I love the cartoon in Tricycle magazine, the Buddhist review, showing one monk saying to another: "Don't worry if you don't understand stuff. It'll probably stay that way."

How interesting that an integral part of the questing and questioning which humans do, creates a tail-chasing phenomenon: it creates the expectation that by merely being persistent, dedicated and disciplined, we will eventually, find the answers and *comprehend*. Yet, there is no guarantee that this will actually happen, so when we bump our noses against incomprehension/lack of understanding, what we are really encountering is the false expectation that crept into the equation. Ha! This wisely sends us back to the only sane possibility, the fundamental tool of acceptance. Now my ego will pat me on the back for having figured that out, I will notice my ego doing it, and I will gently smile to myself. Double ha.

Angels: We think you're taking charge beautifully, if you must know. Continue on handing everything over to us, especially those snarled problems at work. All is well, our angel child. The best next step for you is sweet, deep sleep! We bless you and sing you sweet hymns of peace this gentle spring night. Goodnight, child!

Goodnight angels, thank you!

Tuesday, March 20, 2012, 12:30 pm
Dear Angels,
I am feeling overwhelmed and need your help. I just learned some very sad news. There was a tragic incident on Elm Avenue this morning, a knife attack and suicide at a well-known shop. Angels, what do you make of this brutal incident?

Angels: Pray, dear child, pray. Pray for the harmed ones, pray for the owner, pray for the emergency services and the police, pray for the neighbors and friends of all in your city. A community shows its true spirit by coming together in support, or by shying away in fear, over these sad human occurrences. All humans are on their own paths, and what is inexplicable to you may make sense in higher realms. Do not dwell on this, but bless all and send them peace. They are sadly in need of it, and you have the power to contribute good. Please repeat some protective mantras, and pray again and meditate tonight to shed any energy from this. Above all, be kind and do not slander any of the participants, this is important. Your choice of reaction will show who you are choosing to be in this moment. Take it seriously. Surrounding you with blessings and protection,
Love,
The Angels

Thursday, March 22, 2012
Dear Angels,
Angels, there is another subject I need your help with, please. We have had a pathetically low offer on our remaining property in Florida. The broker is fed up and impatient with us because we are "ridiculously uninformed." He is right, but he doesn't need to be so insulting about it. Can you please arrange a miracle and have a buyer come along and offer more money for this piece? In the meantime, what do we do?

Angels: Blessings of success upon you, child. May all your projects come to fruition. Pray nightly and continue to bless all concerned with this property. Is not this offer 100% more than you have had in the past several years? Even one offer shows that energy is shifting, attention is being attracted, this piece will wind up selling at the right price and to the right person. Go ahead and instruct your broker to proceed, but stand your ground on the price. If the buyer walks away, no harm is done. You have proof that miracles occur, so all that is needed here is a second one. We can provide that easily! Come to us again and again as issues arise, and we will solve them for you. Faith, dear child. You will prevail in the long run. We love being invited to untangle these thorny situations, we love the way you bless the mangroves and pray for their best use and best final solution. You have power — use it for the good, and watch the magic unfold. Yes yes yes ask us to transmute your anxiety, this is a good place to start!

Fantastic, thank you. Such an amazing answer. Sometimes it feels as though I am right back to square one, haven't learned anything from you at all. Fear is a very blocking, obliterating emotion, and it takes such awareness to transcend it. I'm going to do my best. Thank you for this beautiful advice.

I have to run out the door in a minute or two, but just wanted to say thank you for that amazing coincidence today, when a new acquaintance came in the door to say hello, and she turned out to be an "angel." She was open, friendly, chatty – and she was a former bookstore owner – not one store, but two! We had a wonderful conversation, and I discreetly tried to pump her about her business. She was very forthcoming. Both businesses failed, and she talked about how much money they lost, and how impossible to run a bookstore *unless you own the building*. Aha.

I'm just shaking my head in amazement at all of You. Will wonders never cease? Answer: no, they won't!

Angels: We want to encourage you every day in little ways. Forward, brave one, and make that phone call. We loft you with our large, white, sacred wings to the success you deserve. Blessings upon you always,
The Angels — of Bookstores and Properties and Job Situations and Love and Life and Happiness. May it flow for you!

Sunday, March 28, 2012
Dear Angels,
My question for you tonight is sort of rhetorical, but I am curious (always curious). A constant theme in my writing is the various degrees of effort a human goes through in identifying and striving for soul growth. *Trying*, in other words. I think I'll have the words *"Just trying..."* on my tombstone. Seriously, though, my question is this: what if I became lazy, or gave up, or became so discouraged that I just said, "the heck with it" and threw out all my spiritual self-help books, stopped actively inquiring and attempting internal expansion. What if...I just let life go back to being ordinary, stopped talking to you, and basically stopped questioning? If I decided to drop these techniques, and stop the push and the search, would my life stop expanding? Would I become ordinary, plain and content with material, surface phenomena? What happens if I walk away from it all?

Angels: Dear, dear, DEAR Barbara! After all we've been through? We would miss you very much, of course, but since our patience is INFINITE, any decision you made here and now would only mean waiting until you finished this lifetime. We know you are not serious, and are enjoying this process (mostly) too much to act on this supposition. Your life would never be as it was before, you have grown too much to fit back into any previous shape you might have had. Awareness only expands, it does not contract. All the experiences, thoughts, emotions, and practices you have worked on so hard would continue working inside of you. They would leave an afterglow, as it were. Your growth would slow but not stop. Events would occur...which would force you back on your old skills. Truthfully, you can never be "ordinary" again, you have come too far, and your curiosity is too great. You are a great one for running and hiding and pushing away — fairly normal among humans, actually — the difference being that when you make the choice to invite us to help you, it is all so much easier. You might also be a little bored if you dropped the quest — do you not find that you fit in some places but not in others, that your preferred community is more and more with like-minded people?

Yes, I see...but today, for example (at least until my kundalini class) I made no special efforts – no meditation, chanting, kriya, no talking to you, no cocking my head to listen for vibes or special paying attention to signs and events. Just a plain, old domestic day spent drinking tea, reading a 19th C novel and trying to cope with my twingey back. Ordinary.

Angels: And? Then magical kundalini, and this gloriously special and woo-woo writing session! How about naming your bookstore "Woo-Woo Books"? It has a certain ring to it!

Check and mate, angels. Since when do you tease **me** about woo-woo things? You've got me smiling. Okay, I know it was pure conjecture, but we humans just love that future-based thought.

You know, it's weird to be so physically human and yet have this metaphysical potential hanging about all over the place. If my channels and hearing became clearer and clearer, then eventually, do I spend the whole day talking to you? Or the image that comes to mind is that of a child (me) walking around a fairground holding the hand of her parent (you), in an ongoing shared wonderment. It does become like that, doesn't it?

Angels: The parent would be God, yes, and we would be your privileged escorts. Or picture dozens and dozens of your favorite aunts, uncles, cousins, all vying to spoil you and take you on the rides of your choice (even if they made you sick), if they were what you chose. Yes, a bit like that.

And so my biggest challenge is in switching back and forth between the two worlds – it's already starting to cause some hesitation in spots.

Angels, you must love human beings who have insomnia. Imagine if I could stay up all night talking to you. As I do not have insomnia, dear

Angels, I am going to say goodnight, as I am fading fast. Good night, and thank you!

Angels: Bless you, our darling Barbara, and sweet dreams!
Love, the Angels and Faithful John

Tuesday, March 27, 2012, 10:50 am
Dear Angels,
Good morning! Finally, it is March, really *March*. The temps dipped down into the 20's last night, high winds roared, and today we have a typical bright, blustery, sunny, cold dry day, the crisp kind that steals the heat away from your body when you step outside, but makes you glad to be alive. The poor flowers are shivering, and may have been blighted – but at least they had their glory for a week or so.

Went to the special event last night at the yoga studio, Guru Singh's workshop. These educational blasts are so intense, it's like being sprayed with a cosmic fire hose. I soaked it up and marveled at his lucidity, intelligence, power, simplicity. *So that is what it is like to be truly clear*, I thought. He had just come from teaching a course at Kripalu on evolution, and this shortened version touched on some of the main concepts – where we came from (hundreds of thousands of years ago in the mists of time), where we are *now*, where we are *going*, what we have no doubt of *becoming* if we apply ourselves. Such a hopeful message. He spoke as though we, in the room, were the agents of change, the ones who had arrived at this point for a purpose, who could fulfill the promise of enlightenment. He used the visualizations of two arrows, placed in the quiver of our spines, drawn out of our kundalini energy, representing our past and Everything which brought us here; our future and Everything we have the power to visualize and achieve; and shot forward in a huge, cosmic arch.

Putting my life into an evolutionary framework was an extraordinary context for me, something I had only thought about vaguely, if at all.

Taken seriously, it would ultimately mean a shift for me, from humble-student-just-showing-up, to accepting the responsibility for being an agent of change myself. *Oh.*

He also said that evolution is only interested in that one shot in 50,000, and that the rest fall away. Evolution only picks the best and the brightest, the survivors. So if 49,999 times out of 50,000 you feel discouraged or despair, then you must press on until the 50,000ᵗʰ time. This, *this*, I heard. The ahas dawn.

The yoga mats were wall-to-wall last night, and the room was packed. I sat in the back, and Patrice, a kundalini teacher I know, sat next to me. She is sweet and high energy, and was asking me all kinds of friendly questions, such as how long had I been doing kundalini? Had I taken the teacher training yet? Why not? When I said, *oh not I, I couldn't, it's a bit scary, me-student, you-teacher,* she breezily dismissed it saying, "You can handle it! I'm sure you can. No reason not to. Promise – you'll sail through, especially if you've already taken White Tantric. You've got to take teacher training." Then she smiled impishly and said in a teasing singsong, *"I'm-telling-Maaargaret!"*

Oh. Well, this is a message and a half, no doubt about it, and couldn't be clearer, sent straight (as an arrow) to me. And – since I'm a Good Girl, and do what I'm told, I'll (sigh) take this seriously and look into it. Yes, I hear you, Universe. In the context of last night's workshop, this is a literal message that it is time to Evolve. I thought that is what I was doing all along, but perhaps not fast enough.

I need to write to you about the Florida situation, too. Please resolve this Florida situation so that I never have to deal with the realtor or my cousin again, they drag me into the mire, and I have no wish to be there. Please tell me what to do.

Angels: This is the last stretch, the last sprint. You are almost there. You are doing everything right. If it consoles you, please use the Angel Oracle cards tonight or another time to see what message we send to you. Hope, help, healing are here.

You are surrounded by very strong protective energy and all elements are coming together to resolve this in a miraculous way. Use your common sense, talk to your sister, call other realtors if that seems like the right thing to do. Find pity for the realtor and your cousin, know that they speak from unknowing places in their souls. This is not good or bad, it simply is, and you can avoid this in future. Continue praying, meditating, blessing, and all shall be well. We promise!
Sending blessings of love and peace,
The Angels who love you very much!

We Will See You Dance in the Light Yet

Thursday, March 29, 2012, 9:00
Dear Angels,
Okay, this is getting **really** old: the multiplicity of draining, negative work situations. The usual one or two I can bat right out of the court, but now they are piling up and I am sick of it (oops, better be careful of my language or it will manifest). Right – so we sorted out the Smiths and their infinite, entitled requests, which reads like the laundry list from hell for me to micromanage; we sorted out Mindy and the question of the display for the opening. Now we have – TA DA! – the new prospective clients at River Street who are picky, demanding, and are now treating the company like their own private concierge service. I was so furious with their requests that I took myself out of the building and off to see *She Stoops to Conquer* at the arts cinema, live-streamed from the National Theatre in London. That mental health day saved me from sending an email I might regret. Please send away these pushy prospects, do something. I can't handle this. As I have said one hundred times, I am weary of these unpleasant, nit-picky situations that are coming at me one right after another. Working at a fast-food grill is starting to look attractive.

Angels: How clear you are tonight, and how happy we are to be with you right now. That little yoga set you did, plus the meditating, made a difference in your receptivity.

159

*Can you tell? Sweet child, thank you for bringing these troubles to us. We feel your anger and frustration. As with your cousin, you need protection against these strong-willed people. Use EFT for your anger, use acceptance for all your states of mind and heart, ask us to transmute anything else, please go for a long walk if you can — or go sit in a church — and rain blessings on these new clients. Then turn it over to us — don't forget to ask! Grumbling is fine, but don't indulge — get rid of that head-set, move on. Make the active choice about whether or not you **want** this situation to drain you, and act accordingly. You get stuck in, and loop in, the emotions which pet the ego. Ask us to help you disrupt that looping, and we will. You are a **pro** at this, darling, and getting better all the time. Tomorrow is a bright new day and you can make up your mind beforehand that the solutions will simply **pour forth**! How about practicing that thought?*

I need to print your fabulous answer in large print and frame it. Thank you, Angels – your kindness and wisdom never cease to amaze me. In fact, as soon as I finish here, I am going to get a 3 x 5" card and write every one of those statements down, because they are gold, they are the refuge my mind and heart are desperate for. I really look forward to the time when I can remember and use this advice all by myself, without prompting.

So, Angels – about Guru Singh, his second workshop, and his book *Angels Gather Here*. I am overwhelmed by the volume of information I've taken in, over the last 4 days, and have probably overdone it, as I was feeling blue-hopeless-helpless today, on top of it all. But I was so happy to read the title of his book, to buy a copy, to have it inscribed, and then to rush home and do a typical Barbara thing by staying up too late to read it. Or attempt reading it – WHOOSH – is the noise made by all of the esoteric, cosmic concepts he/you wrote about as they rushed in one brain cell and out the other. It was straight discussions on consciousness and human evolution.

But…oh, *Angels*! A space was left after every chapter headed by: NOTES TO MY ANGELS. I wanted to hear him talk into the night, into the dawn, and into the next millennium. Can you tell me a little more about him, the book, and your work with him?

*Angels: He is our child of light, **just as you are**. He is a joy to work with and through, because he walks and talks with us almost at our level. Information streams through him near-effortlessly. You are now connected to him, and will be influenced by his teachings. There is so much beauty awaiting you, child, all these old states of sadness will fall away like the husks they are. You had a beautiful, long, clear dream last night, which became a conversation carried into your waking state, did you not? You have turned a corner; all is accelerated now. Go gently with the intake of knowledge as it does flood your senses. Write letters to Guru Singh — indeed, yes! Tell him how you communicate with us. He will love this, as it validates his teachings and his purpose. Do not be shy, or feel unworthy. Would you not love a student who shared a story of transformation? You have trouble believing that you are special and deserving, you think enlightenment is only for other, special people. No no no! It is for everyone, this is Guru Singh's message. But take it slowly and persist, and we will carry you forward over the parts you struggle with. We're partners, remember? Your spiritual shyness is an asset rather than a liability, though, because it is ultimately easier to overcome than an enlarged egoic state.*

Now the powerful changes begin. You are strong enough now, and you have the skills. Let tomorrow's meeting be simple and straightforward, your main question is enough to build on. A beautiful new day is dawning for you, and the excitement will catch your heart on fire. Look at how far you have come in one year, and be proud of yourself. Your path is extraordinary, you have courage and beauty and wisdom that you have not yet begun to tap, our beautiful kundalini-teacher-bookstore-owner-child-of-nature and child of abundance! We will see you dance in the light yet. We bless you more than ever and eagerly await to hear from you at next writing — for you change with every entry!
Sweet dreams, beloved Barbara —
The Angels, and John — who love you.

Create a Safe Haven

Sunday, April 1, 2012
Dear Angels,
Yesterday was dark, cold and dreary, with rain and sleet first thing

in the morning. I slept late, read for a bit, had a lazy morning – let myself wallow, and then tackled a shortlist.

I am still having trouble shaking the blues, Angels. I am reaching for and practicing more cheerful thoughts, but the mood isn't lifting. It's deep, bad, sad. Angels, I think what wearies me most is when I do *everything* right and it still doesn't work. I feel discouraged and overwhelmed. I dread going into work. I feel like I'm losing control. What happens when I try everything, and it still doesn't work – then what?

Angels: You are brooding a bit, dear. Can you make a choice not to brood? Here's a suggestion: let's go out into the sunshine and play in your garden. You need to restore balance and breathe more more more fresh air! The flowers and birds are calling to you – shall we go? Let's get into your heart and body, and out of your head.

Later, 9:15 pm
Dear Angels,
That was a good suggestion and I took it. I put on my old dungarees, pulled on my gloves, hauled out my garden cart, and tackled the overgrown ivy around the Norway maple. It was really good to get into one project in one location, with one focus. I went right around the tree and pruned all the ivy down to the base. *Ahhh.*

After lunch I tackled a brickwork project, and now it looks much better. Took a shower, meditated for 15 minutes, and went to kundalini yoga class. That class is my lifeline. We did some very intense breathing postures and a particularly luminous meditation, which worked to clear out all that stagnant energy I had.

Angels, when I was weeping and wailing last week, gnashing my teeth over that prospective client problem, why didn't you mention that my overwrought state might be due to after-effects from the kundalini yoga workshop? I lost perspective, totally and utterly, and was desperate for something, *anything*, to set the gyroscope straight again. Why didn't you reassure me that I wasn't unhinged?

Angels: There are many times when we need to let you find things out on your own, times when it is necessary for you to experience an extreme of discomfort.

Which would force me to reach farther and try harder? But in this case it just sent me deeper into the blues. I really do not understand this see-sawing, rollercoaster method of dragging me into the light. I metaphorically bash my head against the wall until it is bloody, and you say, *just a few more bumps now*. I feel like I am never going to be reliably stable again. I'm sorry, I don't mean to be melodramatic, but you must admit this journal is full of pitching and tossing emotions. The good news is, I made a resolve to sit down and write a list of hopeful, encouraging thoughts, so that I could refer to it and add to it when I need a lifeline. I must seem whining and ungrateful sometimes. There, done. I now have a list of eight clear, hopeful, supportive thoughts about ways to correct or re-direct my direction. Thank you, Angels, for helping me. And now it is definitely time for bed.

Angels: We couldn't have said it better ourselves, which is proof of how well you're doing, even though you think you're floundering. Yes, you really did see us in that meditation tonight. Wasn't it beautiful? Turn in, sweet one, and we will visit you in your dreams. Love,
The Angels

April 13, 2012, 8:50 pm
Dear Angels,
At last, the horrific office-sprint with its over-thought components is over. My horizon is clear. The opening was a success, and went like a dream logistically. Angels, thank you so much for helping me pick out an outfit – that was perfect. The clean, white shawl shot through with silver threads was easy and gorgeous, and everyone complimented me on it. How clever to pick something which was extremely light-reflecting.

Now, about this bookstore dream-project. It's starting to take shape, but it has so many facets that I feel like I am trying to catch soap bubbles. Angels, please help me write it all down, think it all through, help me with time management, and help me, period.

Angels: We are here! Together in heart, mind and spirit, yet on the printed page. Such luxury, to flow out through your blessed pen, by your blessed hand. Thank you, dear child, for this privilege! Now, to address this very exciting subject. We are all curled up with you in your cozy chair, tea in hand, wrapper around your shoulders.

First, darling, please get out the oracle cards and we'll have a wonderful reading together. That will reassure you.

Secondly, let's make this sacred. Please choose a time to honor. Light candles and incense, play soft music, gather all of your materials, spread them out, and relax into creating. The creative process is chaotic by definition — make room for that; accept it, recognize it, grow comfortable with it. If you create a safe haven within which to be chaotic, it will not frighten you.

Thirdly, let's refocus on getting clear, energy issues, and time management. You have all the skills, you just need to strengthen your practices: meditation, sensible eating, sensible sleep patterns, and setting intentions and alarm clocks! All will be easy: the season and your rising energy level is with you. Commit to rising a little earlier each day. Your idea of using the morning hours to work on the project is a good one. Just a little bit of intention setting at night (as a habit), once a little in the morning, is all it takes. Can you set yourself 40 days of bookstore dream project intention setting?

*Fourthly: trust, awareness, playfulness, and more more more MORE trust! You feel yourself snagging on fears — have fun — make it a game, trying to catch and release them. You have done it so many times now, you know how to handle every single thing surfacing — you just **think** you don't know how yet. Yes, it's time for the training wheels to fall off. Pedal faster, leave them behind.*

You sense exactly how this amorphous thing inside me is bumping uncomfortably around with a million components, asking for form and solidity. If I can just get it down in tangible form, on paper, it will allay this discomfort. I also have so many questions from the life coaching session to share with you.

Shall we do the angel oracle cards to start the process? The reading turns up: *Focus, Guardian Angels, Music, Miracles,* and *Self-Acceptance.*

This last card reads: "*You are too hard on yourself,*" the angels say. This is where I become more confused. How can I love myself unconditionally, when my heart is so damaged that I can't even feel it? I don't know what the word unconditional even means. I am not an angel and never will be, so how can I "*see myself through the angel's eyes*" as the card says? This is an unrealistic thing to ask of any human. This card of *Self-Acceptance* has actually made me feel worse about myself, because it highlights exactly my handicaps.

I am sad, now, Angels. Here we are again, up against old friend Brick Wall. I am sorry, I am just going to go to bed. Good night.

Never Be Afraid to Ask: Advice from Archangel Gabriel

Wednesday, April 18, 2012, 7:50 pm
Dear Angels,
I am feeling much better following that last, rather blue entry. It frustrates me that I am prone to something I can't figure out and fix. I met with the life coach today, and we talked about the flow chart I had drafted, we talked about financing and fears of failure, and exit strategies. Then we talked about You, Angels, because I am so immensely curious about getting more specific ways of support. The life coach kept turning my questions back on me, and my resource is you, so please answer all my questions about this bookstore dream project.

Angels: Well, my child, I thought you'd never ask! It is I, Gabriel, and it is indeed my honor to guide you through this process. You and I are going to become great friends. This is an exciting time in your life, and you little know how bursting with change you are. All is new and fresh; all is possible; all is miraculous! Let us begin. You wish to know about the power I, and the other angels (whom we will invoke as we go, there will be many experts called in) will bring. We bring you the power to understand your power. You are still taking baby steps and flexing new muscles. With each step we accomplish together — with your asking, our answering, and the manifestation of your desire — you grow in confidence, strength and clarity. This compounds on itself, and as you see the synchronicities, hear our guidance, and shift your actions accordingly, you build into a harmonious flow and alignment. This is the power we bring, and it needs a strong, loyal, committed, caring receptacle to contain it, such as you. We will never let you "fail" because we love you too much, and the way we loft you forward is our proof to you of that. We have great things in store for you — this is just the beginning! And it is ALL play! Can you trust that?

Yes, I can, because of the proof you have brought me before. And I know if I ever wavered in that trust, all I would have to do is ask you to remove the doubt, and you would. I'm slowly starting to realize that co-creation is just pure fun, once one gets past fear and doubt.

Gabriel: Never be afraid to ask, even if it seems such a little question. Both ways work, but I would be honored if you called on me for any and every thing. Truly, let's have conversations, no matter what the topic. We are more helpful to you if all barriers to intimacy are down.

You make it easier for us already, and you meet us halfway with your openness. And we do enjoy the intricate layers of complexity in such projects, which for us is a beautiful thing, like conducting a great orchestra. As a start to ways of thinking about financing, sketch it out in large concepts first. As us to help you come up with creative financing ideas. Don't worry about the micro-subsets yet — those will take care of themselves. That is really all you need to do for now. The most important thing is to flesh out the major components, so that you can ask to have them realized. You have far less doubt and fear now than when you shopped for your car (believe it or not), and so this will go faster.

Magic child, it is my delight to help you with all of the above, and more. Ask, ask, ask! We are brilliant partners, playing in the fields of the Lord. Good night, my beautiful co-creator! Love,
Gabriel and All the Angels of Heaven, and Your beloved, John

April 20, 2012
Dear Gabriel,
I did follow up about the property at 11 Smith Street, and found out that it is under contract, and the closing will be in May. *Zut, alors.* This is the second property I've dragged my feet on, which has been

whisked away. This is the lesson, then – stop dreaming, and **act**. Gabriel, what more can you tell me about timing, trust, acting and whatever else to start getting this bookstore dream off the ground?

Gabriel: Good afternoon dear girl, it is so good to be here with you, as you type rapidly away, and can keep up with me! You are going to have many disappointments along the way, and these were gentle ones. Perhaps you could notice how much you had invested and project into each one and see that practicing detachment would help, at least until the contract is signed. You may have to do some legwork, and view many properties, before the right one comes along. This is a fine balancing act, as you are discovering, as you cannot visualize quite as well, without a physical house to look at. But this also underscores the importance of starting your collage project, and massing lots of images to help the mental picture jell. Yes, buy used magazines at the library, or anywhere. Buy some fresh glue stick, too! The faster you get clear, the faster it will happen. What you need more than anything right now is time and space to draft the big vision and its auxiliary lists. Clarity, clarity, clarity! And prioritizing — yes — ask us to help you with that, especially. All is almost in place — have faith.

As to asking others for help, keep it simple, reduce the input, get your own vision clear before talking to friends. Do you remember how sometimes asking advice about your house renovation just confused the issue? Most practical answers you need are either in books or on websites, and you can dip in and out of those at will. Create a foundation before you start choosing trim colors!

Excellent advice, thank you.

Monday, April 23, 2012, 9:00 pm
Dear Gabriel,
I'm getting a little bit better at work about accepting things that come in, and batting them out of the ballpark without resisting so much, but honestly, the things people ask for! "Clear out the dead mouse under the refrigerator." "Come back a second time to re-do the work you just did." "Bend your rules so that I can get what I want, just because I want it."

And to continue with tonight's theme about everything in my life, thank you for that lovely oracle card reading we just did. It calmed me down after I had made my mega-list of 8+ big worries and was staring at it helplessly. What I hear from you is that I should try to: reconnect and ground, talk to you more often, sit still in nature, release the outcome to you and God, ask for faith to manifest, and remember the miraculous power surrounding me. But this is so much to remember! How can I keep these principles at the forefront of my mind and heart?

Gabriel: Good evening, blessed child, you are excellently clear tonight! Yes, I am right beside you, enjoying this very much. You almost don't need to write, I am that close. Soon we will be speaking to you directly through your auditory channels. Dear child, trying so very hard to remember every little thing and do things right. What you perceive as separate items to remember are actually one energy, the energy of love. Analyzing it and breaking it down into components is your biggest block. All will become much easier as you start to heal your heart, and operate your awareness out of your heart rather than out of your brain. This is shifting already. Miracles are en route. For now, rather than trying to remember all these things as components, simply ask us one thing: to open your heart, and help you perceive with your heart. This will solve your mental dilemmas easily! And the rest will flow like water: enchantment, magic, fun, natural perception, joy — in fact, everything you have asked for.

Gabriel, thank you for this, which truly is an Answer. Which leads to my next serious questions:

Why has so much of my life been consumed with the imbalance of my intellectual fears, and why was my heart so closed down in the first place? Why has it been such a struggle to find even the tiniest degree of understanding and awareness?

Archangel Gabriel: God loves all creatures equally, and his love is very powerful. You already know that at birth you are given the gift of "forgetting" your source, which is God. You already know that the more extreme the contrast, the deeper the appreciation. As an evolutionary being, this is exactly your challenge — to encounter greater and greater contrast, or deepen and deepen "forgetting." If you evolve, or rise to meet the challenge, your soul grows. This is why you recognize the importance of context, and the scale of the struggle — played out on a cosmic trajectory. This is the very wise old part of you that helps to override your fears or justify the pain in a larger sense. Does that help?

Then...what about so many of my family, friends, peers – I seem to be surrounded by happy, well-adjusted people with big, loving hearts who are marching happily along in life with healthy relationships, beautiful children, stable home lives and very high standards of living. This is the norm which is being held up to me, as far as I can see, and I am the exception. This is really painful. I am frustrated because if you count me as a spiritual consumer, then I believed the advertising that happiness is my birthright. If that is the case, then I protest that it is not yet the case for this human. I've tried so hard to do everything right, just like the books say, and the results have been really slow in coming. Or maybe I'm just dense and don't get it. The Game is rigged, there is only one Game in town, and I keep hitting a dead end. Then I sit down hard, with a spiritual concussion – and find I have no choice but to go back to the only Game in town.

*Archangel Gabriel: Would it help you to know that God is experiencing Himself/Herself through your experience of frustration, hurt, sadness, anger, despair and confusion? Together with experiencing the struggle to make sense of it and transcend it? So you see, your process is quite important and valuable, your lifetime and each degree of awareness achieved, is monumental. And very dear to God. **Very** dear.*

Then I think God is a complete masochist.

Archangel Gabriel: Yes, that too. Do you feel better now?

Hmph.

Archangel Gabriel: You're laughing. Do you feel better now?

I suppose...that I feel that's enough now.

Archangel Gabriel: Goodnight, dear Barbara – please write soon, and ask us every moment of the day – we're with you and love to be of service!

April 24, 2012, 8:15 pm
Dear Angels,
My supervisor called me into her office today to confront me about my chronic lateness. She was very nice and neutral about it, and she was right, of course. I am dealing with some feelings of embarrassment, shame, and defensive anger now, trying to breathe through them, sit with them, acknowledge them. My mind is climbing all over itself trying to justify my lateness by pointing out other people's failings. But that is a battle I can fight later (maybe). Therefore, Angels, please help me to go to bed *now*, fall asleep quickly, sleep deeply, rise early and easily, and stick to my morning timetable, and be out the door absolutely at 8:45 tomorrow, not one second later. Please help me with this new discipline.

Angels: Give all your sadness, anger and shame to us, we will transmute it for you. This is the start of new things for you, do you see the significance? This is another subtle turning point, so notice it and welcome it, for it is shifts like this that will pave the way to changes in your work life. Say "yes" to the discipline of early rising, and notice how wonderful it will make you feel about yourself. It is time to let go of old patterns, and this is your opportunity. Be gentle, loving and forgiving, see if you can sustain it for 40 days, and watch your whole life open up. Come, take our hands, we will lead you into this new life, singing and dancing! Sleep now, dear one, and we will wake you in the morning!
Love, the Angels

One, Perfect Rose

Sunday, May 6, 2012, 9:20 am

Dear angels,
Today I slept in until 9, and rushed off to the yoga studio for the mala*
workshop I had signed up for.

---

*Mala: a sacred length of beads strung on silk, held in one hand and used as a meditative tool while chanting mantra or praying, aiding repetition. The length of a mala is specific and it may be made of 108, 54, or 27 beads, culminating in a Guru bead and a tassel.

The mala workshop was led by a kundalini yoga teacher named Gurunater Kaur. She taught us how to use them, and had brought a selection of malas made from different minerals and crystals: jade, turquoise, coral, crystal, quartz, aquamarine – all of which she had made herself, hand-selecting all of the beads. She said that people are intuitively drawn to what they want or need for that time in their lives. I was immediately, strongly drawn to this beautiful garland of 108 rose quartz beads. I was surprised at how distinct the energy was that I felt from the rose quartz mala, during and immediately after the chanting. So I did purchase it. I am so happy with it – it is so beautiful, precious, and sacred. Gurunater blessed it for me. This is another first in my life – and it came into my life on the 40th day of the 40-day abundance meditation we had been assigned.

Angels, please tell me more about this rose quartz mala. What are its properties and significance for me? I love the color pink!

Dearest Barbara,

*Thank you for writing to us to share your wonder at your beautiful pink mala of 108 rose quartz beads. This is another step on your path, another tool for healing, focus, and devotion. It is **perfect** for you. As Gurunater said, anything pink is the color of the heart, and so this mala represents what you need to heal most, together with a tangible form to help remind you that you are already healed, as you have prayed for this for so long. All the symbols and their meanings unite here: your middle name, Rose; the flower and its fragrance, your favorite color of soft pink, the deep healing properties of the mineral itself, and the beauty of the form, simple, pure, tactile, practical. Use this beautiful mala with care, devotion, respect, and an open heart, and it will transmute your pain. So, too, will you blossom, like the rose that you are. Come into your grace and beauty, stand in the sunlight, shed your thorns, yield your fragrance, share your gifts with the world. You have been blessed with gifts of divine origin, welcome them, use them, recognize them. Your precious life is unfolding perfectly. You are "one, perfect, rose." You are **our** one, perfect, rose. Rejoice!*

Beautiful, beautiful, beautiful. *Thank you.* Goodnight my dear angels, please send me sweet dreams and clear intentions.

Wednesday, May 9, 2012
Dear Angels,

It seems all I do is whine and complain, but then there do seem
to be so many incidents in my life which knock the stuffing out of
me. Yesterday was another one. At the staff meeting, Mindy made a
sniping, belittling, remark directed straight at me. I was so shocked by
its viciousness that I went into a kind of PTSD/emotional flooding,
which lasted all day. Tried to write to you last night, but felt too
worthless and full of self-hatred, and I knew it would be the same old
whining all over again. So, I sat and listened. I think something must
have gotten through, because I got out my rose quartz mala, pulled out
my Louise Hay,* which I haven't looked at in years, and started in with
some basic, positive affirmations.

"I'm OKAY" seems to be effective, for some reason, and I seem to
have uncovered a deeply held, mad, bad, sad old belief that I am NOT
okay. It's strange to me that the language/feeling is that simple, but it
is. Something is shifting and I feel ever so slightly better and clearer,
with more energy. I am not destroying myself at every minute of the
day. How did I ever reach such a sad state?

I feel like a pariah at work, and sense the pack instinct starting to edge
me out of the group. I am falling down in dealing with Mindy, my
emotions, and the situation. She has made catty, belittling comments
before, and this is not the first time. I just realized that her technique
is systematically denying another person's reality so that they start to
doubt their sanity. Well, **not I**, **not** this time, and **not** on my watch.
It is all painful and confusing and I need your help.

Please help me Angels Haniel, Gabriel, whomever! I am so tired of
having emotional/spiritual crises, feeling wrong, broken, stupid,
dense, unskilled, clueless, worthless, and any other adjective you
want to throw in. Numb, yes, try numb. Is God enjoying feeling
NUMB? Oh, the incessant, colossal melodrama of pain, in lockstep

*You Can Heal Your Life, by Louise Hay.

waltz with my ego. What would you have me do?

Angels: How clear you are tonight — do you feel it? Yes, the healing has begun. You are gaining distance and making deliberate shifts more easily now, and observing yourself do it. You did it last night — you pulled yourself right out of your emotionally flooded state. Is that not powerful? Have hope! It only gets easier from here.

Well, yes, there was a helpful shift, and it all had to do with using the rose quartz mala. I take no credit for it. I will use it again tonight. I am so full of ICK-ICK-ICK-ANGER-HURT-PAIN-PUNISH, that I am in full flight mode. I don't want to be adult and mature about this – I am having a temper tantrum. Do I just avoid my supervisor for another day or two, and prolong the torture, or what?

Angels: One thing at a time, and back to basics. You are treating all of your emotions as BAD, so that you spiral into tighter, lower, angrier coils. Gently take each emotion, accept it — you know how to do that — breathe through it, and give it full expression. Do this tonight, while you have time, space, and privacy. Use the mala and practice a phrase of acceptance, such as "my emotions are valid, and I accept them." When you feel better — and you will — then you will have the strength to bless Mindy. Come, let us try it. You are so good at these things, and the relief will be so profound! Then you can sleep peacefully, which is the greatest gift. What do you say?

Okay, let's go. Will you please transmute all these awful, ugly emotions, and bring me to a state of greater awareness and maturity?

Angels: We will indeed, because we really, really, really LOVE you! Good night, blessed child! Tomorrow will be the best yet!

Thursday, May 10, 2012
Dear Angels,
Rain all morning, cool and drizzly, giving way to overcast skies, which finally opened up to glorious, clear, sunny skies, and everything dried right off...I could go on with these enjoyable descriptions, but it would be masking the real issue. I know I have to deal with Mindy. Angels, what can I do to get everything out of my system?

*Angels: What you are experiencing is not wrong or bad, and does not necessarily need to be amended. It is uncomfortable, painful, and revealing to you, and causing you to push further for answers. Stay with your feelings as long as you need to. Mindy may need to learn from this as well — perhaps you were sent to her, to help her with some facet of **her** life. It takes great strength to work through emotions on the level you are doing. Keep practicing acceptance, and the situation will clear up of itself. Trust the process. We sent you the oracle cards as a gift to encourage you and let you know that really beautiful things are coming your way. Now the seeds are planted, so do not be surprised when many things manifest. The more you heal, the more energy you free up, the more pours into your life. Your faith will be rewarded. There is nothing more you need do!*

Ah....then there is nothing for it but to practice affirmations with my mala, and go to bed. Thank you, angels, for these gifts and this guidance. Can we have fun now?

Good night, dear girl. May you sleep the sleep of the blessed.
LOVE from the Angels, who adore you!

"Do You Understand?": Wisdom from Kwan Yin

Wednesday May 16, 2012, 9:10 pm
Dear Angels,
Tonight I met with Stephanie for the fourth and last of our sessions. She had agreed to do a reading for me, so we started with that. I had imagined she would use the oracle cards, but what she did, and what happened, was so far out of my experience, that I was unprepared for it. Once again, my life has altered and accelerated. I was stunned by everything that was said. No chance to go back to nice, comfy ordinariness now.

Angels, please help me to remember and write down as much as possible from today's session.

We seated ourselves on folding chairs, face to face, knees practically touching. After a grounding and centering exercise, Stephanie invited the angels to communicate through her, in my best and highest good. Then, after she said, *"and so it is,"* the collective consciousness/her guide began speaking through her.

Stephanie's voice changed and took on a different inflection or accent – it was deeper, more maternal, yet very no-nonsense – as though the bar was being raised, and I was being expected to keep up. The voice/angel spoke in paragraphs, and after each section, said very **directly**:

"Do you UNDERSTAND?"

I felt like 4,000 volts were going through my 20-volt brain, an energy field lasering my whole system from a few inches away. Stephanie said (afterwards) that the presence/voice felt like Kwan Yin,* and I would agree. Here we go:

She – the Kwan Yin energy – started by saying that it was time for me to align myself vibrationally in order to realize the highest purpose of my soul.

She began describing a metaphor: *"Imagine you are on a stage,"* she said, *"and there are no props, no other actors, no audience. You are standing alone on the stage. No one is watching you, it is only you. Imagine you are sitting in the audience, seeing yourself on stage. You can make the image clearer or not, but the control is up to you. You are completely in command. It is up to you what you choose to do on this stage, so what are you going to do? It is up to you whether you fine tune the alignment, in every moment. You can do it at any time, make it louder or softer, less clear or more clear. This is your connection to the Divine, and it is your choice. Now, imagine you go up on stage to talk to yourself, this person you have been watching. What conversation would you have, what would you tell her to do? This is your life, it is only you on stage, and it is all up to you. Do you UNDERSTAND?"*

She talked about the need to breathe, the need to be in nature, the need to take slow, simple walks, and to be by the seashore; I will receive guidance there.

She said that all of my surrounding circumstances were unimportant, they

*Kwan Yin: East Asian goddess of compassion and kindness.

were just surface factors, that they could be set aside, or that I should not be so focused on them. That if I chose to trust in every moment, that all would resolve itself. That my fears and anxieties and confusion come from overthinking and not breathing, trusting, relaxing.

She acknowledged that I have been praying, meditating, and working with the angels and with guidance. I asked about healing, and *She* said it was very complex – body, mind, spirit.

She suggested that maybe the healing I longed for had already taken place, that I was blocking myself because of my choice or worries or lack of connection.

She said, *do you hear the birdsong* (and indeed, a catbird or a robin sang).

She said, *do you hear it in the distance? Listen to the birdsong, it is there.*

Angels, please help me remember what else she said…it almost hurt to hear it, because she really nailed me.

She said that I should simplify my surroundings. I agree with that.

She said that there was no right or wrong, only choices.

She said it was time to listen to my soul and my heart, and follow their guidance. *Ask them*, she said. *What are they saying to you?*

She said something about my need to understand things, and why I was so driven to question them, though she did not use the word "understand."

She said I should use the moment to be in the moment.

She said something about the human timeline, how we were bound by it, but that in actuality, all was time-less and space-less.

(I am beginning to realize that our ordinary, human, tangible reality is the exception, not the rule, and we're such a small percentage of creation that what we go through is, well, maybe not "weird" to Them, but certainly – *sigh* – oh, so *limited*.)

I was spluttering defensively in my mind at these things *She* said, because of course in a tiny corner I had deluded myself that "no one *knew*." Ha. Exposed. I kept spluttering "but I try so hard!" – but that was ignored or swept aside.

What else... *She* said something about choosing to shift my focus.

She kept saying "**D o y o u U N D E R S T A N D?**" and I said yes every time, because it was expected of me, but I am not sure that I really did. I am being asked to jettison my 52-year-old operating system which is so deeply etched into my pea-brain, and no excuses, no explanations, no whining about how hard or impossible it is.

I thought angels were kind and compassionate, but this felt almost stern. I thought I was taking things seriously enough, but this voice and presence made me feel so...shallow.

So...if the analyses and dwelling-upon-things is a choice,

...and the tail-chasing is a choice,

...and it makes me sad, because I get confused, and *that's* a choice,

...then does that mean I should stop asking questions altogether and just trust?

How can I stop asking questions? If there is no right or wrong, why do I feel as though I've been made wrong somehow by this kindly grilling?

So, what do you want from me?

I feel frustrated because I thought I **was** practicing some of these things, but evidently not enough or only superficially. Not good enough, I guess.

This is what drives me crazy – the logic doubles back on itself. If nothing is good or bad, then it shouldn't matter to what degree I choose to participate, it shouldn't matter if I opt not to align myself vibrationally or listen to my heart and soul, or waste my life, or not take walks on the beach.

But the way all of this is couched it feels like that's not really true, that somewhere Someone is saying, *tsk, tsk, you can do better than that.* Or maybe it's just me.

Right. Am working myself into a state. Better stop before someone scolds me for overthinking things. I mean, the nerve.

I'm sorry, Angels, I'm being horrible and rebellious and self-pitying again, on top of being irreverent and hyper-analytical, anxious and self-critical. What a mess. This human pinball will continue to be flipped from one state of mind to the next.

Did I mention that today Mindy marched right up to my desk and demanded to know what was wrong? We worked it out, but I felt sad all day. These details are a serious and real part of my life, angels – how am I supposed to just brush them off, be less focused on them? How do you not focus on a hammer that comes down and smashes your thumb?

But never mind, you have never been in a human body, so you just don't get it. Sorry to trouble you. I will do my mala and go to bed.

Thank you for your help. Good night, angels.

This Is Your Deepest Test

Saturday, May 19, 2012
Dear Angels,
Gorgeous day! The perfect May day.

I requested a copy of *The Findhorn Garden** from the local library and it

*The Findhorn Garden: Pioneering a New Vision of Man and Nature in Cooperation, by The Findhorn Community. The story of a remarkable community in Findhorn, Scotland, where cooperation and communication with the natural elements and devas or nature spirits, created a miraculous garden as "a celebration of life in its divine forms."

came through a couple of days ago. Ancient, battered, circa 1975, edges scraped, binding popping open, binding string exposed...I started it last night and am fascinated. I had no idea. *What* a treasure. Cannot wait to order one of my own.

So this morning's mind-melange is partly to do with the nature cooperation theme – devas, elementals, etc.; partly to do with ongoing sadness and confusion from Wednesday's angel reading; and partly to do with ongoing, ordinary, list-making bizzy-mind. I am sitting outside, angels – *outside* – and the bells of heaven are ringing in birdsong. I am about to go into the garden. What would you have me do?

Angels: Relax and be glad! Let us flow through you! Trust that you are indeed guided, do not doubt. Pause to listen and please ask if you are not sure. Lavish love on your beautiful garden and just talk to every plant you touch. Explain to it first, and apologize if you need to remove it or take its life. Do not feel guilty. You are giving life to so many creatures in your important work, your cherishing is felt and known. The devas and elementals are much assured now, because we have communication, we can reach you, you can hear us. The rest is partnership and it will only improve. Let this day, this time in your garden, heal you. This is all that is necessary. We love you! Shine and be happy, our precious Barbara!
Love,
The Angels

Thank you!

Monday, May 21, 2012
Dear Angels,
I hardly know what to write. I think of all my past entries, and wonder, is there a point? Or I could just delete these words and see what the next moment brings. I am having the blues again, a kind of confusion. All I can do is try not to overthink, overprocess. But then, is a *little* thinking okay, a little analysis? Otherwise, how do I figure things out? My heart hurts.

I do know what the answer is: go sit in nature, by the seaside. Breathe deeply. Not doing so when I have the opportunity is my choice – for example, choosing to focus on petty things like vacuuming the house or running an errand, which I have decided must be done before my houseguest arrives on the 15th. Feeling tired and sad now, I suppose that will change. I guess the problem is that I am not altogether sure that you *can* help with whatever is wrong with me. Maybe I am cracking up. At least I have the option of simply enduring. Angels, if you would like to say anything to me, I will try to hear you now.

*Angels: We are with you now, as we ever will be. You are frustrated because all of your efforts seem to bring you back to the same place, a place of deep hurt that is resistant to healing. You just crave a feeling of normalcy and stability which will allow you to function and carry on in your life. The changes you are going through are unpredictable and seem endless. All the skills you have learned do help, if you remember to apply them — but you get trapped in the emotion of helplessness which saps your willpower. Our dear child, just keep breathing through moment by moment, if that is all you can do. Stay busy if that helps, meditate if that helps, call a friend if that helps, ask us if that helps. Reach for relief any way that you can. Change your thoughts and look for the good. If you can just practice this as a habit daily — try 40 days! — then all will shift for you. This is your deepest test. Only you can decide what grade you will get. Your life is a test, all of it. You are struggling against the responsibility of this, and yes, your illusions are gently being taken from you. Accept this in small doses, give yourself credit for all the things you **have** figured out and gotten through. Then, too, there is trust. Will trusting this moment of blues bring relief? Brave girl, shine through for us. We love you so, and will do all in our power to support you. All is well and all shall be well, no matter what. Blessings of peace upon you, dear child of light —*
Love,
The Angels

Thursday, May 24, 2012
Dear Angels,
More shifting, changing, responding in the world around me as I do. After my experiences of the last couple of weeks, I am shying away from thinking too hard about anything at all, and it is such a pleasure. I know

now when I am in trying-too-hard-mode: straining after interpretation and meaning. I am gingerly allowing my thoughts to flicker over certain concepts: "*trust?*" "*Making an active decision about...?*" but that is **all**.

I think I am getting a teensy bit better (yes, until my next case of cosmic megrims). So tired, so weary. Angels, will you please mow my lawn for me and clean out the gutter?

Thank you.

Angels: We cannot do these things for you, but we can give you strength, courage, and stamina. You are flying high at work and the end of the sprint is in sight. As you resolve these last few housing vacancies, your summer will open up to peace and space. **Then** *we will have many sessions, heart to heart, spirit to spirit, delving into what your life could be like. This is the beginning of the beginning, the new Barbara, as you actively change your thought patterns with deliberation and awareness. Keep taking walks in nature, keep breathing consciously, and please go to bed early so that you can experience the blissful early morning hours. Being sensible has its own rewards, indulging too often does not serve you. You have come so far with us, being brave, true and trying so hard — richness and delight are within your grasp. Soon, soon! Use your lovely mala every night and you will sleep like a baby. You are about to become extraordinary, you just don't realize to what degree. We love you, bless you, and send you and surround you with peace.*

Love,
The Angels

Chapter VI: Beginning to Bloom

The impulse not to suffer is understandable, but there is something else that must accompany genuine inquiry, which is the desire and the willingness to see what is true, to see how we ourselves are putting ourselves into conflict.

– ADYASHANTI, *THE END OF YOUR WORLD*

The Radiance Has Begun

Sunday, June 3, 2012, 8:15 am
Dear Angels,
This morning is bright, fresh, crisp and breezy. There is a mosaic of green shadow dancing and playing outside my window – the many trees – mostly maples – surrounding my house are like a green stadium of activity and motion, sighing, soughing, patting the air, bouncing, conversing, playing in the wind.

I also had $600 worth of gravel delivered for the driveway – and what a difference. I am thrilled. It really makes the house look "proper." Phew! Check, check, check.

Good morning, by the way, Angels – it is so miraculous to sit quietly in my bed and write to you. I have a question about an ongoing problem at work. It's the Smiths again, with their interminable, smug requests for changes to the house. I have indulged in a few private mental scenarios of righteous, melodramatic responses to them. But this is the low road, this is my old ego-driven reaction, and it isn't very mature or interesting or skillful. Therefore, angels, I turn this over to you for solving. Please tell me how to (please) release my extreme irritation with the Smiths. Thank you.

Angels: Dear child of light and hope of our hearts, blessings upon you this gold day. It is I, Gabriel, Please relax and trust that this situation will be solved. As you perceive, it is less the actual fact of what occurred than your reaction to it, which needs transmuting here. You are daily placed in a very difficult situation of needing to enforce strict rules, which conflict with the choices of your clients. You are seeing, more and more often, that this role of policing the clients and constantly educating them and correcting them, goes against your nature, which desires peace and harmony. You do not thrive on conflict, as some people do. Therefore these daily situations distress you. You are becoming increasingly skillful at managing yourself, and the situations, but at the same time, as your true self emerges, you are questioning why you should continue to accept this part of your position. Keep practicing all of your skills with these challenging human interaction — this is what makes you stronger and more flexible. How have your expectations of the Smiths created some degree of your present irritation? Examine that. Recognition of and acceptance of Bob Smith for what he is will help to resolve this irritation. In some cases, you may have to pull out your entire arsenal of skills — and this is a great deal! Detachment, conscious breathing, trust, patience, acceptance, realistic expectations, and yes, even love and blessings. You are right to think that, the greater your skills, the greater the problem you will be sent. This is exactly how it works, and how the soul grows, ever attracting larger means of stretching and expanding. Be proud of yourself that you have come so far and done so well — is it not extraordinary? You are on your way to becoming loving, kind, patient, wise and beautiful, the degrees ever deepening. The radiance has begun.

Dear Gabriel,

Thank you so much for this powerful answer. It must be hard to be a human with such a dominating and ego-driven personality. And perhaps that is my judgment, that I view a large, selfish ego as a bad thing, since it means that one human being may not respect the boundaries of another. So is the ego a bad thing, the way some humans judge it to be, especially in "spiritual" circles?

Gabriel: It is a necessary part of the life force. It is not bad in and of itself — after all, it was created by God, and you have benefitted from it very much in your life as well. It gives you the power to differentiate yourselves, and this creates beautiful diversity of form and expression. When one human's ego disrupts a social pattern, all other surrounding elements rush to balance it. There will always be organisms whose stronger energy supercedes a weaker energy, and this is life force evolving. Read, study, think, feel more on the largeness of this phenomenon and it may help you to stop judging, and be at peace with it. Human social, political and economic systems are highly complex and can be very effective counterbalances to creating stable societies. Do you wish to know more?

Dear Gabriel,

In a bigger sense, yes! I do wish to know more and yes, I do wish to come to terms with the judging side of myself. I am going to wind up here, however, because it is now 9:00 am and I must get on with my beautiful day of activity. Thank you so much for your angel wisdom. O gorgeous day, angels – let's go out and play.

Thank you.

Friday, June 8, 2012, 10:15 pm

Dear Angels,

My question for you tonight, angels, and what I want to leave up to you during Despina's visit, is the sequence, timing and serendipity of all of the encounters and activities with which we will pack our days. Angels, can you please send us wonderful synchronicities and extraordinary opportunities for pleasure and fun, so that Despina has a fabulous time, and does every little thing to her heart's content? That would just be the icing on this huge, super-hostess cake I am baking. Thank you!

Angels: Dear child, we miss these wonderful writing sessions, even though you reach to us with your heart during the day. We, too, love this beautiful connection. The preparation and advent of the visit of your dear friend Despina is yet another instance in your life where the entire package — planning, execution, and actual stay — are a template for and means of flexing your new skills. Has not everything gone smoothly, been timed perfectly, and been completed in exact time? This is a partnership! You are asking for our help, trusting it will come, playing your role in physical manifestation, and then thanking us for it. And so it is, and so it goes, and the proofs build for you, and your awareness of all of the above builds. Thus, dear child, we hear your wish and say "yes!" to it, that your time with Despina will be perfect, and special, and all things will flow in rhythm with a larger pattern. Sleep now,

184

child of our hearts, rest well for your day of accomplishments tomorrow. We love you, and delight in this partnership. Talk to us, ask us, we are here!
Love,
The Angels

Saturday, July 8, 2012, 6 pm
Dear Angels,
I did – it is accomplished. Despina arrived on June 14th, on a sunny mild day at the airport – and we were off and running. Got her settled in, oriented her, gave her the stack of activity literature, drove her here, there, and everywhere, wandered to every beach in the area, gave her the tour of all the high points, including a private garden and Longlawn – and lunch at Bette's, the swanky dockside café of the local marina, whisked her to three cocktail parties in a row on three consecutive evenings, even played tennis with her (her lifelong passion) – and also worked three days a week at the same time. It was wonderful and fun and gratifying – and yes, she met some terrific people – and rather exhausting. She left on the 24th and two weeks later I still haven't had the oomph to vacuum the house. Thank you, angels, for helping everything go so beautifully.

Am sitting on outside on the back deck now, and the birds are all *over*, everywhere, and vocal! Let me see if I can name them: mourning dove, blue jay, wrens, catbird, seagulls, cardinals, robins, and at least one species of sparrow, perhaps some warblers, a woodpecker, and maybe some chickadees. There is cheeping and chittering and twittering and chip-chip-chipping, cooing, cawing (let us not forget crows), tseet-tseet-tseeting, plus the melodious trilling and warbling of cardinal and sparrow. You know, that's a rather extraordinary number of birds in a small backyard, so I do hope my flowers and trees are providing shelter, food, and habitat. It amazes me that there are so many species, and yet none of them has found the delicious concentration of Japanese beetles on my roses. Angels, could you steer some of these birds towards this discovery? I still have not seen

185

a hummingbird recently, though I know he/she must be around, because the red crocosmia is in bloom, as is the clary sage and hosta. The bees are smothering my St. John's wort, and their haunches are fat with pollen – how utterly wonderful.

So many things in my life have been on hold until now, and I am finally picking up the reins again. I am ready to receive your guidance again – where shall we start?

Angels: Beloved Barbara, thank you for writing to us. We enjoy this miracle of communication so much, and cherish it even more than you do! Life is so rich, varied, full and exciting — we want to help you plunge in and experience as much as possible. Even though you have "missed" us in this blink-of-an-eye interim, there has never been a moment when we were not surrounding you, supporting you, responding to you, loving you. Bringing us into your conscious mind and will only makes it that much more alive and enjoyable. You are fermenting with many things that you know are waiting to be articulated, activated, brought forth, not the least of which is your bookstore project. And now, the summer is yours, all yours — though you do see that people are now attracted to you more than ever before, and are showing up in your life: Bettie, Adrienne, Sonia, Josh — just to start! The love you are learning on the inside is beginning to manifest on the outside. All that comes into your life will hold richness and reason for you. We will help you find time and energy to enjoy these wonders, as they come. Dear child, go now and enjoy your evening with your excellent friend Prim, and write to us soon, for we are excited to start getting into the creative details of all that you wish for and dream of!
Love, the Angels!

July 12, 2012
Dear Angels,
It has been such a long time since I have sat quietly and listened to hear you.

Among the jumble of little life things and big life things, I suppose the most prominent on my mind is the thought of renewing attention to the bookstore project. I continue to visually shop for a store location. Thus, what do you know, a sweet little cottage on Main Street came on the market, for a minor $279,000. I printed out the RE flyer and am eyeing it. This is where the courage comes in. Dare I? I have not refined my vision on paper or graphically yet, and have nothing approaching a business plan or budget. So here we are – can you help to make it happen?

Angels: Dearest Barbara, this is wonderful! Yes, make the appointment, and do go see it. If nothing else, it will be good practice. Taking action, making the phone call, seizing the moment — this is where success occurs. If this is the one it will happen for you; if not you need to build practical field knowledge and also overcome your hesitation and reluctance. Taking action dissolves doubt, dissolving doubt builds trust, building trust helps you open yourself to miracles. Do you see? Your part of the partnership happens in real time with tangible objects, and we cannot do it for you. If you are leery of a real estate agent chatting about you to his colleagues, explain to him/her that you wish the viewing to be confidential. He will understand, and that will overcome much of your hesitation. Yes, you live in a very public sphere and are wise to practice discretion. Think how disappointed you will be if this sells without your having seen it. Better yet, think how EXCITING it will be to walk into a space and project your bookstore plans into it! This will motivate you further. Take our hands, dear girl, let us guide you and help you fly. What were those words you said to little Amelia when she was so afraid to jump off the diving board? We coach you to use those words, too: "Yes, I can!"

Thank you for this incredible support. I see now...that with a little awareness, I can catch my little doubts as they flicker through my mind, acknowledge them, and vaporize them back into nothing. Or transmute them, or replace them with a mantra or affirmation. There's a regular swarm of them, like gnats, to handle.

Angels, please help me find the time, space and motivation to spread out again and get creative, to pick up where I left off and find the courage to push my heart's dream to the next level...

Angels: Easily done! Let us sit down to play soon — ask, ask, ask. And perhaps try the oracle cards? You are closer than you think, all is flowing towards you now and your golden era is arriving. We love and cherish you, blessed child.
Love,
The Angels

July 17, 2012
Dear Angels,
The worry this week is the social awkwardness of fellow beachgoers who bring their dogs down to the beach during swimming hours, even board members – which breaks the rules the rest of us abide by. How can I send a message that carries to everyone, and encourage them to cooperate with the rules?

Angels: You know the answer to this, dear girl — bless them and bless the problem. Sit quietly and bring it to mind, and as you pray for a solution, bless the participants. You will feel your heart softening immediately and the fear dissolving. Once the fear dissolves, you will be able to speak to each kindly and honestly about your feelings. If it helps, write out what you want to say first, and rehearse it. Call each one on the phone when you feel comfortable about it. You may be surprised at how simple and effective that is — you are blocked with a little bit of fear right now which makes you feel defensive. Find your strength and your truth, and have faith that the solution will come. Release this to us, dear one, and we will help you. It is our privilege and our joy to do so.

I will do this tonight, because I am tired of carrying this around in my heart, and it is so very petty. It is hard to find one's way in a world full of rules which people are always breaking. How on earth can law enforcers stand their jobs, which is nothing but trying to stop the overflow of rule-breakers?

Good night angels, I will write anon.

Sunday, July

29, 2012, 12:40 pm
Dear Angels,The mental exercise I am tackling today is that of paying down my mortgage in full. Angels, will you please help me pay down my house mortgage in full, $49,000, as quickly and as easily as possible?

Angels: Dear one we hear you and rejoice with you, and feel your happiness as financial freedom looms on the horizon. Things may start to happen very fast now, but you are well-prepared. As your faith and trust and fearlessness increase, the spiritual wheels are lubricated and spin faster — so to speak — for your benefit. You already know that all is well and all shall be well; you already know that your will for you, is God's will for you; so it shall be manifested with joy and pleasure. Your golden age is upon you, and in turn, you will become a compassionate, caring, sharing force for good. You will radiate your kindness and giving outward, and create your own magical ripple effect. This is dynamic grace at its highest, best realization. The request you pose — as you know now — is a tiny, easy energy shift for the cosmos, and is granted willingly and with joy. Accept and watch it happen, with equal willingness and joy, and then you align yourself with us. Do you begin to see?

Yes. I do begin to see, and understand in the most modest of ways, an inkling of what is meant by "power and glory." Thank you, angels.

Choosing Awareness, Grace, Wisdom, Peace

Saturday, August 11, 2012, 6:30 pm
Dear Angels,
O hammock time, sweet, peaceful, excellent hammock time! Angels, please help me write an ode to hammocks and their therapeutic qualities.

The last two days or so we – the region – have been saturated in ultra-heavy, moist tropical air, 94% humidity, with tissue clouds scudding by immediately overhead. A tornado watch was in effect, and it was definitely a nerve-wracking, flukey weather system that could have delivered anything. After I got home last night, I was sleepy but restless, so I walked slowly down to the beach and watched the concentric, frilly rings of breakers echo in, with racing buff and gray tissues of fleece overhead, near touchable. Thrilling!

Thank you for helping me get out of the house, angels. That was good for me.

Today, however, woke groggy and late, to hot, saturated, stuffy stillness. Moved slowly until noon – had a strong cup of coffee. Enjoyed running some errands on my bike. Gardened a bit, made some phone calls. Went to the beach about 2:30 – good idea. High tide and luscious satiny water, 74 degrees, and the beach was half full of people giving off a sense of low energy and relaxation.

Then home, shower, missed 5 pm yoga, so in a peaceful mood I propped myself up in the hammock and meditated for about 10 minutes on the question, *what am I seeking?*

The answers: healing, understanding, transformation, reunion of my body mind and spirit, and – equilibrium.

Which struck me like this: E Q U I L I B R I U M

I did not know until this moment, suspended in this hammock, how deeply and powerfully my Libra nature drives me. That I am literally hanging in balance right now, bringing a physical release and sense of aha! to my soul. I had a profound visceral sensation of being the physical pole between the arms of the two scales, ever striving to reduce the wild oscillations of those scale arms, to bring them to stillness, peace, and yes, equilibrium. It is the oscillations I feel most keenly; it is the oscillations I see when I look back at everything I've ever been driven to do in my life. And it finally makes sense to me why I am so entirely happy in a hammock, because the physical suspension is in perfect harmony and alignment with everything in my nature. When the oscillations have stilled, there is perfect safety, there is perfect relaxation, which leads to all other perfections: harmony, healing, completion, etc.

Angels, all my life I have had fluid writing skills, but not necessarily the creative imagination to spin stories, narrative, themes, characters. This question lies like an unresolved lump in my psyche, a stone I continually stub my toe on. Can she, can't she? Please tell me about my creativity and what I could do to stimulate it.

Angels: It is I, Gabriel, bringing you blessings of love and peace. Thank you so much for opening up to my message tonight. This questions of your creative ability is an excellent one, for you are the channel through which God's creativity flows. You know this, now as fact, and you know it takes many billion-billion-fold forms. Therefore you are creative, yes — this is inescapable. The blocks, fears and doubts are like so many boulders and logs blocking a stream — they never stop the water, but they can divert it to a different shape. You have a belief that the imaginative capacity to tell stories is somehow innate, inherited — one has it or one doesn't. Question this belief: is it really true? Question your motives: why do you want to tell a story in novel form? Curiosity and compassion are a necessary part of the motivating drive. Time, willingness, desire — what part do these play? Yes, you can write stories, but do you want to? The time may not be right yet. You are slowly discovering a more powerful, organic base to your life, which is pure, simple contact with nature. The process of your healing and the return of your joy and emotional body will ultimately answer all of your questions about creativity, because the urge will then arise so naturally that explanations are unnecessary. It simply becomes Doing. This urge will lead you to study, experiment, take classes and workshops, expand your curiosity — and the day will come when you won't believe you could have ever doubted yourself so. Every facet of this process can be turned into a request to your Angels — please ask us! You are our blossoming child of light, which is pouring through you and you know it not. Please, darling Barbara, let us expand and explore your wish for greater creativity! Let us fold it into your life in a natural, joyous, harmonious way. We can transform your life — but you have to ask us to.

Gabriel (hi), thank you. I am starting to get it. My "observer nature" is surfacing, and more frequently now I have a sense of being calmly detached, especially if it is a situation where you and God are working through me. I am enjoying the distance that creates the audience and the stage. This is a sacred state, I sense.

Last night I read *A House in France* by Gully Wells. Towards the end she writes of her sweet three-year old boy wreaking havoc with crayons on the walls of a room. When asked why he did it he says, *"iss my essitement!"* Beautifully put. Yes, dear Gabriel, *iss my essitement!* That makes me want to take your hand and unite, in my mind, body, soul, memory, viscera, all the lovely things of this world. Please help me channel my essitement! into writing well, expressively, imaginatively. If it is God's will for me. This would be fun to share. Help me find my voice. Help me start.

Good night, dear Gabriel, and thank you for your presence, wisdom, and company. I love your company.

Goodnight, blessed child!

Sunday, August 19, 2012, 11:00 am
Dear Angels,
The life snarls seem to come at me one right after another. A work problem is preying on my mind.

It's Felicia, the marketing manager who has been in place one year. Now that she is sure of herself, she is making power moves.

I am alarmed, anxious, confused. I have a *deep* desire to pack my bags and flee. She is plain bad news, and she dislikes me enough to do me harm – and she does not appear to have scruples.

Angels, what do I do? Starting a job hunt would be such an upheaval. I am comfortable where I am, and reluctant to make the huge heave-ho effort. Nor is there much out there on offer. Please help me to handle these roiling emotions and plot a course of action which is strong and wise. Fearful and melodramatic scenes are starting to loop in my head. Please help me shift my thoughts and actions to a higher plane. This one is very scary and very bad.

It is hard to figure out the reality of this – is it a genuine threat, should I bolt, or can it be worked out and resolved naturally? Thank you, angels for your guidance.

Angels: We are here to help, and it is our joy to lead you into the light using all of the skills you've been learning. The excellent draft list you made about making the transition from ambiguity to clarity, is your map. We were with you and helped to guide you in writing it. Does it not calm you and give you a brilliant plan of action? It can be infinitely expanded on, but we don't need to make it too complicated. Yes, please add, "shower blessings on Felicia and all company staff" as an important component.

*This is all you need to do. Consult this every day and practice whatever items on it call to you or seem necessary. Whether or not the work situation is a real threat is not so much the question — the question is, as always, your response to the situation and your choices. You are choosing awareness, grace, wisdom, peace. Even if you do not actively feel these qualities in your body, mind, or soul, they are there and growing. Sleep now, dear one, and be refreshed and happy in the morning, knowing we are always besides you and always so close! We cherish these opportunities to help your soul grow. **Nothing** is more important. Goodnight, shining star of our hearts —*

Love,
The Angels

Friday, August 31, 2012
Dear Angels,
A peaceful, sweet summer evening. We have dodged hurricanes so far, miraculously – one year ago we had Irene and that created quite a mess. Knowing what it could have been makes me grateful.

My office alarm of ten days ago abated somewhat, but I still feel the tension and disapproval at work. I feel so angry and helpless, which is why I feel blue tonight. I was kidding myself that the situation might have calmed down. I just want to march in and put my resignation letter on Mindy's desk. A typical employee fantasy, I suppose. Is this the spark to get me started on a new path? Please help me, angels, I am sad and confused.

Angels: Trust your higher reactions, darling child! You know what to do! Think about it — you're already there. First — you are writing to us. Secondly, you're ready to revise the strategy you drafted earlier. Thirdly, you have the oracle cards ready. Fourthly, your mind is already casting around for solutions: meditation. Acceptance of hurtful emotions. Making a list of positive effects.

Trying affirmations. Re-reading past entries for encouragement. Now, what else can you do for yourself that is loving and accepting? Remember, this is a process, and may take some time, so recognize that practicing all of these skills may be a weekly, or monthly need — just as when you bought your new car. Imagine now, if you got a beautiful, shiny fantastic new dream job, just as unbelievably perfect and sexy as your car? Would not all the pain and ambiguity be worth it?

That's an excellent way to put it – perspective, I need perspective. I think I will start right away on my list of positive aspects. I have to repeat here what Anita Moorjani wrote in her beautiful book, *Dying to Be Me:*

"My aim is to feel good enough about myself to get to a point of trust, and in that state, let go of the outcome. When I began observing my own flawlessness, I started to notice my external world reflecting this."

This says it all so simply, and get to the heart of what I struggle with – negative emotions which generate judgements about myself, creating a spiraling-down pattern – almost like a pincer movement between the mind and the emotions which harms the soul.

Here's what I feel good about today:

- Meeting with those kind clients and former bookstore owners, who gave me hope and curiosity about my own interests in a bookstore
- Just getting to my hammock at the end of the day
- The success, oh the huge success, of waking up with clarity and energy, effortlessly at 7:00 am, then doing 45 min worth of breathing exercises and yoga
- Being aware of how much cleaner and happier my body feels after doing weeks of intensive yoga
- It's payday
- Receiving the arborists' bill for a full $500 less than I thought it would be
- It's a soft, soft night, the crickets are chirping and thrumming, and I may just be able to get up early and go to 8:30 yoga

That is enough to start with. Thank you, angels, for teaching me how to be kinder and kinder to myself.

Let All Doubt Dissolve

Saturday, October 5, 2012
8th anniversary of Yogi Bhajan's passing.
Dear Angels,
I am back again after September's kundalini yoga multi-weekend workshop, which finished today. Once more, it was four hours of chanting, sweating, philosophy, mantra, breathwork – and so we stumble out at 5 pm on an October afternoon, wondering what we have just been through, what we can learn from it.

Personally, I found the meditation on the Divine Mother to be incredibly powerful. I poured myself into it, and demanded to be healed, unified, reunited with my whole soul, have my joy returned to me.

Now, tonight, I am feeling a little blue. I know this place, this feeling, this phenomenon where Old Stuff surfaces after an intense kundalini yoga practice. I very nearly went for a walk to the convenience store to buy a pint of ice cream, but I didn't. Instead, I let my feelings surface, cradled a pillow as if it were a baby, and welcomed and accepted them all in. Wow, I did it: I caught myself in time, sat myself down and worked it through instead of acting on it. Was that *healing*? I don't know. But a victory of sorts, I think.

Monday, October 1, 2012, 9:15 pm
Dear Angels,
I am not sure why I am writing tonight – I have combined sense of overwhelmment and exhaustion. I am continuing to get these bouts of deep, numb lassitude, like a low-blood-pressure, low-blood-sugar, one-two punch. Why is it so hard to stay on an even keel when it seems all I do is monitor and maintain my little health issues? Yes, I know, I should see a doctor. Blah!

There is so much more to go on about, but I really just need some kind words of wisdom and guidance from you, please, about the current confusions and anxieties in my life. Thank you.

Angels: Darling girl, we are so pleased you are writing to us again! So often now you are tired, busy, or distracted. This is a wonderful therapy and we encourage you to pick up your pen more often. Your life is full to overflowing, and when you proceed without knowing the questions clearly, the answers may likewise be unclear, and thus less helpful. When you write, you are always clear, even if you think you are not, because the single-pointedness of the activity forces you to articulate the issue you need to know about most. Also, it keeps some helpful tools in the forefront of your mind. You are a little low on energy because your thoughts and feelings are tending toward the fearful. Notice the anxieties around your health — acknowledge them and accept them. Otherwise, they will accumulate and build into a reality. You are getting glimpses of detachment now, your observer-nature, which is incredibly useful. Practice expanding this and resting in it. We are so proud of how strong and fit and determined you are to increase your health! Your fantastic walks at lunchtime in the park-like cemetery, your increased yoga classes, your walking and biking around town, this is a huge success that has already given you tangible, active hope every day. You are reinforcing your own radiance this way, and we are cheering you on. Building your confidence and self-esteem this way is exactly what you need to do right now, and you are very aware of it.

*As for your fatigue and intestinal disorder, you need to solve this as soon as possible, because the confusion and anxiety it generates depletes all the lovely energy you had built up from your other activities. Yes, do more tai chi to build your energy. We would like you to see a doctor. A physical checkup is very important. A diagnosis of either condition or both would bring you great relief just in the knowing. You are surrounded by many kind, sensible friends who know the medical field firsthand, who can easily support and guide you. Please, darling Barbara, from your angels who love you so, please release your fear and resistance to us and ask us to help you make an appointment. You **know** we will wing you through the rest! It is larger in your mind than it need be, let it come down to earth and be a very normal ordinary part of your life.*

Dear Angels,

It makes it so much easier when you just "tell" me what to do. Thank you, dear angels, and good night.

Sunday, October 21, 2012 3:45 pm

Dear Angels,

It has been an extraordinarily perfect weekend. I am so grateful and relieved (and aware) that my energy level has been stable throughout both days. I really appreciate this, given how many dips, flatlines, and kneecapped energy states I have had lately.

And now this luxury – capping perfection. To sit here in my snuggly spa robe in a clean and bright, cozy room writing to you angels. Let me pick up where we left off last night with the angel oracle cards, which I had laid out but nearly fell asleep over. I drew the cards: *Manifestation, New Love, Ideas and Inspiration.*

The last action I had taken was to tour the property on Main Street, but I don't have the cash, and am not in a position to buy it right now. The upcoming months should be quiet for me, so maybe I could re-ignite the project? Please give me guidance or suggestions. Thank you, angels.

*Angels: Dear Barbara, we are so happy to hear from you and engage in this creative, fun dialogue about your bookstore. Thank you for writing to us. We write to you about manifestation, ideas and inspiration and new love, because we love you so much and want to help you succeed with great joy, happiness, and satisfaction. Your soul craves it, and the craving grows as your fears lessen, and your confidence increases. The manifestation card reads: "You nourish your newborn idea by believing in it and by following the step-by-step guidance that God and the Angels give to you through your feelings, dreams, and visions." And also by the answers you receive from us here! So far, so good. You are resting in a little bit of a plateau, catching your breath, looking around, seeing how far you have come, and wondering which path to strike off on next. It's not altogether clear, it may be a bit murky, but you **feel good** and have clarity about the rightness of what you are doing,* *and faith that the next step will be revealed. We have arrived together with you, and we send you a gentle reminder that even when it doesn't "feel" like anything is happening, great divine machinations are always occurring. Enjoy this peace, this lull, because once the active manifestation starts, you will be a busy girl! As for steps to take next, continue exactly as you are doing now. Scout locations, research books, add to your database, look for opportunities. This would be a good time to talk to a small business administration organization or start-up consultation. Start drafting a business plan if you feel like it. Review and revive your initial creative studies. Lay the groundwork before you go to Kripalu and perhaps make the bookstore your creative/manifesting intention theme for the weekend. This is enough to start with — it is plenty, in fact. Dive in and make every exploration a pleasure. You are right where you are supposed to be — know this, and let all doubt dissolve.*

Thank you so much for this reassurance. I feel better and stronger already. Thank you angels!

Letting Joy Seep Back In

November 25, 2012, 4:20 pm
Dear Angels,
I have not written in so long – I am saving up my subjects, as it were. Of all my major issues, the one for which I have the greatest desire to heal, is the question of soul retrieval. The sad episode of nineteen or so years ago, when some vital, beautiful and vivacious part of my soul, fled physically, bodily from me in a great "whoosh" in response to an abusive encounter, is a driving motivator in my quest for healing, as you know. My visit to Kripalu and shamanic workshop reawakened this desire/issue/unresolved part of me, and so with this in my heart I turn to you with my questions.

After the teacher's presentation I went up to him and asked, "Can a fragmented soul rejoin or reunite without doing a soul-retrieval?" He said yes, absolutely. *Aha.*

I walked away musing on this hope-candy, this answer to my burning need. Which brings me to here, now, me, and You, angels. *Has* my fragment of soul reunited with the rest of me? It would be a new dawn in my life if my soul was united, whole, and joyous again.

*Angels: Dear child, we love thee so. Yes, you are right, a new day is dawning for you, and your long years of fears and tears can be put behind you now. You are our courageous one, our dawning star and shining child of bliss. Your soul is whole, your soul is whole, your soul is whole! We feel your uncertainty — which is natural. You have lived for so long in a fractured state that it will take you a little time to let the joy seep back in, as you begin to find your increasing degrees of expansion. We say, do go and see Stephanie anyway, she will confirm for you what you already sense. It is no coincidence that your renewal is occurring at the end of the year, at the death of 2012 you will emerge into a beautiful, stronger, reborn Barbara, with clarity, purpose, strength, joy, and life skills for managing all that is sent to you. The gifts are coming, the gifts are here, the gifts always were. Find excitement in this miraculous expansion of your being. Watch with awe as you attract, faster and faster, people, abundance, miracles, loved ones, into your life. Meteor showers of blessings can be as much of a roller coaster ride as 'bad' things in troubled times. Can you accept this magnificence? You can always turn to us when things become overwhelming. The times are changing faster than you know, and you — you, dear Barbara — are part of the rising population of enlightened ones, the torch carriers. As you accept your miracle, you will observe, and see with clarity, that every minute, fraction, degree, or molecule of previously experienced anguish which was necessary to generate its being, to generate the growth response in you, which in turn brought you to this place of healed wholeness. It may just be, dear child, that nothing will ever be the same again — can you feel this? No fear, you are ready! Ah, yes, dear one, you have it: this, **this**, is THANKSGIVING.*

It is already communicated, from my heart to yours, but my pen keeps moving, and I will just say, *thank you*, angels.

December 18, 2012
Dear Angels,
Bit of a hectic day today…I am re-reading my entry from August 31st and your answer to me, and so I think there is nothing better to do, than repeat that lesson:

Solutions:

- meditation
- acceptances of painful emotions
- making a list of positive effects
- repeating affirmations
- re-reading past entries for encouragement
- making a list of what I feel good about
- breathing deeply
- practicing "Let's see what happens!" to expand my Self
- step into the realm of ambiguity
- coming up with an ask the angels list

Wow – I just found my notes from three months ago – it's all there. Just need to practice the skills, I think. Angels, please tell me anything else I need to do or practice in this new period of uncertainty.

Angels: Darling girl, we love you, you're a star! The beauty of this is that you've already figured it out and have beaten us to the punch. It's right there under your nose – transformation of the situation is yours for the making. Pull it all together – try a little bit of each of these, every day if you can, and see what happens. Could it be that this is merely a test to see if you can shape your destiny? You know, deep down, that no matter the outcome, you will be more than fine, in fact, you know that a new horizon holds no fears for you. How far far far you have come, brave girl, brave heart. Once you feel confident enough about rising above the situation, you could even become **curious** *about a new job, or start to* **enjoy** *a job search. This is where you want to be, expanding in positive attitudes and positive emotions. It feels GOOD! And you're there! So please, darling one, do dip into the Louise Hay and the Abraham-Hicks book, and enjoy your sense of positive power, or would that be power positivity? We're right by your side, enjoying the ride. Your growth into a realized human being occurs at these very moments, these delicate moments of choice. It is an honor to work through this consciously and willfully with you, and a joy to see it unfold. O blessed child, success is thine!*
Love,
The Angels,
And John, with a big kiss!

Saturday, December 29, 2012, 10:40 pm
Dear Angels,
In spite of all my experiences with you, my nearly two years of
intimate communication and constant exchange of thought-energy,
in spite of the multitude of miracles you have bowled me over with,
in spite of my factual knowledge that our partnership works and
manifests itself in tangible form, I am still shaken to my core every
time another such miracle lands in my lap. And here we are again,
angels, in a late-night writing session, when I am coming down off
a miracle-high, feeling overwhelmed, and grateful.

Today I went on a wintertime road trip/escapade to a local industrial
town with my dear friends, the Williams family. We drove to a funky
neighborhood known for its architectural salvage warehouses, and
had fun poking around – punctuated by stops to pop in and out of
local restaurants. On the way home, it began snowing. When we
began fish-tailing on the slushy roads, in the cozy confines of the car
with white snow pouring down around us, I taught them the *ad guray
nameh* protective mantra. The kids loved it, and recorded our chanting
on their mobile phones. We laughed all the way home.

A charmed day turned into a charmed night. We were all cramped
from too much sitting in the car, but believe it or not, everyone was
hungry again, so at 6:30 we set off for the local chic bistro, which
was happenin' and bustling. We sat down, ordered a Napa Cab Sav,
and had a delightful time puzzling over the luscious menu. I chose
the pappardelle with chanterelles – heaven. The four of us chatted of
this and that, and the conversation turned to books. One thing led
to another – and maybe it was the wine – and I found myself telling
them about my dream of a little second hand bookstore. They all
became very excited, and the conversation took off, as they entered
into the vision and proposed names, themes, buildings...I couldn't
keep up with the excited stream of comments.

My eyes were swimming with tears at this loving support, and I think
my heart ping-ponged between my brain and my throat, because there

was *this loud angelic thunderclap* when Joe said casually, "I think it's a great idea, and you're right, it's just what our town needs."

We had dessert, and we left the bistro, they drove me home, and off they drove into the night and into the snow and now it's almost midnight and I am still writing – but barely – having writer's cramp and still feeling wobbly and awed.

Off now, to my meditation and my pillow, and sweet dreams to me – Love,
Barbara

*Angels: Darling Barbara, sunshine of our hearts, bless you always and thank you for writing to us. The magic is picking up speed, it will happen faster and faster now, because you are ready and the timing is right. We love raining miracles upon you because you recognize them not only for what they are, but recognize the context and also the conditions that brought them forth, which **you** helped to create. You are in awe of yourself — this is what is really happening — the eternal You, the divine source at the center of your being. Yes, you are starting to get faint intimations of the Diamond Mind of Pure Being. We are delighted with the new thoughts you are choosing which help you to align with Divine Creation. As you choose these thoughts more consistently, your reality will become ever more flawless as the Universe moves to support your think about yourself. And your awareness is growing incrementally by leaps and bounds as you make direct associations with the thought you think and the resultant events in your life. Oh, yes, very much "if A, then B." You now know how to actively, deliberately, self-reinforce positive thoughts. **You're there! You're there!** The rest is just a matter of degree. As for your miraculous dinner last night, why we enjoyed that very much. It was a complete set-up, our favorite kind. Could you grow accustomed to more of the same? You may want to prepare yourself... Do not be shy about calling in or using the services of other earth angels — and you recognize your friend as one. They are strongly empowered to do great good, and they derive much joy from this involvement. A door has been opened... you are peeking through it... only you can push it open and step across the threshold. With all of your skills, openness, willingness, courage, grace and desire, how can you possibly fail? Trust the perfection! You are part of the perfection! We count on you to walk in your own radiance and report your experience of it to us. This is vital! This is everything! Be our witness of*

Divinity, laugh with us down the days, years, eons... for flawlessness is the Cosmic rule of Being.

Precious one, we love and cherish your smallest to-do and planning list, as the tiny building block that becomes your glory. You are at play in the fields of the Lord — and so it is.

Blessings upon you child, from the Heavenly Host of Angels — and John for these real moments of human and Divine perfection.
Love,
All of Us!

One day, I hope I can learn to write back to you as wisely, lovingly and magnificently – but for now, I simply say all that it is in my heart to say, which is thank you.

Coming into Wholeness

Friday, January 24, 2013, 10:30 am
Dear Angels,
I called in sick today and am taking the day off, because this is a milestone in my life, a kind of birth-day. For I finally made the appointment with Stephanie for a soul retrieval session. Please tell me about this upcoming soul retrieval session, and if there is anything I need to do to prepare myself emotionally or spiritually. Thank you.

Angels: Dearest Barbara, we rejoice for you! All is well, you are ready for this. Meditate for a few minutes if you can, be calm, centered and neutral at the time of the appointment. Breathe beautifully, as you have learned to do. Invoke us, trust, and bless darling Stephanie for this serious work. If you can take 15 minutes beforehand to bring yourself into a state of reverence, the process will be strengthened and Stephanie will be assisted. Then...let go. We will be with you every moment. Your soul does rejoice at this day, believe us!
Beautiful beautiful and beloved child, go forth trusting into this magical day!
The Angels, who love you!

Saturday, January 26, 2013

Dear Angels,

I met Stephanie as planned, at 3:30 at the yoga studio. We sat facing each other on chairs. The room was cold, I felt a little nervous. Stephanie questioned me about my experiences and reasons for wanting a soul retrieval. I explained the "hole in the soul" I'd been carrying around for 20 years since the soul-splintering episode I had experienced in my thirties. I added, parenthetically, and to fill out my energy anomalies, the weird, parasitic energy that had descended on me after the violent deaths of my aunt and uncle – what I have always thought of as "the evil miasma." Also mentioned the nighttime visitations of malicious, preying entities.

What happened next took me by surprise. Without explanation, other than to say she would be using the depth-hypnosis model, Stephanie talked me down into a light trance. She asked me where I *felt* this parasitic energy, I realized it was residing between my shoulder blades, behind my heart. Odd! It was a kind of clotted, dark area. She asked me to keep focusing on it, saying what does it *feel* like? Where is it? What shape? It was hard to put words to it. And then, there was a shift, and she said, if this dark energy had a name, what would it be called? "CLOUD" it said! From that point on, she talked to "Cloud" – asked it why it was there, if it knew it could move on and be somewhere else. She asked it a whole series of questions which "Cloud" answered through me. Then she took her drum and her feather and drummed it into the Light. I felt a shudder as it rose through me and out of me, and a sensation at the top of my head. Whoa. Weird and woo-woo, and not at all what I expected. Stephanie then counted down, bringing me back to the present. I was conscious the whole time, but "I" had moved aside. I am still astounded today, at what transpired in that session. I asked Stephanie about the soul-retrieval, and she paused, thought about it, and said I should write to you about ways of coming into wholeness. Good idea. So here I am, back again. Stephanie also asked me to monitor how I felt post-cloud-removal, and let her know what shifts or changes occur in the next few days.

As it was, I already felt a clear space in my back, a kind of tingly emptiness. I was very sleepy and woozy after the session, so I went straight home, made some dinner, curled up in bed with a book on angels, and fell asleep over it. I was exhausted. Slept like a baby, deeply and straight through. Woke up to fresh, sparkling white snowfall and a gorgeous, sunny day. Pulled myself together and headed back to the yoga studio for the kundalini workshop starting at 10:30.

Yes, I would definitely say that today, I felt lighter, cleaner, relieved, happier, clearer. *Normal*, in fact.

Dear Angels, I have to come back to the topic of the soul retrieval. You had told me that my soul was, in fact all together and rejoined inside me, but that perhaps it would take some time for me to experience it again. I feel that I would like a ritual to definitively mark this event, which is why I am preoccupied with the idea of a soul retrieval. It would be a bookend, put a stamp on things as it were, give me an experiential memory to reassure me. Is this so crazy or wrong? Please tell me all, tell me as much as you want about this important life-event for me. It is sometimes a little tough to be human and not quite know or understand the subtleties of what is going on all around us. Thank you for helping me understand this a little more. Also, please tell me, are there any **other** parasitic energies in my body I need to clear out? Sheesh.

Angels: Dear, dear Barbara, precious and lovely girl, thank you so much for writing to us. We feel so very close to you when you write — as do you — is it not a miracle that we can touch each other this way? You have many serious questions, and though you are ever cheerful and brave, know that these are real energies and entities which flow through you — we do not, cannot take their treatment lightly. It is such important work you are doing, if you only knew! Yes, that is a protective ego strategy you practice — the cheerfulness — and we love you for it.

Dear child, it is I, Raphael. Blessings of healing upon you child, and thank you for calling on me today. You ask about the unification of your soul and coming into Wholeness. You wish for a ritual to complete your rejoining, to honor the return of your soul fragments. For we did indeed today pour them back into you, your soul is once again complete. Joy will come back to you slowly, it is like re-learning to use a sedentary muscle. Practice by watching as many sunsets, sunrises and moonrises as you can (truly, this is your assignment) — and being outdoors at every possible moment. You can create your own ritual to celebrate your soul — ask us, and we will help you. Trust this wholeness and completion! Look for this principle in all that you observe, see wholeness and completion in all around you, and it will become reality. Remember the example of the five dissonant koshas, moving out of sync? Well, your mind has fastened onto the idea that you were in pieces. Now your job is to coax the mind into agreement with the soul, the body, and the breath, and the witness consciousness. And please, child, give yourself permission to cry, allow yourself to be strongly moved by all that you experience. There are iron bands across your heart and it is safe now to undo them. In the privacy of your home, be moved to deep emotion and let it well up and overflow in your safe sanctuary. You have built a strong, resilient container for your emotions, now sound them deeply. Your heart yearns for this expansion.

Dear Raphael,

Thank you for your extraordinary presence. I see this now – that I could have a really beautiful, special ritual for my soul, with candles, music, flowers, poetry, blessing, incense and prayers…on the next full moon. I will make it magical, and I will cry, gladly, on this day, and any other day you want me to, as I feel that beloved, long-lost soul-fizz returning to my circulation. Why, I could have a crying *festival*. Anything you want, Raphael.

Please don't go yet, because I do have one more question for you, regarding that parasitic, dark "cloud" that had settled on me and which is now gone, thank god. I have learned to call this "energetic interference" in shamanic terms, which I will abbreviate to EI.

Clearly, this EI was some kind of entity which had settled quite happily into me, and had done it so successfully that I continued to operate "as normal," even though at some level I knew I was always subpar. I am amazed that I carried this parasite for so long. What I don't understand, is why did none of my other energy work budge it at all? Why did not the kundalini yoga or the tai chi, or working with you angels, or repeatedly visiting the healing halls of Kripalu, just discourage it so much that it would leave? Would not light, positive, healing energy dislocate something like that? If I had realized something like that was so completely resident in me, I would have done something about it sooner. Brrrr! It makes me wonder how many ordinary people are walking around with small, medium or large energy parasites like tape worms, and have no idea that they are hosts. Double brrr!

Dear child (still Raphael),

Excellent question. The answer is somewhat complicated metaphysically, but the simplest way to explain would be to draw parallels to earth–plane parasitic organisms, which have evolved to lodge, stick, adhere, intertwine, hide, and integrate successfully with their hosts, deriving just enough energy to perpetuate themselves without draining the host's vitality to the point of death/loss of host. The host would have to become aware of, or uncomfortable enough, about the parasite, to take action to dislodge it, such as pulling off a tick. In the case of your "cloud" your energy disciplines and practices made you, the host, stronger, so you could bear its presence more easily. You needed a third party to assist with its removal precisely because it had so successfully found a niche where it could reside.

Raphael, in future, if something similar happened again, and I were aware of it, could I flush it out myself by willfully ejecting it or banning it from my body?

*Raphael: There is no simple, clear answer to your question because it would depend on the conditions, your energetic state, and the strength of whatever energy invaded your body/mind/ spirit. You have strengthened your aura considerably since that event, and your protective chanting, invocations and practices all help to guard you from such energies. If you were an advanced shaman you might be able to cast it out yourself, but it would be much better to have a human, angelic, or spirit ally to assist. This energy work is what angels **do**, as guardians of the many many forms of energy which weave in and out of the cosmos.*

At some level I can see that yes, I had to be ready to receive the energy healing, and that certain stages had to be accomplished in my growth and understanding before it was possible. Still, I have to wonder – why didn't you angels give me bigger hints that this foreign body was draining me? I feel frustrated that I could not have had it removed sooner – I feel like my time and energy was quite literally wasted. Or was it a case of all the signs being there but I just didn't see them or understand them?

*Raphael: You have answered your own question, but I will expand on it. Remember the concept of Divine Timing. You are progressing on one strand of an intricate web which intersects with many others. We angels cannot interfere by informing you, especially if the progress is organic and healthy and the result is inevitable. Do not confuse your disgust at having been "invaded" with the steps you take on the path. In spite of your frustration, remember too, how much **you** increased your own energy willfully, by choosing positive thoughts and feelings. Consider that perhaps you made your body sufficiently unpleasant for the entity, that it left easily — which might not have been the case if you had attempted it some years ago. Remember, child, how fragile and easily upset you were, just three years ago. Please trust us — trust me — when I say that you were handling just about as much as you could at the time. The timing of this removal was exactly right, and we are so proud of you. Again, this is major work, do not take it lightly. It is a miracle that you are working so beautifully, so closely with us, that for every question you ask, you seek the answer, and you take action by finding the answers in the books we send to you (when not writing or communicating directly!).*

Yes, I suppose I am a bit of a greedy sponge that way, I want to know it all, and I want to know it all right now! By reading the right book. Yes, it *is* a miracle the way you send me books to answer my questions. Thank you for answering my previous questions and putting it into context. You are right, of course, but I have to indulge my human "what-ifs" too. Goodnight, dear Raphael, on paper at least, and thank you!

We love you, child...!

Friday, March 1, 2013, 9:45 pm
Dear Angels,
One month and many, many inner adventures later, I'm back with more questions than ever.

The weeks after the entity removal (that was a serious watershed) have been wonderful – I am brighter, clearer, stronger, normal, in fact: normal, the way I remember being nine years ago. It is miraculous just to sense my body working back at its ordinary capacity, to know that I have joined the ranks of the living again. February was a crazy, busy time, with a major blizzard and a power outage, subsequent heavy snowfalls, true winter weather; unpleasant conditions. But I have been so wrapped up in my internal life that I barely notice what was going on outdoors. I was entirely focused on bringing myself up to a certain level of conditioning for the combined shamanic/yoga workshop at Kripalu, which I took in late February.

I knew it would be intense but – how naïve! I didn't realize it would turn me inside out and profoundly alter my reality. Ordinarily I would go into great depth and give a blow-by-blow description of my experience, but here I am going to fast forward to when I arrived home. Sunday: fine, feeling woozy and exhausted, I unpacked, had a quiet night and went to bed. Monday came, work was easy and I felt positively feisty. Monday night came…went to bed still feeling the high vibrations from all of the weekend, feeling emotions wash through me as though they were brand new sensations. I had felt strong and powerful all day, but wondered when I would feel the effects of the chakra opening. BAM! In the middle of the night I was overcome with energy flooding: a textbook first chakra opening. This was overwhelming enough, but then what happened, in my fuzzy, half-dream confusion, was that a great big snake came slithering along, with the teacher's head. And he spoke to me telepathically, and we had a conversation. I think he said, "Don't worry, don't be afraid, it's just me." This was overpowering and intimate, and something clicked in me and I thought, "Duh, Barbara, he's *journeying*, of COURSE he's journeying, he's a shaman."

I don't remember much of the rest, but believe me, that was enough. I have spent the last four days trying to recoup my psychic boundaries, make sense of what happened, try to sort out my feelings, but did not have the discipline to untangle those threads too well. Thus, my head was a mess, an utter mess.

But one of the other miracles to come out of this was the skill to offer clients, friends or family the shamanic techniques we were taught. I realized that this was something I could do well, with great satisfaction and joy in the offering. I felt so clear and calm, so self-assured – all utterly novel feelings for me. In fact, this whole week I have been chiming like a bell. This has been the strangest week of my life, hands down. A revolution has occurred, and I am reeling with the healing.

Please tell me more about this session – over to you, angels.

Dear child, light of our hearts, this is a triumph. A triumph, a triumph, a triumph! We are singing joyful alleluias for you on this day, because you have gone from being wounded, to healed, to HEALING! You now embody the sacred path, and the divinity that is in every cell of your being will now become apparent to all who see you. Love thyself, child, for thy bright magnificence.

You are very tired, dear girl – in spite of your excitement, would you like to continue tomorrow?

Sunday, March 3, 2013, 7:30 am
Dear Angels,
Yes, I would like to continue this! Now that it is Sunday, and I am relaxed, refreshed, spacious, grateful.

Almost every night now, just before I fall asleep, there is another kind of visitation. It is the same phenomenon as my first chakra clearing. It is this moving, humming, strong frequency which travels up my body, going from chakra to chakra and lighting them up. It is like electromagnetic love, and I am overwhelmed by it. Angels, please tell me, is this Divine Love moving through me? I am trying to relax and allow, but I am also intensely curious.

Angels: Dear child, alleluia and blessing upon you this day. Is not life miraculous? We adore your willingness to partner with us. Alleluia! We are happy to answer your questions about the chakra illumination. Yes, this is a blessing that comes through your teacher, who is journeying. Your instincts are correct. He is a powerful teacher who is deeply connected to his students. Every time you experience the illumination you heal a little bit more. You cannot initiate this yourself just yet, but yes, you can invite it. Do not be afraid, for although this feels invasive, it is more a channeling of Divine Energy than an individually willed event. Your teacher is an instrument of God's love, just as you are, dear. Enjoy the beautiful sensation and use it to increase your internal awareness. You are more ready than you know, for what is to come. Write to us often with any confusion or questions, for you will have much of both!

To continue with questions about my friend and her healing...the chakra illumination seemed to go well. So this is what empowerment feels like – a quiet inner strength. Fifty-two years and it's my first experience of it. Many formerly abstract words have meaning now. Angels, please tell me more about this session and how I can help other clients again.

*Angels: You and other friends have been concerned about her for many years, because of the outwardly manifesting signs of her woundedness, in her chaotic lifestyle. Also, you have been sad and puzzled at how stuck she has been, and her evident fears of taking any steps to change her life, despite her loving heart and intuitive nature. You have been on parallel courses in many ways, and you have been a strong and shining example for her, a pathfinder. You carry with you now residue of the magnetism from the practices, and yes, you are attracting people who need to heal. Notice that this is because **you** have made the shift into healer, and are no longer being perceived by people and friends as seeker-wounded-I-want. It is the shift in **you** that has changed the chemistry. Please give this some thought, for it is significant. Yes, it is an initiation. The trickle will become a stream, which will become a river. Prepare yourself. There is much, much work ahead, but your foundations are rock solid and you have incredibly strong protection. Your fearlessness will increase, and joy will flow in proportionately (how we love it when you find the right word!). Regarding the healing you did on your friend, it was perfect. She sets the paradigm of your trusting loving friends, who will now seek you out. She has set one foot on the path of healing and **yes!** Rejoice with us in your heart, because as you know, it is that first willingness that starts the healing ripple. Alleluia!*

Alleluia, indeed. I begin to see...the ripple has no beginning and no end, but when it comes through me, I can watch it flow out.

One week later, having processed some of these post-workshop energy effects and projections onto the teacher, I am sitting in a place of detachment, which may be the biggest miracle of all. I feel as though I have come out the other side of a tunnel. All my past relationship experiences now sit there, watching me, waiting to see how I'll handle this. I seem to be drawn to complex men – the workshop teacher was right up there, same pattern. The irony is, the more wonderful a human being you are, the higher you go, the more people you attract, the more you have to manage – and can one fit it all in? I send the workshop teacher big blessings.

Angels, please tell me about everything I am wondering about.

*Angels: You may find some of the answers to your questions in Guru Singh's book on relationships. But we know that what you are asking for is reassurance in this moment. Yes, he represents healing issues in your life, of course —you have figured these out precisely. And he does mirror back your assumptions and projections, so all of these things are psychological and emotional quicksand pits, if you are not alert and aware. Heavily use the radical acceptance techniques you learned, as you go. This will serve you well, and keep you centered, wise, and calm. Pay attention to the Little Girl In Class, raising her hand, who wants and needs so badly to be special. Is this a samskara? Use **every facet** of this encounter, all your feelings, all your psychological analysis and social awareness, to pull more and more samskaras from this. His presence is a great gift in your life, and you are ready to embrace the challenge. Whether or not this leads to continued study, friendship, or something more, is **up to you**. Do not be afraid of bothering him too much with questions. This is his role, and you do not need to charm him. Take it seriously, be respectful, pull out as soon as you are uncomfortable. Unwrap this beautiful present with love and attention, and call upon us at every stage. You are unaware of your beauty, inner and outer, and the effect you have on people. Unfold your petals, your fragrance, your velvet softness, Rose of our hearts!*

With love and sweet blessings,
The Angels and John!

Chapter VII: Expanding

Provide an enormous song and phenomenal dance before you fly into the Sun.
– GURU SINGH, *ANGELS GATHER HERE*

Loving My Wounds

Sunday, March 31, 2013, 6 pm, Easter
Dear Angels,
The unbalanced times continue like so many incoming curveballs.

Two weeks ago, when I was at the low point of exhaustion and tension, I decided to take a hot bath with Epsom salts. It was excellent in theory, and mostly excellent in practice, as I slept like a baby and was sweetly, deeply relaxed. However, I stupidly brought up a kettle of boiling water to the tub, thinking to augment the hot water, and accidentally spilled some on my right shin. Ow. I immediately invoked you all, put on an ice pack, and carefully covered it. It did blister, but seemed to be healing nicely and shrinking without infection. Well, dummy me. I left the bandage off and must have bumped it, because this morning it started throbbing painfully. I took a peek and the pus had turned green. Oh dear. And it really hurt, and looked nasty. I realized it was *nicht gut*, really *nicht gut*, and so have spent the entire day with my leg propped up, alternately blessing it with healing, sending it love and light, and putting on cold packs and crystals. And invoking you, Archangel Raphael. It is now 6 pm and it looks a little better, but I can't really walk and have been immobilized all day. Angels, help! What would you like me to do, do I need to go to the emergency room? This is giving me a bad scare, a wake-up call. It has my full attention. I am trying to dwell on the healing side, not on the fearful side, but am not succeeding completely.

Angels,

*Darling girl, we are surrounding you now with love and light and healing. All shall be well. You did not recognize the moment this happened that this wound was an object lesson for you — what does it reflect, what does it represent, what do you need to learn from it? What are you ignoring, or pushing away? We are working with you to heal it as soon and completely as possible. At the moment it is stable and healing, **but** please do monitor it carefully and treat it very gently and lovingly. Is this gentle and loving treatment something you could bring to your own self-care more often? If you loved Barbara the way we do, every day would be a love-bath!*

Thank you for the reassurance about this frightening burn wound. Above all, thank you for helping me to heal it. I am trying to send it love-baths, but as you know, angels, I have been so shut down for so long that the emotion "love" is just a mental construct for me, not something that throbs in my 4th chakra. I have no idea how to overcome this. Perhaps this is a good lead-up to talk about samskaras. What do I work on next: anger, sense of worthlessness, being unloved, terror on so many occasions, lack of boundaries, fear of intimacy? There is at least a year's worth of chakra illumination sessions in me, lined up like 747s at JFK airport. It would be nice if I could just do my whole childhood at one fell swoop and clear about ten of them.

Angels: Dear, dear Barbara, please see the dawning light and have hope in this miracle! Do not be overwhelmed by the enormity of it. You have a miraculous healing modality at your fingertips, and all you have to do is stay the course and you will be free! Please hold this joyful attitude in your heart and mind, and see if you can treat it as a treasure hunt. We say to you again, you are handling quite as much as you need to right now. All is perfect and unfolding organically. Love these wounds as you release them, for they are indeed gone and the new you is growing into place. As for the next samskara to heal, trust your intuition. What feels old, stale, heavy, ready to be cleaned or cleared?

Thank you, this is so true and right. I need to meditate or write some affirmations to shift my mood, this burn wound has brought me down with a bump. Thank you, dear angels, thank you.

Sunday, April 14, 2013
Dear Angels,
Much has happened in the last two weeks, but the most significant event of all was the miracle of my healed leg. I have been very careful in the past two weeks, have left it pretty much alone unless I needed to change the specialized burn bandage dressing. This morning peeled off the bandage and...wow. Healed skin. Beautiful, clean, new, tender, skin under the icky, dried-up layers. There is still a small patch, maybe 2"x 2", which still needs to clear up, but it's there. Miracle, miracle, miracle. I am flooded with relief, gratitude, and amazement. It could have turned out so differently, don't want to even think about it. So thank you for this extraordinary object lesson and privilege. Please, angels, if I ever get above myself or too cocky, would you just remind me of this episode? I am so thrilled by this healing miracle that I want to run around showing it to everyone (but I won't). So *today* feels like Easter!

That's my news for now. The song sparrow is tweetling outside my window with an echoing friend in another tree, it feels like my own private concert.

September 14, 2013
Dear Angels,
How things have changed at work. For the first time in years, my incoming workload has suddenly simplified and diminished. My days have been quiet and peaceful, mini-crises have not materialized. I extracted myself from the special-event fundraiser, and the office energy is quiet, orderly, and calm. It may not last, but I am amazed

by it and enjoying it. In the wake of that last crisis, I started using a new affirmation: "I LOVE MY NEW JOB!", saying it silently to myself 100 times a day, or as many times as something irritated me. It was extraordinary how it immediately dissolved the feeling and shifted me into a place where I could cope. In short, it worked like a charm, so that I am beginning to suspect that my "new job" is actually my old one, reborn. Hmm, so many miracles and mysteries...at this point I just smile and say, "thank you."

I start kundalini yoga teacher training next Thursday, September 19th. While I know I am ready, I have no idea what to expect, and am apprehensive. The Good-Girl-Student in me wants to rush out and buy new notebooks and pencils and exercise clothes...angels, please tell me about this major transformation I am about to undergo – if you can.

Angels: Darling girl, here we are, in full force loving you and loving the way you write to us. The miracle of it! It never grows old, this divine connectedness, your receiving our messages and turning to us again and again. Blessed child, we surround you with joy and happiness, and all the love we have!

*What we can tell you about your upcoming kundalini teacher training is this — which you already know. You are on a sacred path (as are all humans). It is about to intensify. However, all of your previous experiences, disciplines, practices and embodied knowledge have prepared you well. There is nothing to be anxious about, because you are more than ready. You are so beloved, protected, guided and supported, that we hope you will enjoy this process and drink deeply from this magnificent fountain. Yes, you are more than ready. Yes, you will be transformed. You have every skill at your disposal for navigating the deep waters, and any new "experiences" may be familiar to you from what you went through after the shamanic weekend workshop. So you see, this is not new to you, you know this already. What will be surprising to you, perhaps, is that it only gets better from here — life becomes richer, and your healing accelerated, the blessing more manifold. The process has begun already. **Finally!** you say. So, darling heart of ours, lay out the angel cards if you wish. There is nothing more to do but trust, relax , enjoy — and ask and write and bless and thank!*

We love you, always and always!

The Angels

Friday, September 27, 2013
Dear Angels,
Well, you were right. There was nothing I needed to do but show up
and bring my full willingness and attention and openness to class.

You were right: the 4-day intensive was transforming. But that word is
an abstraction, and cannot describe the molecular reorganization I am
undergoing now.

That last entry, 9/14, was before I had received my spiritual name
from 3HO,* which was on Monday, September 16th. Maybe the most
miraculous day of my life, ever.

My spiritual name is *Sarandayal Kaur.* I am pierced, I am humbled, I
am turned inside out, I am reborn. I had no idea. No one told me. I
have gone completely into some kind of chemical mush inside, and am
reorganizing at a cellular level, as does the good little caterpillar in her
chrysalis. *No one talks about these things.* Perhaps it is for the best, then when
one is blindsided, all resistance is down, and you have no ego defenses
left to fight with.

So I have spent the last week in a state of raw, new-skin confusion,
wonder and wide-eyed astonishment, grace, bafflement, vulnerability.
No one told me.

And it's all in The Plan, isn't it?

I am perhaps doubly bowled over, because I have never known such
real intimacy – Divine Intimacy.

All these things were just little black and white descriptive words before.

In class they brought up ...Prana (cosmic) and prana (human). I think
I am experiencing this, but am not sure. I have this high pitched,
singing vibration around me. At this moment it is fairly strong, so
I am thinking hmm, maybe I have overdone it this week, between

---

*3HO is the lead organization which oversees and disseminates the teachings of Kundalini Yoga as taught by Yogi Bhajan. The acronym stands for "Healthy, Happy, Holy Organization." All mantras, meditations and kriyas mentioned are available on the 3HO website.

the 4-day intensive, tai chi on Wednesday, kundalini yoga class on Thursday, and then this morning my first ever, full-length home kriya? Which actually, left quite an impact on me today. Plus – nearly forgot – at least two 20-minute crystal-grid meditations. Plus having a sore throat and sniffles.

So yes, maybe I am pushing the lab effect too hard (as in experimenting on myself), because I am *hummin'*. Am I going to blow a gasket?

Angels, please tell me about prana, the pranic body, and anything I need to know that will keep me grounded and sensible. I had two outbursts of giggles this week – drunk on energy. Help.

Dear Barbara: We love you so! Please turn to us and write at every opportunity. We can answer every single question you have (or point you to an earth-plane information source) and we can give you oceans of reassurance. You are aware of being in an expanding, fragile, vulnerable and tender state now. All is new, and changing fast. Old paradigms and shells of your previous existence are being shed. Yes, you are newly hatched, and glowing with new-life prana. We are here to incubate you. Nothing is more serious, real, or important. You are our baby, our beloved, and we are fierce in protecting you while you grow your new spiritual identity and persona-to-be. Your bewilderment is normal and natural. We love you for it. The extreme mix of sensations will continue, perhaps for months. Please, dear one, when you reach a point of fear or confusion, please either turn to us or turn to one of your teachers. Yes, you may be overdoing it, and you could overload your system, simply through eagerness or not-knowing. Energy — Life-force energy — does not discriminate, and will flow where there is a channel or an opening. So, although you are strong, you are still a novice, and do not have perfect control of the taps which regulate the prana. If you are ever unsure, take your hands off the taps, or skip some days in your practice. You will still reach the place and level you are destined to reach.

As for the individual vibration you feel, try to separate it out from other things going on in your life — it is independent of them, in a way. Your mild anxiety about your trip tomorrow is preying on you, and making things worse. You are ready for action — all else is abstraction. Please sleep now, dearest one, and we will wake you early in the morning with songs of joy. Don't forget to invite us in and ask us for all you could wish on your trip!

If prana is life-force energy, and it is a regular part of me now, shouldn't I be able to hear/perceive/feel/sense you angels more clearly? I mean, my "hearing" has speeded up and strengthened a great deal, and I can now just "ask" in my head and hear you. But I would have thought stronger prana would have refined that perception even more, no?

*Angels: We are laughing at your eagerness, your yearning to connect and student desire to get it right. Patience, patience! You are doing so beautifully already, so fast, so willing, trying so hard, **always**. The gifts come when the gifts come, and are not to be rushed. All is carefully calibrated to raise you to the point of readiness. "Seeing" or "hearing" us more vividly might only confuse you more at this point. Our little fire-hydrant-drinker, you do not know how much you have already ingested. Precious girl, trust. Trust us, trust the prana, trust the timing, trust this very moment and everything in it. We can talk about "presence" and choices another time. Simply observe, and know that **you** are perfect, and the moment is perfect. We send you to sleep with sweet blessings, and we surround you with Divine light, love, and protection, our precious chick!*

Thank you, angels, thank you!

There is a 6-month gap in my journal, from the end of September 2013 through March 2014. I had to stop writing to the angels during that time, because KYTT was so all-consuming. I return to writing again with the entry from March 25, 2014.

You Know What to Do Now

Tuesday, March 25, 2014
Dear Angels,
I'm back, finally back! and here we are again, just like old times.
Thank you for guiding me through everything during KYTT, through
every minute of the last outrageously transformational seven months.
I dropped off the planet, I had no spare energy or time to write to you
with such a packed schedule.

There was just an odd incident at work in the office of a colleague.
The postage meter went flying off the filing cabinet and landed on the
floor several feet away, startling both people in the room.

I went up to check it out, and definitely got a distinct shivery
sensation. In fact, I still have the sensation. I hope no "energy" landed
on me – ugh. I've had enough of that. Please write and tell me what
happened, and that I am safe and protected.
Thank you, angels.
Barbara

*Angels: Dear child and precious child of god, we love you and so miss your writing to us.
Please begin again if you can, we have so much to tell you and to share with you. Now that
you have completed most of the KYTT, you will find some time, a corner of your life, to
communicate again. We can help with your pain and confusion, just reach out and we'll be there!*

*Regarding the recent incident, do not fear. Yes, there is a wandering energy which expressed itself
in a burst of energy, but it is not harmful or malicious. It has not settled on you, but you feel it
because of your increased sensitivity. The energy is lonely and wants attention. Your building is
old and some of the past life still vibrates in the walls. We will console these energies, and if you
wish to clear the building, you can ask us to work with you in sending them into the light.*

Heaven knows I have enough issues to work out regarding KYTT.
Did I really just go through that? I think my soul and I ought to get
gold stars, that was *rough*. And yet the teachers say, it never ends,
the unfolding, unveiling, learning, growing.

I've just come through eight months of spiritual pummeling, and I don't understand anything any better. Angels, something has to give. Can you tell me anything at all that will give me real hope? Above all else – and you *know* this – I loathe the feeling "I am trying so hard and it hurts and I am doing everything they've told me to do and it still hurts and I don't get it and nothing is getting better and I am trying so hard and I don't know how to try any harder." That is the worst, feeling sad, forlorn, and hopeless. Over to you.

Angels: This is why we ask you to start again to work actively with us. Not only can we help you with your personal pain, but in a bigger perspective, we can educate you so that you can help others with their pain. You have already started doing this in significant ways, as you did with your niece. Do you realize that your healing actions have a ripple effect, an impact on the world? Please begin to notice and appreciate and foster this! It is so important, and you have come so far. We know that there is no panacea, no easy solution or aspirin for those dark episodes. What you can continue to do, is pray, ask, and keep up your spiritual discipline to strengthen your own vessel. You are starting to become aware of how weakening it can be to isolate yourself. You are ready to come out and hatch a little, as they say. We would say, ready to bloom a little, ready to bloom a lot, our beautiful, precious flower! Rely on your healing instincts, which are strengthened now: praying, going for a walk, talking to us, getting out of the dark space physically and mentally: shift it! Choose to play some music, this is easy now! You have all the tools, assemble them. Truly assemble them. Make a list if you need to: what can I reach for that will shift this energy? Last night you did beautifully! You cut cords with your teacher. You see —you knew just what to do, and you did it.

Please tell me about what happened in class. On the one hand, my teacher listened sympathetically to my story. She – deliberately or not – misunderstood my question and twisted it into a personal situation, which was done publicly in front of the whole class. While I respect her teaching, whatever happened to me via her energy on Sunday, felt targeted. What is going on?

Angels: This is highly complex, playing out at many levels, and we cannot give you a simple answer, just that it is something you have to go through right now. If it is any consolation,

know that you were chosen because you were the strongest and could withstand it the best. You are now keenly aware of how easily a teacher crosses the line with his/her power, and you will remember this.
With blessing of our eternal love,
The Angels

Monday, March 31, 2014, 9:00 pm
Dear Angels,
I want to talk to you angels again about the triggering events in class of last weekend, which spiraled me into an emotional cavern. It has taken me a full week to start to escape from their psychological effects. Dark thoughts started circling like sharks, and I could not shake the black mood.

Please tell me about what I perceived as a power play by the teacher. As you say, now I have had a taste of it, and I will not forget it quickly. Thank you for guiding me to try the Divine Shield meditation, which has saved me completely – 11 minutes of meditation tonight, and I could feel the black cloud lifting. Thank you, angels, that was really a close one.

Angels: Precious Barbara, can you feel us now? The other effect of the Divine Shield meditation is that your awareness of us will be heightened. This is so exciting — we grow closer and closer, or perhaps to say it correctly, more and more apparent to you.

*The incidents of the past week — emotional, psychological, spiritual and developmental — are a turning point for you. It was your crisis. We could not warn you about it because you needed to battle it fully and completely, in order to be victorious and vanquish it. You were never alone, though you may have felt far from us at many points. You need to know that there will be more battles, but **you know what to do now**.*

But angels, that felt like such a close call. I mean, the negativity was just waiting for any weakness to burrow into my brain. If even I, who have umpteen spiritual skills and knowledge and legions to call upon – if someone like I cannot withstand it, what earthly chance does a human have, who does *not* have all of these resources? It took everything I knew to turn the tide. I mean, that is some tenacious darkness, or whatever you would call it. No wonder so many people succumb – it is like a siren call to the ego – pure fear is like pure crack, you can get high on it. These states have all been so confusing.

And the only reason I can write to you tonight with any degree of clarity or sanity – instead of self-pity – is because of that Divine Shield meditation. Can you tell me more about my teacher's role in this?

Angels: When you come to a boulder in the path, and it blocks the way, you must use dynamite to clear the path and destroy the block. Your teacher is the dynamite — or rather, she lights the fuse. The blessing is that she is so aware, and so conscious, that she does so with great skill and care. If it had not been her, it would have been another teacher. She cannot afford likes and dislikes with her students, so yes, you received her personal-impersonal treatment. She knows that you know, just what she is doing and has done. Can this be easy for her?

How will you use this as a teacher? Think...will this make you softer, kinder, more tolerant? She may have done you a favor in the long run — because you will never want a student to experience what you did at her hands. Perspective will come in time — and you will heal from this, as you have healed from all things. You did a powerful thing when you blessed her. Continue to do this and it will have good consequences.

Okay, angels, you have coaxed me out of my carping mood, and answered my question – so thank you. Can we talk about the other things now? I was told I need to strengthen my aura – evidently I am not doing enough meditation. Angels, don't you think my life is ascetic enough already? You do keep sending me angel oracle cards about the inner child and being playful and getting out into nature and finding my soul mate – sorry, but I can't do that and meditate at the same time. If all of my practices have not strengthened my aura, then what *would*? You already know that my good-girl, over-achiever mode takes me too far, so that isn't the answer either. I know! I'll QUIT. How about that? I am so fucking tired of trying.

We know you are not really serious, and are just blowing off steam. We think your biggest difficulty is that you have no one intimate in your life, to celebrate you, to hug you and hold you and tell you how terrific you are. If we were substantial and tangible you would have received a million hugs from us by now, at the very least! And we feel you trying to be brave when you are so lonely and hurt inside — and this weakens your aura. You see the situation, you know what needs to happen.

Why is it so hard to love myself? I cannot scrape up any semblance of this emotion for myself. I feel sadly, wretchedly stuck. Oh, well, I'll just have to go through life with a crumpled aura. Maybe it will be better in my next life. Will that do, angels?

This is serious, please do not degrade yourself with dismissive humor. This is a pattern you have been repeating for years. It is your choice, to change it or not. We can help you become unstuck. You will never do a more courageous thing in your lifetime than this. You do have it within you.

I DON'T KNOW WHAT IT FEELS LIKE.

Ah, radio silence.

Never! Nice try! Give your anger and hurt and sadness to us, over and over again. **You're sooo** *close, if you only knew. What would you say to continuing this another day? You're fading a bit, you can't hear us showering you with loving words and support anymore.*

Yes, I agree, I am suddenly exhausted. Thank you angels, I'll keep trying. Thank you for everything.

Dear Yogi Bhajan

Sunday, April 27, 2014
Dear Yogi Bhajan,
Today I graduated from Kundalini Yoga Teacher Training, Level One. Which means I am an instructor now. An Aquarian instructor. It has not hit me yet.

Eight months of intensely surfacing psycho-emotional garbage. Eight months of trying to be brave about looking into the mirror being held up to me. Eight months of keeping up and "being delivered to my experience."

The ceremony today was so beautiful, exactly right, perfectly powerful, deeply blessing, intense and significant. It made me very happy. I **love** the quotation for my teacher-consciousness slip. Thank you very much for that.

And after all was said and done, and the party was over, I came home and the emotional cocktail hit. I felt blue, then sad, then angry, and the whole time was compulsively head-talking, in scenarios. Awful. So, went for a long walk, sat by the water, watched the April clouds. Came back and did my 90-day meditation, which worked to clear out the gunk.

But really, I think today was all about you – or God, or all of us. Not really sure. But I thought I would write to you anyway and thank you for everything. There have been many messy moments, and many miracles, along the way. I know that the real adventure is just beginning. Before I fall asleep over this page, over to you, dear Yogiji! The page and the pen are all yours.

My dear,

I am honored that you should write to me. Congratulations on graduating today. I am very proud of you. Everyone around you has been telling you what a fine teacher you will be, but you will not feel or experience this until you have taught a few classes. Nonetheless it is the truth. Your teacher has a careful eye on you and you are in her prayers. Do not be afraid of her — these fears are your phantoms still to be cleared. The first hurdle is achieved, and though you can catch your breath for a moment, the race is still being run. Now all accelerates — but I anticipate. My dear, there is much I could say here, but nothing that is not documented elsewhere. My private message to you is, may God go with you always, and bless you at every turn. Remember your pratyahar! Turn again and again and again to God, to me, to the angels, until it becomes your very breath. Then will you know peace, and bounty and bliss.

Sleep now, dear one. Sleep is healing too. Write to me again — we have much to share and discuss.

Yogi Bhajan

May 8, 2014, 9:00 pm
Dear Angels,
Here we are, on the page again – just like old times. But what a different Barbara is writing these words – how far I have come.

Angels: Dear Barbara, Here we are in full force, overjoyed to be at your side and helping again, our magical wonderful human being, Barbara! If only you knew how brightly you shine these days – you'll be blinding us, if you're not careful! But you must allow us our little joke. We love it when you call upon us, and love it even more when you write to us. This beautiful faith of yours is a very powerful thing. One day you will see this. We love your lists, and this is child's play to us! We will loft you through every task with grace, ease, poise and calm – even mowing. Remember, dear child, it is only May 8th and there actually is abundant calendar time for you. Let's sit down this weekend and decide on a kriya for the class you will teach, that will go a long way toward calming you down. You will have to work continuously in upcoming weeks to achieve much on your list, but it doesn't have to be difficult. Efficiency is your best friend, and we'll help you find pockets of time and energy. You are an excellent strategist, and all will happen smoothly, we promise. Remember, dear one, to please focus on the positive positive positive side of things, to keep your aura bright and energized. You've already figured out how to manage your fear – that was masterful!

The one thing you will have to be careful of is going to bed at a reasonable hour (like right now). Work on a slightly earlier sadhana, and do both the sat kriya and the 11-minute in the morning to free you up for evening projects and evening pleasures.

And now, dear one, please enjoy sweet dreams and know that we adore you, and will be helping you at every step.

With love, light, and blessings,
The Angels

Dear Angels,
You are amazing and I love you. Thank you for everything.

Sunday, June 8, 2014, 9:30 pm
Dear Angels,
Last week I laid out the angel oracle cards and on my second layout
– on instinct – I drew just one card, and it was *Archangel Michael*. This
was very moving for me – we had a conversation, and I put the card
on the altar downstairs. Two days later, Aynsley emailed me to ask if
I wanted to have the archangels visit me. I said...well, why not... and
so she emailed me the same list of instructions for your visit I had
gotten four years ago, when I first invited you to this house

Please tell me a little more about this seeming "form" or chain
letter? For example, this concept of "hosting." I mean, since you
all transcend time and space, can you really reside for x period at
y time? Are these conditions really necessary for your arrival, stay,
and departure, or are they conventions, terms and limits for the sake
of humans, so that we can grasp and embrace the concept of hosting
a non-physical energy? That was quite a pen-full. I will be quiet now
so you can answer.

*Angels: Dear Barbara, beloved heart of ours, you are very tired and we are not sure how
clearly we will come through to you. You try so hard for us, and we love you for it!*

*Yes, this is a long list of questions, which we will try to answer for you before you nod off.
Darling one, it is not possible to go into the metaphysics of angel energy in this limited
space. Yes, we are beings of light and love who transcend time and space. At the same time,
we must work with the human experience of linear time and physical space. We channeled
the letter through a human, and so please do not doubt its validity, even though it may
appear like a chain letter. This form also ensures that only those who are open, trusting,
and have faith will receive this message clearly — and thus receive our "visit." Yes, while
the time–space limitations and rituals may seem unnecessary for you — who have grown so
miraculously comfortable with us over the years — please don't forget how many humans
have little or no idea about how to work with angels. Structure and ritual are comforting
— they also give the host a format to follow, because humans need to feel that they are
doing something. Strictly speaking, no, one does not have to open the door right at 10:30
pm, SINCE WE ARE ALREADY HERE WITH YOU NOW! OUR DARLING GIRL!*

AND VERY HAPPILY SO! But doesn't it give you a nice sense of beginning, middle, and end, a physicality to an unphysical event? Without definition, there is simply vague nothingness. So you are welcome to follow as much or as little of the script as you wish, but we did write it, and think it is a helpful guideline even for a seasoned angel-friend like you, We love you to the ends of the earth, dear one, and are thrilled to be here in force for you. Think about writing to each of us individually by name — with as many questions as you like! Because we love you.

But, deare one, you also need your sleep, and to complete your meditation. Invite us in to your meditation, see if you can sense a difference! Beloved heart, write to us again tomorrow.

June 10, 2014
Dear Archangel Gabriel,
Today is the 10th and according to the invitation, you will only be with me 3 more days, so I had better hustle if I am going to write to each of you in turn.

Let's see. You are the angel of communicating and carrying prayers to God.

What can you tell me about my role as a kundalini yoga teacher? This kundalini ride is all at once way too much for me, and not enough for me. My ego keeps patting me on the back, telling me to relax, I'm doing fine, I have it all (ALL) figured out.

How do I find balance and make sense of this flood? I get confused between making an extreme effort, which then tips into being too hard on myself. Then that realization breeds other emotions, and I am just a mess.

Dearest Barbara: What a privilege it is to communicate with you. Please never make light of this — we angels absolutely do not. It is a God-given gift and utterly precious to us. Your willingness and fluency is a joy. So know that we are your ultimate penpals, that THIS, this writing, is Reality and a sacred practice.

With some of your questions above, your internal line of reasoning has become circular and you are trapping yourself without knowing it. Hence your confusion and frustration.

Try once again the method of finding a healing image for each of your confusions or frustrations. That will break the cycle.

Is there such a thing as a healing image to diminish the ego?

Archangel Gabriel: It would be worth trying to receive one, which might become like a mental mala to be used a thousand times a day. Its effect would be not so much healing, as bringing you into the Present. Many of your emotions are by-products of the ego, so the end result is toward the same goal.

Your Greatest Strength and Secret Weapon

Sunday, June 15, 2014, 8:15 pm
Dear Angels,
Seven days short of solstice, and it's still quite light out. A fine breeze is blowing, the crickets are singing, the birds are making their sleepy good-night-calls, and here I am in my heavenly hammock looking out on a lush, green summer world.

Archangel Gabriel, please give me your wise counsel on my upcoming kundalini yoga class teaching. I am much calmer in recent days and feeling more confident and hopeful, so it is as if some dark, stubborn stain of insecurity has been healed out of me. I am trying to practice humility affirmations, and that is helping as well. Please tell me what I need to know as I go into this new adventure of teaching.

Archangel Gabriel: Peace be upon you, dear girl. Good evening on this lovely summer night. In the 50-50 partnership that exists between God and humans, you have fulfilled your part of the bargain excellently. In other words, you have executed the physical, tangible, logistical earth plane side to a tee. Our part comes during the actual class, when we protect, guide, bless and assist at all levels. Thus we create the harmonious effect together of more elevated, more healed humans. There is really very little left for you to do, except enjoy the next 36 hours — and continue with your preparations. Know that teaching will become a deep joy to you as you progress, deepen your knowledge and skills, and allow God's light to flow through you.

Turning to us with your questions, doubts and fears at every opportunity has become your greatest strength and secret weapon. We know you are curious about the communication theme, and how this will translate in the moment. Trust us once again, dear one, you are a rose that is unfolding. Do not hasten the sweet uncurling of the petals!

Thank you, Archangel Gabriel, thank you. Oh, you are so patient! When I did my kriya practicum, my teacher said that I had "so much wisdom." This puzzled me, because I certainly don't feel wise. In fact, much of the time I feel like a clueless dope, just going through the motions and hoping that something will feel real, true and innate one of these days. What did she see in me, that I don't see in myself?

Archangel Gabriel: She sees your soul, dear child, she sees your soul. She sees more of your pain than you know, and understands your struggles. You know that as a Saturn teacher she cannot praise you — at least, not highly — without risking triggering your ego and spiritual pride. So she is in a difficult position — she walks a tightrope. How do you let a student know their depth and strength, let them know they are exceptional and can go far, without contributing to the ego? It's a delicate task. So she has to find words which are strong, true, supportive, and neutral — which touch on your depth and allow you to carry on, but give you an idea of direction and potential. And oh, does she see your potential, both negative and positive. She gave you a sample of that foresight. Her third eye is open and she has clear vision. She could be an extremely powerful mentor to you if you had the courage to take that step. Your fears are understandable — she is a forceful personality and not to be trifled with. She knows you have strong guidance and respects you for that — it makes the road much smoother and easier, it resolves problems faster.

For now, dear girl, let that same wisdom guide you on the little things — prepare yourself for sleep, do what is right in front of you in the moment, and trust in tomorrow.
Peace, light and blessings —
Gabriel

Such a lovely, thorough answer...It gives me much to think about and truly answers my questions. Dear Gabriel, let us have a talk about the elements of Nature – the *tattvas* – sometime, I never really got that. Off to bed, then – goodnight angels!

August 17, 2014
Soul statement. Afternoon swim at Hopewater Bay...shimmering light, Caribbean softness in the air. Soul basked.

"I know and believe that I have wealth and abundance beyond calculation, beyond my wildest imaginings. It is true for me now, in this moment, and always. I know and I believe that the universe supports my every action, thought, decision, and belief."

Life adjectives that Soul craves: spacious abundant softness. Gentleness. Slowness. Grace. Little-girl-humming-to-herself-happiness. Surrender into It. Boundlessness. Drinking, soaking, steeping in Gorgeousness.

The Kilimanjaro of the Heart

August 31, 2014, 11:30 am
Labor Day Weekend
Dear Angels,

Sunday morning on Labor Day weekend and I am moving oh-so-slowly. Gave myself permission to sleep in – so woke up about 8:45. In a perfect world I would have gotten up at 4 am to go to sadhana at the yoga studio...but somehow resting deeply is important to me these days. This is what I would like to write to you about, my energy levels.

Let's take today as an example. I feel sluggish, sleepy, and fatigued....when these states repeat so continually, I want to diagnose this chronic depletion, find out what I need to do to fix it, and HAVE DONE WITH IT.

I need high, clear, stable, reliable energy to accomplish my life! You know this. And is it: solve-able, heal-able, diagnosable? Or should I resign myself to this lowered state of energy as my new, regular set point, from now on?

You see Angels, the problem is the not-knowing. I can throw all the attitudes you want at this vague state, but then it becomes a game, *"what-mindset-should-Barbara-choose-now?"* which is exhausting in itself. I am baffled that after doing everything I have been doing, having done it so right, so well, so obediently, that the energy promises of my practices are not manifesting. It seems endless.

Here we are in the hammock, together again. You know I joke about suspension therapy, but it's real, it works.

Wearily over to you, Angels.

Angels: Dear Barbara, Our beloved girl, thank you for writing to us. We understand your weariness and bafflement. From a human standpoint, with linear human thinking, you're perfectly right. The effort you have exerted, the work and discipline you have committed to and sustained, should logically result in the healed body-mind-spirit you so reasonably and ardently desire. But we are working on a Divine Schedule, within Divine time, all the more so since you are in active partnership with All That Is, and working to make conscious choices. Your label and metaphor of tortoise energy is a good one — but as always, beware of creating a label, a story, a thought pattern. Your struggle is to discern between what seems to be an enduring state (it is not) and a temporary state which you can choose to alter by shifting an attitude or belief. This is very sophisticated work, and please do not be hard on yourself for being confused about how to handle it. Go back to basics and start using imagery from "The Five Minute Miracle." There is a reason you re-read this journal this morning. **You are your own surgeon.** *Take the tools, apply them. You may have to cut deep. You are correct that there is an energy block still in your left hip/pelvis, related to past and current life, reproductive wounds. Continue the work — yes, the metaphor of the final slog up the slopes of Kilimanjaro, in the deepest dark, with only headlamps, in a raging storm, is an excellent one (courtesy of your beautiful friend Carol who experienced that trek and described it to you). Know that we are your loving sherpas, and you WILL make the summit. Bear the goal in mind, do not falter. Never resign yourself to anything! The universe does not recognize this* *word. Work with the knowledge you have now that the universe is a giant copy machine (what you project will be duplicated back to you) and see what you can shift.*

Your greatest fear is of opening your heart. You know the answer, you know the path. It does not have to happen all at once, but it is up to you to recognize, and to seize opportunities to open, to soften, to allow.

Your open heart will solve all energy problems once and for all. Let that be your Kilimanjaro.

Oh joyous girl, how we love thee!
With peace and blessings,
The Angels

August 31 2014, 11:30 pm
Dear Angels,
Well! That was an astonishing exchange I just had over at the Williams'. After a lovely dinner with the parents and children, after much laughter and food and teenage silliness, poker, backgammon and ping-pong, the Dales went home, the boys went to bed, and Lydia, Liddy, Isabelle and I were alone in the living room. Joe headed to bed early, and after he left Lydia mentioned a nightmare she had had. For some reason, (oh yes, how these things pop out of me at opportune moments) I said to Lydia and the girls, "Can I tell you about a strange nighttime experience I had?" I then told them about the dream of the operation on my beloved, passed, pet dog Cyrus, Archangel Raphael, my participation, etc. I had their full attention and they were spellbound. There followed a Q and A about past lives and angels, and I volunteered to bring over my angel oracle cards tomorrow morning and do a reading. They were thrilled, and said yes. I know exactly what got into me – it was you, but it was fascinating the way it just unfolded, and I found myself Confessing All and talking plainly about this deep private side, and working with angelic energy. I've become much stronger, haven't I?

So here we go, angels, venturing forth to educate two willing and open teenage girls. What a huge privilege – thank you for the trust.

I was of course curious to see what you would say to me tonight, so I laid out the angel oracle cards and the card that turned up was *Soulmate*. In spite of all of my work with you, this card's appearance has never made any sense to me. Please tell me what you intend by sending it to me in the context of my question to you about the girls.

Angels: Deare One, Blessings! Hallelujah! We love you! Thank you for being our messenger and earth angel. This is indeed exciting, and we are thrilled to work through you tomorrow. Your real work on this Earth is beginning, you feel your authority and your strength. So much will start to become clear to you in upcoming months, all of your trust and faith will be rewarded.

As for the card that turned up, Soulmate — ah, we have your attention now (not that we didn't before). It is not (though it might) that this will manifest in the near future, but what is happening is that the So Purkh* meditation is changing your vibration. You know this, yes? So remember that these vibrational shifts have consequences, that is all. Your linear mind has not caught up with your intuitive one. Every time you experience the feeling of bafflement, look to this discrepancy, and resolve it.

Thank you, angels...You're so right, I go blindly along doing these little practices, and them am surprised by the consequences and vibrational shifts. Must start putting two and two together a bit more. But for now I will set attempts at interpretation aside.

Good night, angels!

Can You Grant Me That? An Exchange with God

September 4, 2014

Questions for God:
Why am I so shy of you?
Why am I so afraid of love?

---

*So Purkh: In the kundalini yoga tradition, a meditative composition called a *shabad*, whose vibration opens consciousness to the Infinite. So Purkh is specifically attuned to healing human relationships, particularly male relationships, and for the men in one's life.

How can I find a balance between pushing myself adequately to receive the benefits of kundalini practice, and the tipping point of punishing myself? How do I talk to my soul, and listen to my soul? Everything is going so well in my life. Why do I sometimes feel so tired and numb?

Please tell me all about that remarkable dream I had about chasing a man on a mountain path, then slipping off the path, right off the edge, and the mountain suddenly became a solid, enormous cake of *lavender buds,* all adhered together. As I fell off the mountain and gravity carried me down, down, **down**! a voice guided me to make my hands into claws and slow my descent by clawing the lavender bud surface with my fingers. This, plus the wind updraft, lifted my lower body, so that it floated out at an angle to the lavender bud mountain, and my clawing into the surface acted as enough of a brake that I was safely lowered to the ground where I immediately began pursuing that man again. There was no sensation of falling, no fear.

"I am goodness and mercy and compassion and understanding. I am peace and joy and light. I am forgiveness and patience, strength and courage, a helper in time of injury, a teacher in times of confusion. I am the deepest wisdom and the highest truth, the greatest peace and the grandest love. I AM these things and I choose to know myself as these things always." *CWG*

"...come to me along the path of your heart...." *CWG*
How can someone who has been through genuinely damaging events, who is wounded, scarred, and emotionally traumatized, come to you on the path of the heart when the heart is shut down permanently in trauma and deep terror? How can someone so damaged and in pain, create themselves when their judgment and abilities are clouded by pain?

And: "What I resist, persists." Okay, God, this is a good one. Let's talk about resistance and my resisting *You.*

God: Ah, my love. So long have I waited to join you in your mind, heart, soul and body — to flow — even in these limited words — to join, to be able to come through you and be heard. So often have you written to my angels and I have longed for you to write to me.

You are my child, and I love you infinitely infinitely infinitely! You give me great joy to converse and commune with you now.

You say you don't feel that joy, you're not there yet...the raptures will come, fear not. For your present purposes you are perfect right here, right now, in this moment, tonight. Truly. Now this question of resistance. There are degrees, and degrees — can you grant me that?

Mmm, yes, I suppose one could grant God a minor point.

*God: Good. So the degrees of resistance are calibrated to your inner energy, strength, prejudices, emotions, etc. In other words, degrees of fear. If you **look** at that fear squarely, it will dissolve. So, you fear to let me in, as you fear you will drown or be swept away by the emotion. Know, first, that there is no hurry here. I am the most patient of Lovers. Having read much literature written by mystics, you have formed the idea that being possessed by Divine Love is a desirable, albeit somewhat overwhelming thing to possibly experience. Therefore, your mental construct says, "Not me. No way. That's fine for other people, but that is just too risky." So you pigeonhole it as "something-that-happens-to-other-people." Granted, humans typically do not like to lose control, so this is a fairly normal reaction.*

Yet here we are, my dear having a wonderful coeur-a-coeur*. Is this so bad, so scary? Can we not continue doing this, and get to know each other better?

But you're **God**. You already know me.

God: I can only know as much of you as you allow out.

So this is a courtship.

God: Absolutely.

Is this new clarity and courage a result of my chanting the shabad *So Purkh?*

God: Ah, my love, this is the poem to open your poor wounded heart wide open, to heal it finally, once and for all, to bring balm to your soul and resolution to your lifetimes upon lifetimes of seeking. This is the golden key you have been waiting for. Let me put it

*French for heart-to-heart.

this way — in taking your courage into your own hands, in agreeing in this lifetime to heal as much as you could of past trauma; in agreeing to do everything possible to expand and heal your soul, however necessary, you attracted the greatest, most powerful healing tools directly to you. By humbling yourself and accepting not only the guidance, but the celestial partnership, you activated all energies to surround you, support you, and guide you on your path. In other words, if I may make a pun, you don't realize it, but you are Self-Realized.

I love making you laugh.

That was a beautiful and clear answer. Thank you. Now, could you please tell me about the dream of the lavender mountain?

God: The lavender signifies being cleansed…yet it is granular and tangible and must be climbed, so it is arduous. The color, of course, is the color of the 7ᵗʰ chakra, symbolizing your climb to enlightenment. More importantly, the medium or material is friendly and life affirming, fragrant, healing and calming, neutral and non-threatening — so you must know that even if you appear to fall off the path in your pursuit, **all** *forces support you lovingly, so much so that you will not even feel the sensation of falling. The lavender also reaches to your deepest memories of childhood and being soothed. Clawing your hands into the mountain is your part of the partnership, that you listen, hear, obey and trust, and hold on — thus gaining the proof for yourself that you are safely delivered to the next stage of the pursuit. The man you are chasing can be any positive image you want — your soul, Me — but it is elusive. So the question is: what do you Really Want?*

Ah, I love this question. Wish I could answer it. I think my most immediate and rather horrifically pressing wants and needs of recent decades – 1) reuniting with my soul, and 2) healing all traumas – are healing or healed, so I can finally look around, breathe, and assess. There's always the path of kundalini and service –but is the path of kundalini yoga what I really want? Or is this one of those Metaphysical questions with Lots of Capitals That is Never Quite Answered in One Lifetime?

God: You are right, of course — it is an open-ended question designed to make you seek out experiences for your Soul. But I — or the angels — we are always standing by if you turn to us for clarification.

So at some level, I never really have to figure out anything again – at least in the furrowed-brow manner I used to adopt. What a relief.

Which leads me to my question about the Soul. Now, Soul and I have just started getting re-acquainted after our bumpy re-introduction last January. Can you believe I am able to joke about it? That was an outrageous experience, you know.

God: I know. And Soul LOVED it. Yes, even the separation and the pain and the yearning. What extremes, what great contrast, what clear definition, what amazingly strong emotions and motivation! Can you begin to appreciate this now, with a little perspective?

Ha. It was a setup! Yes, I can appreciate it.

God: Have I told you I adore you? I **adore** *you! Now, dear one, time for bed. I wish to spend every moment of every hour of every day, of the rest of your natural body-life, communing and communicating with you, and adoring you. For this, I Live. So, to sleep, to sweet dreams, to wake, and begin anew my precious Beloved Barbara. I will teach you how to remember to love thyself, myself, all selves — and we shall know Glory, you and I.*

Can I say, God, that it's *really* amazing and fine to finally feel healed and normal, not freakishly wounded, damaged, and effed-up? That really was exhausting, you know. Could I please now start to enjoy some of the perks and benefits of just having normal energy levels like I used to?

God: Create it! You know how, no need to ask. This is the beauty of the system. You're gold. Everything else is a refinement and a detail.

Oui, mon capitaine. Bonne nuit...

Friday, September 5, 2014, 8:30 pm
Dear God,
There have been some pretty glorious days lately, of softness, splendor, miraculous peace, and astonishment. The angels sent the *Emerging* card, and I get it. It's true, it is finally true, it finally *feels* true,

not some theoretical pipedream word on a piece of cardboard. I am sitting in my hammock by moonlight, writing by flashlight, and a thousand chirps and trills surround me.

Last night, my chakras must have been opened by the yoga class, because I had a middle-of-the-night energy visitation that feels like a column of humming light coming up through my first chakra. Please tell me about that – was that "kundalini-mata-shakti" – or was that You? Why does it only come sometimes? I notice that the KR (kundalini rising) visitations never leave any cell-memory imprint in my body.

God: Hello, my best beloved, writing to me surrounded by peace and magic. Perfect lover's conditions, perfect for intimacy. You are a lover at heart, though you don't know it yet. But let us not anticipate. Oh, how I embrace you in my million ways. You and I are merging – not just e-merging, but merging. Watch for it, notice it, welcome it. Is it not sweet?

As for the kundalini rising, this is one of the crown glories of my creation. For it is both "I" and mother energy; oh yes, good term – velvet vibration – and what is it? It is a column of pure love energy, actually. Which is why it is sexy, and why your body opens to it and begs for it. Each visitation raises the vibration of your subtle bodies. I know you are sometimes relieved on nights when there are no special effects (they are less frequent now) because those energy vibrations can be so outlandish and baffling. You have no earthly, physical context for them – but the great wheel of evolution is slowly tracking across humankind's development.

So all I can do is lie there and let it wash through me, whenever it comes – or can I invoke it? I am so stuck in my human conditioning of wanting to fix, control, embrace, improve, and follow instructions, that I can't get past the sense that I should "do" something about it...or participate somehow. Being utterly passive and receptive is a challenge.

*God: You've described it exactly. Yet, you are **not** passive, since you have put in the hard work and commitment to raising your vibration and healing your systems – so in that light, can you see it as your reward?*

Oh. Oh! A *reward*? Also a little foreign to my mindset. Isn't my soul the one drinking it all in? I just wish I could get to a place where the velvet visitations are slightly less peculiar to me. Or, maybe I need to embrace peculiarity.

Do those velvet visitations ever last a long time – is that the ecstatic experience yogis describe? Double V, what an apt term. Don't you just love moi?

God: You keep answering your own questions. Yes, I just love toi, Absolutely in the most absolute sense. Let's enjoy some moonlight, shall we?

I Am Ready!

Sunday, September 14, 2014, 1:00 pm
Dear Angels,
More miraculous weather. Hot sunshine, stillness, no wind. Dry, crisp clear days like a California chardonnay crossed with Kodachrome. The greens pop, the blues pop, all sparkles. I am sitting at the beach on September 14th! My inner beach bunny glories. The beach is deserted except for 5 families. The water is crystalline – high tide, flat as a lake, lapping gently with no swells or waves. What gorgeousness. I have brought my journal to the beach, and grains of sand cover the page so there is a gritty quality to my writing.

You have gotten my attention by twice sending me the card *New Beginnings*, and I wish to make a list of the main "new beginning" events of these recent September weeks:

1. Beautiful angel oracle card reading with Liddy and Isabelle;

2. Powerful class with Guru Singh, after which I had a quick opportunity to speak with him, and mentioned #1. He then closed his eyes, "communicated," told me that I had a gift the angels were grateful for, and then, delivered my assignment: I am to write and publish a book on communicating with the angels. This stunned me, woke me up, this cosmic nudge – but

boy, did I have it coming. And it could not have been delivered more accurately, more kindly, auspiciously or authoritatively. Definitely a command from on high. Wow. More on this later;

3. Melinda and John got married on the 6th;

4. A new yoga apparel boutique and studio opened last night;

5. KYTT teacher training for the next class started on the 11th with Guru Singh leading it;

6. Both local gas stations shut down suddenly for different reasons, in the same week, so there is astonishing, non-combustion-engine peace on the island;

7. I finished my 40th day of *So Purkh* last night.

So I sit here, with a Thermos of hot tea and an apple, already dry from my swim and my salty skin crisping up. I log these conditions because I know from reading past entries how important these tactile qualities of the here and now, are. Skipjacks are shoaling in the shallows; an occasional splash is an exclamation point in the shimmering flatness. Crickets chirp in the grasses. *Shazam!* I am in love with this day.

So, new beginnings. Angels, let's talk, we're overdue. It is time I became the high priestess of my own life. No more energy issues, no more limiting beliefs, no more driving myself forward with shaming shoulds. I accept the assignment of writing a book with you, about you, and about invoking divine help for human needs on this planet. I am excited about this, I think we could have great fun together. It just remains for me to provide the tangible transferal into media for human perception. So, angels, let us celebrate this new beginning on this fourteenth day of September, 2014, and consider this the first entry. I will next want to know about concepts, outlines, rough drafts, visualizing, etc. Oh, and that new laptop – it's time. Please help me launch my new life. And please tell me what you said to my teacher at the time, or is that private? I cannot help but be curious.

Over to you, angels.

Dear Barbara: Wahe guru!* We can hardly wait to spill onto the page with you in this joyous acknowledgement of your accepting the heavenly assignment. Oh, child, child, child, there is laughter and singing in heaven, you have no idea. Adoration is being showered upon you this very moment.

We told him [Guru Singh] we had been working with you for a few years, that we love you, loved your gift, were grateful for it, and were encouraging you to expand and share the gift. We said it was time for you to put it into a format which would reach other humans, to help the planet heal. And that it had to happen soon. We blessed him, and blessed you, and blessed the work to be. We are joyed beyond joy to have made this transmission. All will happen quickly now, and we require you to pay closer attention to everything and be especially opportunistic. We could even help you to write this within a year if you really work with us. What do you say?

I say, I am *ready*. These are three words I could not have conceived of a year ago. Let us get to work. First, brainstorming the style, tone, format and message. I have a vague idea about writing the book as a how-to-help-thyself book, quasi-biographical, but really as a step-by-step guide to invoking you, hearing you, and then following the guidance, yet illustrated heavily with passages from my own writings, so that people can read for themselves the power of solid guidance. Basically I'd take what has already been written and re-format it. What do you think?

Dear girl, we have some ideas to add to this. Since you're at the beach and — reasonably enough — a little distracted — we need not get into specific outline details here. Yes, we feel your general thought is strong and workable. You know that the book must make sense, flow easily and have a logical sequence that people can grasp. Your biggest struggle will be with revealing intimate parts of yourself. Yet, the abundant creativity that together we shall generate, will make this fly from your fingertips. It will be the first of many, this is our way. You are the channel, and you agree to the flow, so all shall be abundance and ease from here on.

I am excited, because I **get it**. And it so much fun to think about the thousand ways I can turn to you to share the fun – as in, please help me

---

*Wahe guru: In the Sikh tradition, a mantra or vibrational phrase meaning cosmic ecstasy, or dwelling in God. It expresses the journey from dark to light, from ignorance to understanding.

invoke the angel of writing, the angel of book publishing, the angel of authors, the angel of all the crystals I can work with to pull out the best of my best. HA. I just remembered that my very first 40-day kundalini yoga meditation in KYTT was for self-authorization. Oh, ha ha *ha*. Oh angels, let's fill the book with lots of humor.

I have to tear myself away, but this entry is very gratifying. It's a START. Blessed angels, thank you!

Our joy and our delight, shine forward and lead the way. Write soon, let us keep up the momentum. Showering you with blessed love and radiant beingness, we send you on your way. The Angels

From You, Through Me

Sunday, September 21, 2014
Dear Angels,
I must leave for yoga in about 10 minutes, but I promised myself I would begin The Angel Book **today**, as transmitted through your agent. So let the trumpets sound and the starting bell be rung – I declare this project begun. I have this yellow legal pad and two blocks of artist's sketch newsprint pads – and my own willing heart. I have no idea how this will take shape, but that is the fun of it, because this creative project will be *from* you, *through* me and all of my human filters. Therefore, there will be no blocks, no doubt, no hesitation – it is already done, already completed – I am just coloring inside the lines. Ever possible question I could have will be answered by you, and even if there were some moments of artistic waffling or agony, even that would only be fodder for the book. So all is well, all shall be well, and…

THANK you.
Love,
Barbara

Angels: We love you unto infinity, blessed child, and the bells of heaven are ringing out for this celebration. Thank you **so** *much for hearing us, and for choosing to accept the assignment of the book. We are silent until we have one such as yourself to speak for us, so your gift is incredibly precious and important, you know not how important. Your energy becomes higher and higher, finer and finer, with every prayer, meditation, chant and kriya you do — and you feel this flow, too! Soon it will become a gushing river, and your life will expand exponentially. But for the time being, let us get to work. Your question is about the oracle card Nature, and our message for you. This is one of many, many messages we will lovingly send to you. The reason for this card is — as you know — you are very receptive and open to us and the nature spirits when you walk outside or sit by the sea. Your soul drinks it in. We can send your best ideas when you are outdoors, which you can then go home and write about (or bring a notebook with you). You've truly worked so hard and steadily at hearing us under* **all** *circumstances, that we know you'll hear, no matter what. But for the purest inspiration, try taking your book project thoughts and questions outdoors. Work with us, and see what happens! Oh, we are so overjoyed!*

The Aquarian Human is Hatching Out

Thursday, September 25, 2014
Dear Angels,
I feel as though things are quietly accelerating and I need to pay attention. Last Friday I drove up to Millis, to spend the night at the ashram, so I could be there in cozy time for the Fall Fest on Saturday. Good decision. The minute I drove onto the property I felt calm, calmer, *calmest*. Saturday was so relaxed I felt high, a kind of divine well-being, with no desire to move from my spot in the tent. All that sacred earth energy soaked into my bones. I see now why people love festivals and practicing directly on the earth-surface — wow. I was happy-happy-happy all day.

Then followed a packed week of more vinyasa and kundalini yoga, tai chi, swimming, celebrating the equinox...all reveling in September energies. But I want to cut to the chase with a question about the energy this is moving through my body as a result, particularly at night.

These nighttime energy visitations come in different forms, flows, intensities, and entrance points in my body/energy field. Lately these have had a *very* different quality to them, in a different way from kundalini rising.

What happens is that the humming energy "prepares" me, insofar as I become extremely still, like I am being held steady for some kind of cellular hookup or docking. In this utterly still state, a data stream pours into me, in a kind of soft, direct fast beaming river like a soft, blunt laser. I can *feel* the data; *feel* the bits and bytes and shape. It is always directed into one of my chakras. Last night the beam seemed to go from my under-chin, through my upper palate, up into my forehead. It *pushed* my tongue into my upper palate, and I felt as though an energy axis or wire was stringing all those parts together firmly, like a light suture. And then, as always, it was over suddenly and my body parts relaxed.

I know I have written about this phenomenon before, but in my overwhelmment, confusion or naivete, it never really occurred to me to question where this energy came from. Then last night, or this morning, the word "Pleiades" came to me. And I began to wonder, is this energy extra-terrestrial? Yes, okay, I know, I AM naïve, but I'm trying to work *with* what is happening, not resist it.

Angels, please tell me: what is this information, where does it come from, why is it being poured into me, and will it make me brighter, more conscious, anything? If I flipped out and decided to shut off my willingness, would the data stream stop? You can hardly blame me for asking so many questions. Thank you, angels.

Angels: Dear Barbara, Beloved heart of ours, please fear not! We sense your alarm and distrust, and wariness of these phenomena. These reactions are normal, and we hope to write answers to you that put everything in perspective, and which allay your fears.

First of all, we must always begin by telling you how much we love you. This is a constant and will never change. Your ability to transcribe for us is as miracle which we will do anything to foster and encourage. It's such a beautiful gift! Thank you for coming to us, again and again.

*As for the nighttime visitations and the data streams you receive, at some level you do know and understand what is happening. Your ongoing use of crystals has definitely facilitated the delivery into you of this information. Yes, there are beings outside the Earth's sphere which are watching events on your planet, beneficial beings who are part of the great unfolding. You should not view them as frightening, alien or threatening. They are galactic — or cosmic, if you will — custodians, with a very serious purpose. If the peoples of the Earth self-destruct through fear and hatred, some souls must be saved, and some souls must be tapped to be the first responders, just as with your EMT and firemen. All hangs in balance now — this you know. The data being fed into you is creating a kind of repository or bank account in your superconsciousness. We cannot say if you will draw on this in your lifetime, or in 100 lifetimes from now. The information does not harm you and does not affect your daily life. However, as you rise up through the layers of the kundalini ladder, some of it may be accessible to you. Trust your common sense and inner knowing. Do you not, after all, feel quite normal despite all of the times that this has happened? You have borne everything remarkably well and are absorbing everything easily. All beings appreciate your willingness and cooperation. Even though you feel as though you are "just" human, and it's "just" little old you (to use your term), please, dear one, re-read Yogi Bhajan on the magnificence, destiny and infinite nature of the human. The eggshell is cracking across the globe, and the Aquarian human is hatching out. Stranger and stranger times will come: hold fast! Have faith! Turn to us. You will be calm and knowing and steady when all others are confused. **We need you**. What else would you like to know?*

Oh oh oh oh oh! Angels, what can I say. It is very WEIRD to be in a limited body but be told of unlimitedness. I am having an oil and water moment. So why don't other intense spiritual practitioners go slightly mad, trying to process their experiences? I imagine at some point it is too much for the psyche to handle. So…these data streams – will they keep occurring, or will they finish at some point, like the Encyclopedia Britanica, A-Z?

It will keep coming. The information is infinite.

What does God have to do with the kundalini energy, the data streams, and the cosmic guardians? My goodness the universe is a complicated place.

We are smiling because there is no simple answer to that question. When you converse with God, that is primal source energy — the One Creator. Doubt this not! It is easiest to use a metaphor which perhaps you can understand — that if God had a body, prana would be his breath, and kundalini his electromagnetic field. Work on this metaphor with your intuition — and it will become plain to you.

So... God's voltage is essentially streaming through me, or sometimes coming in a cloud, or bursts, or in different frequencies. Why only sometimes, then, not every night (not that I would want it to) – what primes a human body for being a conduit?

As above, so below! It's precise. Think on what physical resistance does to physical energy transfer. The metaphor holds for human bodies. There are multiple frequencies and forms of energy — and just so, the blocks to those energies can be deeply embedded. You have recently had almost two years of intensive block removal, week by week, class by class, experience by experience. But how much did it take to bring you to this state of clarity? Phenomenal effort! Phenomenal persistence! Phenomenal commitment! And now your body is sweetly humming the way it was designed to. What you view as unusual and special, is actually the normal level at which humans can operate all the time. This is the point of Yogi Bhajan's teachings. Do you begin to appreciate the miracle?

Yes. Yes. Yes. One more question (I think) and then I'll let you go because I must do my meditation. Please tell me about the way the energy shot through my hands and came out through my wrists and palm bases last Saturday. Was that what they call Reiki? That was cool – I could feel the healing power.

Yes, that was Reiki energy, and it was perfectly natural and normal. Work with us and keep intensifying your kundalini practice, and you'll be able to direct yours with intent. You healed your left hip, you know.

I wondered about that – how exciting. I would love to develop this latent healing ability. Please show me how, and lead me to what I need to know. I know – one more question regarding my 40-day meditations. For example, how long should I do my current one, "Conquering Self-Animosity"? Part of me thinks I should do it for the rest of my life.

*Sweet one, we surround you with joy and reassurance. You are moving into a period of great stability and intuition. Fears and blocks will drop rapidly from you now. The current meditation is good for polishing. A few more nudges of self-confidence and you will be flying. You tend to regard **all** other teachers as more experienced and knowing than you — but this is not so. You **do** deserve to be in the pantheon of Teachers — that is with a capital T. Even though you may not have embodied the knowledge yet, this will come. Stay the course and open your heart to us, as ever our dearest Barbara and Sarandayal Kaur. Trust!*
We love you!
The Angels

Tuesday, October 7, 2014
Dear Angels,
Here I am, at the ready, my pen is at your service.

Angels: We fly to your side to be with you in this miracle of written communication. Little you know of how subtle and sophisticated you have become. All the more reason that it is increasingly important that you write to us whenever you can. This will add material for your book, there is no time to lose. Please let us pick up again and we will provide the time and space for it. Time, space leisure —yes, these things are comforting and desirable. But do not let yourself become too slack, as it wastes time. This is your challenge in maintaining your Libra balance. What questions do you have for us today, dear child?

My question is relatively minor, put in context with all of the outrageous things I've been through with you. But here goes. For a long time now, I've noticed that whenever I go into a yoga studio, I have to guard my tongue carefully, and watch my words and conversations. There is a strange energy which kicks in, which sometimes causes unwise or unaware words to pop out of my mouth. Or, old socialized patterns of ego defense mechanisms or domination crop up. Please tell me about this social immaturity which seems to be mirrored uncomfortably back to me.

The phenomenon you mention in yoga studios and other sacred places is commonplace, and happens to everyone, even your senior teachers. Sacred presence does not tolerate lower levels of consciousness, and so whatever is in you, will rise to the surface. It explains why, for example, your senior teacher frequently says what-you-perceive-as unkind remarks. Her lower levels of consciousness are being tested, as well as yours. Notice this carefully, and you will see that occasional lapses in tact, are simply this — like a mental burp that needs clearing. What you can do to correct this in yourself, are things like pausing for a few moments before you go into a room, setting an intention to only say kind or positive things, blessing the occupants of a room, and continually noticing the places or people who trigger the lapses. You already do a number of these things — you just need to tighten up your consistency.

Thank you angels, how helpful. If I'm honest, I suspect what I am really reacting to is the ego's affrontedness at being caught out. This mirroring is so uncomfortable. Do other people also feel the itchiness, is that why many people melt away right after class – do only the fools, the ignorant, the courageous and the conscious remain behind to socialize? I usually feel as though I am walking into the lion's den, depending on whom I anticipate being there. I didn't even realize, until last night, that my feelings were strong enough to count as a lesser degree of woundedness. And knowing what I know by now, I definitely want to avoid:

- Overthinking
- Storymaking
- Identifying with
- Furthering, strengthening, or in any way prolonging the hurt

Yet, it is there, the Ouch, the icky memories and associations. What do I do to clear it?

Do an illumination session with your friend Brian! Also, cut energy cords with all yoga teachers you feel any power differential with, and any students. You have also now discovered the subtle body portal and communication link with ascended masters.

Do use this. As you have experienced, with a crystal-clear question and earnest petition for help, and the holding of sacred space plus your willingness to receive, this is a very powerful healing opportunity.

Thank you. Even having been in these environments for years, I have an assumption that yoga environments are all healing, all the time – and that healing is by definition a *soothing* phenomenon. But the deeper you go, the grittier it gets, and so it is understandable that people drift away or fall back, the closer you get to the source of the pain. I think that does it for now – was there anything else you wanted to tell me?

Only that we would like to write to you forever and ever about your splendor as a human. Please do follow through on purchasing the laptop so we can begin the book in earnest. And write to us on your birthday, and ask for a miracle! Guru Ram Das* must grant it for you! Sending, surrounding, and embracing you with all of the blessings of the Divine —
The Angels

Tuesday, October 14, 2014
Dear Angels,
Tonight I went to Kyla's class at her kundalini yoga studio-boutique. I hadn't been in about three weeks, and I'd forgotten how upbeat the energy is there. Kyla worked us hard in a tiring set – she always does – but then the energy afterwards is off the charts. After we finished singing Long Time Sun and chanted a long *sat nam*, everyone just sat there, stunned. And continued sitting there, stunned. No one moved. I think it was a good three minutes before anyone budged.

This sacred space, this community, is such an electric blessing in my life – and it contrasts highly with my own quiet life here on the island, especially after this sleepy weekend. So I was musing on the way home on the nature of creativity and the the high vibration of this studio. My thought was, "I want to be in this kind of community more often.

---

*Guru Ram Das: the fourth of the great teachers in Sikh Dharma. Kundalini yoga is considered a Raj, or royal yoga, which is passed down through the lineage of the ten Sikh gurus. The consciousness, principles and values of Raj yoga are inherited from the teaching of the ten Sikh gurus.

What will *my* potential create?"

Which is why my question to you, angels, is "what next?" And you sent me the card, *Signs*.

That's all... just looking at my current tendencies, stories, preferences and resources, and wondering if I will break out of Sleeping Beauty mode, or if I'll just go quietly into the sunset on a chaise longue by the pool (what is it about that lazy, hedonistic side of me?). Over to you...

Dear Barbara: How we love you, and laugh at your self-deprecating humor. Your book will be very funny, you know!

We feel your wonderings, your experience of this contrast — is it not superb? Both of your lives are highly defined, but obviously, in different ways. You offer the complementary style to your teacher's — instead of action, you offer rest. This is part of your inner nature, and will not change. It is an important component in your focus on creating sanctuary for yourself and others. Sanctuary can be just as vibrant, social and energizing as a yoga studio with much activity.

There are no final answers — your questions are open-ended. The important part is that you are re-examining the nature of creativity, and are intrigued by it. Now that your own is blooming again, fear not, your energy will increase, and more and more good will flow into your life. It is law — it is inevitable. You are beginning to appreciate the power of re-creating your story in the moment, and doing so daily — this is where your power and your glory will come from.

Cherish the contrast, cherish the inspiration that a leader like this teacher provides. Keep asking those questions, and keep re-inventing yourself. Your motive is the love of the teachings and the community — let this seed grow big, fat, and strong! The rest — that will happen, because you shall make it so, with our help and with trust and faith in God. Desire! Foster and fan that desire — and we shall support your every move. Does that help, dear one?

Yes yes yes! Thank you! Must go do meditation before I fall asleeeep... thank you angels.

Saturday, October 25, 2014

Dear Angels,

Glory day – another glory day in a month of glories. Late October, hot sunshine, in the 60's. The day so magical and packed with incident I hardly know where to begin. First, I taught Thursday night's sub class for Harpiar Kaur and had five students. The class was brilliant, insofar as You All came through, and the way the students went into deeeep-far-away meditation was awe-inspiring. All shiny faces and joy, coming up to thank me after. Something shifted in that class, because today, Saturday, I woke with such clear, high-functioning energy, I finally felt *human*. Afterwards, ran into a friend and she mentioned the haz-waste disposal day over at the middle school. On a complete whim I ran down into the basement and took about 20 cans of ancient paint that had been sitting in my basement for twelve years. Drove them over to the middle school, the men whisked them away in 2 minutes flat, and off I drove. A huge wave of relief washed over me and I burst into tears as I drove away. This was the true sign to me that the physical and metaphysical sludge was healed and cleared away.

Miracle #2 was that I went to town for a minor errand at the car dealership, but wound up marching into the office supply store to purchase a laptop. This item has been on my list for a few months now, have had a few stories and resistance and fears around it, and whoosh! You were there in full force, escorting me through by sending me Nate the Great salesperson, and something like $550 later I walked out with the deal done and all systems loaded, protected, cleaned up and started up, readied by the tech for me in a couple of days' time.

THANK YOU. These tech things are so mysterious – thank God for techy guys who find it child's play.

So now we start writing in earnest, and I can at least start transcribing the Angel Diaries into electronic format.

The rest of the miracle day...took a bike ride to the beach in the blazing sun of a late October day. Sat on the jumble of sea wall rip-rap, curled up in a little rock nest, and there I peacefully let the questions rise up. I think the most import one was about Mother Mary. That was surprising when She came through the other night, primed by my having read Andrew Harvey. So, when I teach KY, shall I invoke only one presence such as Mother Mary, would that be more powerful? At this point it is starting to feel like an *embarasse de richesse* – how on earth do I know who to call on, and when?

Over to you, angels.

*Angels: Dearest Barbara, light of our lives. How we adore you. You may resist these words, but write them anyway. We worship you. Yes, worship. Why? Because with every healing that occurs, every elevation of your consciousness and soul, the divinity within shines brighter and brighter. Until you become one with God. Just accept this for the time being and keep writing, please. The more brightly you shine, the easier it is for you to contact all ascended divinities in other realms, and the more they are attracted to you. They are, of course, **absolutely** accessible to all humans everywhere, always – but – the energy attraction strengthens as you purify yourself. So even though Mother Mary may never have been in your cultural consciousness or religious beliefs, except in the vaguest way, she can now be extremely present for you. In fact, she longs to be. And though you do not know it, you have need of her. In your grief at the loss of your mother thirty years ago this November, you shut down your belief in mother love and mother energy. You have wandered as a lost little girl ever since, relying on a tough exterior to get you through your struggles to survive. If you will work with us and with Mother Mary, we can gently transform your wounded, little girl's heart. It is true that the many many divine beings available to call upon can present you with an almost baffling array of choices. Is it not miraculous? So we understand your question very well! Yes, dear one, your kundalini classes will be more powerful if you work with and invoke one deity or divine being – or two or three. A host would probably be confusing. We can help you! Ask us as you rehearse and practice and it will become very simple and clear who shall be your most effective divine helper.*

Dear angels, thank you.

Saturday, November 15, 2014, 9:00 pm
Dear Angels,
I am sitting here studded with crystals for a meditation session, because I want to ask you a very serious question about The Soul. *My* Soul. And perhaps it is unnecessary, but I have placed blue lace agate and angelite at my heart chakra, sugilite at my throat, and danburite and aqua aura at my crown, and am holding a piece of selenite. Should probably have something to ground me. But I find these stones very comforting, and you know me, I am Determined to Get It Right. How funny I am.

Anyway, angels, I stopped off at the library today and checked out the website of a famous spiritual teacher, as I have recently re-read her vivid spiritual autobiography. This author firmly asserts that her soul goes by a name.

I want to know more about my soul. In a previous entry of mine, I had written to my soul and it said, "souls never have names." Which is it?

And if my soul has a name, how do I find it out; and why don't I feel the same passion this author feels for her soul? Her book is clearly a love story. After all I've been through, I am still pretty much myself, calm, cool and collected, and really don't feel strong emotions about things.

So...do I just have to be patient for another two dozen lifetimes, or what? Not that I am asking for things to change – me, I love love love my comfort zones, breathers, rest spots, and peaceful days. I should stop right here and NOT STIR UP THE MUD.

Hm, think it's time to take the crystals off now, I'm cooked. Angels, I know this is a ramble, but please tell me more about aligning with my soul, or whatever it is that is supposed to be happening.

Angels: Blessings on you, dear girl. Thank you for writing to us! Your soul is trying to reach you, all the time, every day. You do not need to write to us to ask about your soul, you can write to yourself directly. But we will answer your questions for you because this is serious work and it is time you started understanding the gravity of your transformation.

You have been guided to re-read this author's book, just as you were guided to buy it. Messages are being sent to you at every level to encourage you down the path of soul exploration. Most humans — as do you — have a somewhat confused, generalized idea about what the soul is, based on vague and inaccurate societal/cultural notions. Therefore you have to re-educate yourself about the very nature of your soul. It must be something that you never take for granted, as you know the agony of separation. You have come very, very far but must not turn slack now. Time is crucial. Every day is an opportunity to explore, expand, and investigate. We will help you, but please continue to ask, ask, ask.

Then why do I still feel so shallow and ordinary? My soul has come back into my body in a quite extraordinary way. Why does it have to be such an active task – why can't it just unfold naturally and organically as I live my daily life? Honestly, the stuff I do would choke a horse. Oh for pete's sake, what does a girl have to do? (hm, are we hitting a bit of resistance here?)

If I were a good girl, I'd say, "right you are, angels" and trot off and do ten kriyas to unfold the soul. And lastly, why are you so patient with me?

Dearest Barbara, We are patient because we are angels! And we love you, truly. We see past your ego, which is fighting for recognition, and seems to guide your pen and mind from time to time. What would your entries look like if you wrote from your soul?

I don't know, angels – my ego seems to be ever on the ascendant. And I don't think it wants my soul to be uncovered. What a sick game. Okay, angels, I think I've written enough for tonight. We've touched on the subject, at least. Am too tired to continue and must get up early – I am looking forward to taking Dharm's class tomorrow.
xx Barbara

Jubilation!

November 16, 2014, 9:30 pm
Dear Angels,
A great Sunday...Dharm's class was about breaking through blocks.
The meditation was potent and physical, to open up the heart center.
I am still working on the not-blurting thing – he just brings out my
little ego tricks, it's amazing. I told him I was teaching, and his eyes
lit up. Yay.

Later today I took Heidi's fantastic four o'clock vinyasa class, which was
packed on a cold, gloomily perfect November-esque day. You know this,
but I will record it – that you or some divine agency nudged me with a
reminder to invite a conversation with my soul during savasana. Brilliant –
it worked. Soul came through so clearly, and we had a lovely dialogue.
The breakthrough was, soul said something to the effect of *"this is what we've
waited lifetimes for—to be a priestess"* – referring to my kundalini yoga teaching role.
Rather, my role as a Teacher. Because soul was quite clear that this is the
mission, the core arrival at beingness. I had an immediate response of,
this is THE gold nugget within my heart-which-is-within-the-body-heart.

Oh oh oh joy, oh validation. Oh consolidation and confirmation
and conglomeration and gold-stamped, gold-plated, finalized
actualization! That message unified all the free-floating schtuff that
has been mucking around my life for decades now. It is as though the
core has formed, or has jelled and manifested.

Hallelujah.

Walking home, I was quietly jubilant under the flaming-gold tree
canopies and streetlight glow of a dark November night. So much
anxiety fell away from me with that declaration by my soul, I did not
even know I had had so much vague, doubtful unease.

But this, *this*, I get. The Priestess archetype – this, I can do. This makes sense to me. This gives me something to work toward enriching and developing.

What a luxury now to look back at yesterday's sad whining and send out showers of gratitude for the contrast. *Ha ha.*

I am especially thrilled to know that it is so easy to hear my soul during savasana. And as you say, I have a lot to learn about the soul, its mission, and how I bring it forth in my life – and in doing so need to re-educate myself and stay humble and open. Please send constant reminders. Over to you, angels –

*Angels: Dear Barbara, Jubilation! The skies ring with song and praises and celebration and the sounds of celestial joy. Oh, dear child, we are so **glad with you!** And bless you a thousand times unto infinity, that you noticed and embraced and laughed at — THE CONTRAST — between your despondency and frustration one day, and the relief, joy, knowingness, and heart celebration the next day. This is your spiritual growth, manifested. You are a wise child and growing ever wiser. You are a joy to guide, you have no idea how much we rejoice over you, every day, beloved of our angel hearts.*

*You shall feel flat and stale and ordinary no longer, for your soul has called to you, and you have heard. The path is clear and shining, and laid before you. This is not to say it will not be difficult — your challenges are only just beginning. But having the core **knowing**, the inner unshakeable glowing, that ignited ember, will be a light beacon, anchor, and container for all your days. Dear child, please go to bed and dream the sweetest dreams of your life. We stand watch and guard you ever, with joyous love and blessings,*
The Angels

Soul and I

November 26, 2014, 5:00 pm
Thanksgiving Day
Dear Angels,
Angel card reading: Guardian Angels

Thank you for this love letter of the Guardian Angel card. I feel as though I am one big wonder right now, so much is going on. But also, so much has smoothed out, and I feel as though I may be getting a taste of cruising altitude, now that the turbulence seems to be past.

To recap the day: 9 am vigorous yoga with Nancy, which unlocked my sulky hip and pelvis. Home to luscious rose-petal tea and toasted crumpets with cream cheese, scallions and smoked salmon, sitting in the watery, bright November light surrounded by my radiant, softly respiring, fragrant and blooming plants. I drank a whole pot of tea, peacefully and happily spending the whole morning at the table, reading a library book. At about 2:30 I took my tablet, bundled up and drove out to Southpoint Park. I put Sirgun Kaur's chant *Ma** on repeat and just walked around the road tracing the rocky point of the lighthouse.

Here is where it become interesting, subtle, and hard to describe. For the past few months – well, all summer, really, I have sensed my soul budding and rising and growing in me, asking asking asking for the conditions to bloom. I have heard and have done my best to respond. Frequent visits to the local beach seem to quench the thirst. With this yearning state going on all the time in the background, I have gotten on with my surface life, but privately using every tool, technique, opportunity and situation to nurture this deep longing.

Then, a week ago, I attended Sat Kartar Kaur's special kundalini yoga workshop on blessing and healing ourselves. In this class, she played Sirgun Kaur's *Ma* during relaxation.

---

*Ma: "The sound of MAAA calls on compassion and protection. It is the sound that a baby uses to call on the mother. Here, your soul is the child, and the universe becomes the Mother. If you call, She will come to your aid and comfort... when the shield is strong, you become protected from the impact of your own past actions." From The Aquarian Teacher™ Level One Instructor Yoga Manual, by Yogi Bhajan, PhD.

It was the time, the place, the moment, the vehicle, and the intersection of all that had risen before. During relaxation I had a nebulous vision of my SOUL, sort of ephemeral but with a shape like a human-amoeba, sort of pulsing, vaguely conforming to a human shape. My soul was *SINGING MA*. Over and over and over. My ego-intellect jumped in and began firing doubt and questions. SOUL ignored them, in a distinct way that was loving and inviting, and simply meant: SING WITH ME. Ego-intellect was very hesitant, but started to, a little bit, here and there. SOUL ruled, SOUL was victorious. It reminded me very much of Captain von Trapp inviting everyone to sing "*Edelweiss*." There was no resisting it, and no reason to resist. So we flowed, finally.

So now I have had a glimpse of my Soul, and I cannot get *Maaa* out of my head, heart, skin, or any other part of my Being, pacing to the chanted sound pouring into my ears.

What happened during my walk today? Some kind of communion, some kind of one-ness joy as we walked and sang and blessed. The cadence of the song exactly suited a blessing-stride. And I understood suddenly how the Aborigines sang everything into being. And Soul and I watched the giant gray combers roll in like liquid marble, and form perfect hair-curler tubes, and merge and foam and suddenly be peppered with sea birds popping up after the wave had crested. "I" yielded. On that walk, "I" yielded to Soul; it was her time, her domain, her wisdom. Yet intellect kept burbling quietly underneath, occasionally surfacing with questions and respectful queries, trying to find the DMZ where we two blended, shared or exchanged.

On the final, eastern side of the mile loop, I consciously invited all of you to come along. I invited *you*, angels; and all my power animals, and JC and Mother Mary. It was...a land of invited unity. And I sensed you all.

Then I realized...Ego-intellect does not need to be the one summoning. Soul knows all these energies and beings very well. Soul is right at home in this dimension. And another piece of the puzzle fell into place.

No longer do "I" need to worry about duality and the peculiar sense of being half in, half out, like Mary Poppins and the sidewalk chalk art. Now that Soul presides, that connection, that gap is bridged. Soul is the rainbow which reaches from side to side, from Earth to Ether. It is as though I was trying too hard to play hostess, and I thought I had to put my guests at ease, but they were already settled down to the feast.

Oh Angels, this is huge. This Thanksgiving Day, this feast of One Soul, this quiet glory. I have asked God for more understanding, and I have received it. Thank you.

And that is my entry for today, really. Topped off with drawing the *Guardian Angel* card. Angels, over to you.

Angels: Dearest Barbara, We are here with you in force. Your joy is our joy. Your soul is risen, and your holy, sacred path now shines and beckons before you. Flow now commences. Be prepared for change. Enjoy all with awareness and radiating blessings from your heart. Welcome each new shift as the miracle it is, for you will watch them through the coming years, washing through, over, and with you, just as you watched the combers at Southpoint today.

This is our own Thanksgiving gift to you; and in turn we shower you, beloved girl, with our rainfall of celestial angel thanks for the path you have kept to, in turning to us, listening to us, working with us, praying with us, and blessing with us. For all goes straight through to the Ultimate Divine Glory of God, and though you are shy of this magnificence, you will one day come to know it in yourself.

Today was a larger step than you know, an unfolding occurred. Be patient and these sacred states will begin to move through you. You yourself know all too well that overwhelming experiences do not necessarily foster growth. Fire your vessel in the kiln of time just a little longer, dear child of our angel hearts.

Now, angels, I think I shall have just a bit of Thanksgiving dinner – roasted potatoes, and salmon baked with scallions, garlic and ginger. Then to return and work on the book. Thank you, Angels!

Sunday, November 30, 2014, 7:30 pm
Dear Angels,
This has been such a gratifying weekend, with all things in good balance. After gardening and making a run to the transfer station, suddenly I was pole-axed and woozy again, so I just took a nap before 4 pm yoga class. The fatigue passed during the quietly miraculous class. I feel my scattered pieces coming together.

Which brings us up to tonight, angels. The card you sent me for tonight is *Healing*. Please, what would you like me to know about this card?

Dear Barbara, Ah, how clear you are tonight. And we love you, this is why we sent you the card of Healing. In truth, you are always healing, but at certain junctions energies intersect and you experience a more powerful clearing than at other times. This was your achy-tired-sleepy-wooziness today, the point at which many energies were flowing through you. You did well to just relax and let them stream, and to consciously breathe. We tell you this so that you will know and not be fearful, and will deepen your understanding and trust when these states occur. Healing may not always feel like clarity, light and energy. It is important for you to know that these uncomfortable physio-spiritual states which alarm you a little, are actually something which you can embrace and link with a positive outcome. They are not something to cause fear or worry, nor are they abnormal. They are merely uncomfortable, and because they can be sustained over time, projecting "wrongness" onto them can be an easy, human reaction. Therefore, rejoice! In the beauty and excellence of the life you lead at this moment!

Thank you, angels! Help me rejoice...it's a bit of a puzzle to feel weary and rejoice, but will try...Oh dear, am yawning now...

You are weary, dear one. Would it be best to continue this tomorrow?

States of Healing and Grace

Monday, December 8, 2014, 10:30 pm
Dear Angels,
I have just completed my daily 11-minute meditation of the Mahan Mudra, just laid out the oracle cards, and drew *Divine Guidance*. I am happily curled up in bed under 5 layers of covers, plus a little electric pad. It was freezing today, in the 20s, and I came home chilled like gazpacho. Much better now! I am all pen and ears, please tell me more.

Angels: Dearest one, Bless you, heart of our hearts. We love you to the reaches of Infinity for your writing gift. We send you the message in this card of Divine Guidance to show you, to demonstrate how true and straight, clear and accurate you have become. You are quite right in knowing that the Mahan Mudra meditation is a communication position. When you let celestial energy flow around you in a directed way, it completes a healing circuit. As with all of these meditations, the effects are small and subtle, but do strengthen your vessel incrementally. It would be better to do this meditation for 90 days or longer. The saintliness Yogi Bhajan is referring to is the refinement of all of your systems. Yes, it helps to balance your chakras. And, as you observe, it makes you clearer so that you can communicate with us.

Mahan Mudra meditation is also a position of blessing and transmission. It goes both ways. Do not forget, you are Divine, too. So the completed circuit from the Universe, which interacts with your physical, limited embodied Divinity, makes a kind of double-linked chain. It is a tandem effect, a linking of earthly and divine. It is a very beautiful position.

So the meditation is about communication, devotion, guidance receptivity, and raised vibration. Like a spiritual tuning fork. Angels, good night, and thank you!

Saturday, December 13, 2014 (note symmetry of 12-13-14), 9:30 pm
Dear Angels,
Almost time for a new journal. Today – more splendor. The weather was clear, bright, sunny and still. I had stayed in bed until 9:30, and then decided to start my day with a crystal meditation. That got me off to a calm and centered start. Spent an hour doing sadhana to prepare for

tonight's shamanic journey* with Aynsley and Rene at the local yoga studio.

Arrived at the studio and settled in for the shamanic journey to the underworld. The room was fragrant with sacred *palo santo* wood smoke. Rene and Aynsley, who were leading the shamanic journey, smudged and feathered everyone. They began the guided meditation...we journeyed... up into space, zooming about, to a green world, looking down on a path cutting through tall grasslands. Looking at my bare feet, I felt the soft, powdery dust under my toes. Found the tree, a giant redwood with buttress roots, which I had to walk way, way, way around in order to find the entry crack. Descended down, down, down – felt like something out of Tolkien, fable-like. Came to underground cavern. Met Crone again, was not afraid of her this time. She said, "How are you, my dear?" We went to the river and got into a boat – I called it cockleshell in my journey, but it was wooden, like a skiff. We floated downstream and *cool* – we were accompanied on the right by a giant, zig-zagging anaconda snake with a flat, triangular head. I am sure it was my former shamanic teacher – it was like a nod to me – "we've got you covered." Arrived at a sandy shore and got out with Crone. I saw, standing there, "MA" - Mother Earth or Changing Woman, who shimmered and shifted appearance constantly. She greeted me with open arms. Her gown was diaphanous and blowing in the wind. I was supposed to give her my burden but I didn't know what it was supposed to be (I had a clear crystal in my hand), so I just gestured at my pelvic region, where I store my pain. "MA" reached forward and her fingers translucently went into my pelvis to pull it all out. At this point, in real time, I felt a tangible tugging sensation in my pelvis and arched right off the mat. Tears trickled down my face. Whoa, that was **real**. That crossed worlds. Wild. The journey experience became physical sensation on the earth plane. How the...?

Then MA embraced me, looked into my eyes, and said, "You can trust me," but I think what she meant was "you can trust this." Then she gave me a gold ring. As we left to retrace our steps, I had a sense that she was

---

*Shamanic journey: a guided meditation led by a shamanic practitioner.

Galadriel. When I stepped back onto the path, I was no longer barefoot, but was wearing sandals with a single strap, decorated with jewels. I am curious about this metaphor – why the difference between barefoot and jeweled sandals?…and so, we were brought back to the present, into the yoga studio and our mats, and we shared our experiences. I was buzzy with Presence and everything that had happened on my journey. Said good bye to Heidi, Rene and Aynsley, and sped home under a crystalline, starry sky.

Did my 11-minute meditation of Mahan Mudra. Sitting in meditation afterwards, musing on the journey, I realized: the *ring*. The ring of power. She gave me my power back. This, after I had done the second chakra kriya this afternoon, specifically for power.

This is my Christmas present, the ending gift of a year of outrageous transformation, starting with the soul retrieval in January.

It's all really working. I have come so far in one year. And angels, you have sent me the *Power* card on several occasions. Journeys within journeys within journeys.

Oooh. Drinking good, strong, peppermint tea. This hits the spot.

Oh, that anaconda.

I am thinking about the next rising generation like Aynsley and Brian, who are utterly at ease and at home with traveling between worlds, and who straddle both seamlessly, making the shift organically as they respond to circumstances. Aynsley is a paragon of grace and poise, and she seems to blend the two – earth-plane and non-earth plane – effortlessly and naturally. I think the upcoming generations will be increasingly fluent and fluid, and my astonished reactions will read as a quaint historical footnote someday. The new norms for rising young sophisticates will include not only an assumption of multilingual and multicultural facility, but multi-planal fluency.

Angels, it has been such a perfect day, I almost can't come up with any questions for you. But please tell me about the commitment to teaching kundalini yoga.

Dearest, beloved Barbara: Every time you write to us, it is a journey, and you are crossing or accessing a different realm. **You** *are just as beautiful, poised, graceful and intuitive as your peers. We tell you this only because you are not yet assessing yourself as truly as you might, and external validation gives you valuable context. Part of regaining your power will be to strengthen your ability to assess yourself. You deeply admire many of your peers on their healing paths. Consider how many of them might admire* **you***. We know this never occurs to you — which at one level is fine, as it supports a humble attitude. Yet you must find your footing at this professional level, with your peers. You are keenly aware of power imbalances such as those you experience with your senior teachers. This motivates you to correct it by working on your second chakra — excellent. Look carefully at what is making you uncomfortable right now. You ask us about your level of commitment on your teaching path. How we love you, dear girl!*

Tuesday, December 16, 2014, 1:36 pm
Dear Angels,
Quiet day at work, everyone scattered to the four winds, and a brief, welcome interlude with no UPS deliveries. Angels, you are so gently relentless, I can feel you nudging me down the road, millimeter by millimeter. In short, Aynsley just emailed me with her idea of hosting an angel-reading evening in the Verdant Vineyard tasting room, this coming February, with me as hostess. *Moi?* But-but-but-but…!

You know, oh wise ones, that one day, I will look back, read this page, and smile at my reaction of inadequacy. But, I am not there yet, at that "one day" destination.

I know what you want me to do (answer Aynsley with a resounding YES). I know my initial reaction of panic will wear off. It still astounds me that people can see my abilities more clearly than I can, and are ready and willing to encourage me. You know I am not used to having a human cheering squad, and find it a peculiar sensation. Angels, why is it so hard for me to take these things into the public realm? Other people have no difficulty whatsoever.

Angels: Dear Barbara, Blessings on you, sweet girl and angel friend, for listening and hearing, loving and trusting, asking and receiving. These are powerful modes which you will understand better one day. Each time you pick up the pen, you create a miracle with us, and it cannot be said enough that we love you, and love you for it.

This proposed event which is startling you, will be very easy and natural. It is why we speak through Aynsley — the pieces are already in place, the talents and skills are there, the willingness is all that is needed. Ask us to remove your fears, dear child, you are so ready for this! You have done far more difficult and fearsome things. Your courage is deep: call on it. Your friends are true: call on them. We send this message again to you: we need you. We need you to begin the long process of softening hearts and accessing minds and spirits, to counter the terrible energies rife on the planet today. All soldiers are being called. It is time to enlist; the battle is on. We need you. All efforts, no matter how small, have an effect. All blessings, no matter how gentle, radiate out. Please, put aside your personal concerns and step forth as part of this team of beings of light. It is time for you to evolve to the next stage of your life and commitment as a human being. These steps will happen in small, incremental stages, but they must happen. Take your old habits, fears, attitudes and beliefs to the mat for dissolving; and to the pyre for burning. 2014 is finishing — it is time. Move on with us, dear child, and stretch your wings! It is time to fly.
Love,
The Angels

Wednesday, December 17, 2014, 2:45
Dear Angels,
My protests are feeble and pretty silly in light of this response. Sigh. As always, you put things in perspective. It is time for me to take a long, hard look at my motives, and re-assess them. I am still coming out of the fog of "*I-did-it-I-made-it,*" so I've been enjoying lying flat on the ground at metaphorical base camp, so to speak. Or the camp at 15,000 feet, whatever the altitude is I've achieved. Hard to peel myself off the ground and start up the mountain again. The directive has changed – it is no longer unbending intent to unify and heal this fractured mind-body-soul. So, what *is* my motivation, angels? I'm not sure I know. I can only start putting one foot in front of another, and hope that it will become apparent.

My list of things to examine in myself, then are:

- personal power, energy levels, daily vitality
- commitment to kundalini yoga teaching, discipline, and sadhana
- motivation, desire and willpower
- outdated beliefs and attitudes: the laziness of wanting it to be easy and on my terms
- reluctance, rationalizing and protesting
- ongoing reinvention of self: positive new stories, new stories, new stories

That should do it for now.

Your Treasure Hoard

Tuesday, December 23, 2014, 8:30 pm

Dear Angels,

Dozy day at work – things quiet, no phones, staff restless because of piles of chocolate and pre-Christmas, ready-to-bolt, get-me-out-of-here energy. Went to staff holiday lunch at local pub restaurant on the wharf – eight of us making small talk in a grubby, cheap atmosphere. Everything greasy, salty, overspiced. The director ordered tater tots swimming in cheese, and deep-fried pickles. My turkey burger was actually tasty, though I suspect it was due to half a bottle of MSG. The other staff seemed quite happy with the choice of restaurant. What an interesting object lesson – if I had made up my mind to be positive about the exercise, what could I have focused on to shift my perspective? I just find it strange that no one in the group seemed to find the atmosphere repellent, the music obnoxious, and the food second-rate. The tab for the meal wasn't even affordable, it was expensive.

Over the past weekend, I conserved my energy and stayed quiet. At some point during a meditation, a light bulb went off: *power retrieval*. It's as though I turned a corner and everything in me said: do *this*. *This* is your next focus. So, among other things, I have been doing full-body crystal meditations using garnets. I now suddenly see this theme of power loss and power retrieval, all around me and in everything I do. Walking down supermarket aisles and scanning the food packages and products, I whisper to myself, "will this build my personal power?" For 90% of the supermarket items, the answer is no! Power retrieval: am I drinking enough water? Getting enough sleep? Refraining from sugar? Connecting those consequences with the deflated, depletion state I find myself in?

I am drafting a personal program whose sole, overriding theme is: *personal power*. It is my new lens, and everything is now being assessed in terms of whether it builds me, or does not build me. I am trimming my budget and cancelling subscriptions, plugging little leaking financial holes. I am replacing batteries and burned out light bulbs. It has been a very illuminating 4-5 days in concert with the season of the solstice. Interestingly, the gadfly that stung me into reassessment was my irritation with my yoga teacher's breezy holding forth about his private life, with (of course) no inquiry about me or mine. It is a weird dynamic between us – I cannot tell if we are competing, or he is trying to keep me in my place with condescending pats on the head, or what. Note to self, cut energy cords again with him.

This brings me more or less to where I am now, sitting propped up in bed, writing to you, angels, and just having pulled the oracle card *Harmony*, in response to my question to you about ways to retrieve personal power. Hm, Harmony. "*Conflict is resolved in a situation that was troubling you. Know that you deserve this peace and happiness, and accept it graciously.*" Angels, please tell me more.

Dear Barbara: We love you very much! We send you the Harmony card as a reminder that states of conflict do not need to last long to achieve their goal, the friction to create the spark to light and ignite. Once achieved, do not stay in conflict! There is no need. Use the igniting power and move on. It is good that you can recapitulate these events for the sake of your personal record, and so that you understand them fully. Now you have had the experience and can internalize it as a tool and call upon it another day when your motivation wanes.

We are very proud of you, too, truly. You have slogged through many miles of murky emotional and psychic debris, and have been very patient with yourself in times of darkness and confusion. Your energy field is already clearing up very quickly due to the events of the last two weeks — in combination with all of the healing events of the year. How many more miracles can you handle in the next week, before the year turns? There is still time to bring this cycle into completion with a downpouring of blessings.

As for personal power, and your new focus, we say hallelujah in the most tender, divine, and joyous way, to you, dearest one. This is the normal operating framework for humans, what is normal and necessary to achieve and create and build and have a life on the planet. You have had so many blows to your personal power system throughout your life, that this breakthrough in your awareness is a signal lifetime achievement. Yet the humility you have learned along the way — and will continue to learn — gives you a spiritual grounding which is hard for many humans to reach. Bless those years of pain and searching, dear one, they are your treasure hoard. Recalculate your life in terms of all the joyful events that have happened, and watch your personal power increase. And then, my dear, come to us with your courage in both your hands, and let us help you open up your heart. This is the last, greatest, biggest, best challenge. You will rise to it, as you have risen to all other challenges, for are you not Sarandayal Kaur? Blessed girl, the time is on, and you are galloping down the finish line. But for now, real time calls you to bed, to restore your weary body. Let us take the next two days to celebrate your peace, joy, love, harmony and grace — tangibly, actually, and together. We await your next writing with smiles and angel arms.

Come to us!

Blessing of peace, love, and light —
The Angels

Chapter VIII: Bearing Fruit

Rebellion is a sign of self-love.

– ANONYMOUS

Dear Reader

October 18, 2018

Dear Reader: And now, it's your turn.

For the first time in this book, I, Barbara, am going to happily, recklessly blend both italics and non-italic fonts, because these modes are now indistinguishably blended inside of me.

Dear reader, this book is designed to simply show and share. These human reachings and *angelic teachings* are designed to turn you back *into* your Self, in both senses of the phrase. The infinite, unspooling path, should you choose to walk it, leads you to turn *in*-ward for guidance, in order that you may turn *in*-to your highest Self. In other words, choosing to come into your own self-authority.

In the preceding pages, you may have noticed that I, Barbara, am a recovering "give-it-to-me-in-one-tidy-understandable-package-with-no-further-effort-on-my-part" seeker. My recovery is mostly accomplished, with occasional blind spots and lapses.

For myself, although the path was long and rocky, all of its stages were necessary. I was helped along by remarkable guides, teachers and friends. I honor and humbly acknowledge the powerful, life-changing wisdom which many talented teachers have shared with me over the decades. I especially appreciate the teachers and ascended masters who continue the golden chain of teachings of kundalini yoga, and who have not let me slide again into the comfort zone of unawareness.

However, having also walked this road, I understand the temptation to project authority onto a teacher, author, book, or dogmatic system, to then expect full, final achieved external results from said teacher, author, book or system – and then be confused when few or no results occur. This is the temptation, and the pitfall, I would caution you to look out for.

Why?

Because the truth, dear reader, *is that you will be **so much stronger and more glorious** if you figure it out for yourself! We are here for you, on both planes, earthly and heavenly. Will you join us on the path?*

With blessings of love and light from
Barbara
The Angels
and
John!

Epilogue: Harvest

"...So many miracles and mysteries...at this point I just smile and say, 'thank you.'"

- BARBARA SCHLUBACH

One early morning, in a pre-awakening doze, this message came through: *The point of the journals has been achieved.*

The angel journals healed me. They provided the material for this book. Together with my disciplines and practices, over time I changed habits and patterns. My consciousness shifted. I began to breathe more slowly and deeply, from a centered place. Formerly unknown states like confidence, tranquility, and detached observation began to form the background of my personality.

The intervening years, between the December 2014 entries and now, have brought many more rich learning experiences, whose human-angelic journal entries await transcription.

After four wonderful years, in 2017 I had to trade in my VW Golf TDI, which I always thought of as "The Minx." This was my automotive heart's desire, but I decided to trade it in for a gas model. I cried all the way to the dealership and startled the salesman by saying fiercely, "Make sure you find a GOOD owner for that car." Farewell, my faithful lovely...I bought a new Golf TSI in silver, slightly larger, more sedate in handling – but oh, yes – still standard transmission. I named her Edelweiss. She is the perfect size for packing up cases of newly-printed books, and taking them on the road.

Of all the adventures I went through, the dream of the bookstore was the one thing which did not manifest – as such – during the time-frame of the journals. At that time, with a pang, I let it go, thinking the results had to be literal. Now rereading those entries, I know that this creative underground guidance-river flowed powerfully into this book and its production, and that the web of human involvement is expanding like the sun.

Energy and health imbalances have tapered off, but still occasionally knock me to my yoga mat and provide a stiff learning curve ("Angels, *really*? Oh, oookay.") And then I take action: I listen, bless, invoke help, take action, surrender, accept the healing – and then we're fine again until the next time. I am much faster on the draw these days, but sometimes enjoy a moment of protestation before I buckle down to the healing partnership.

My skill of hearing angelic frequencies has shifted to a slightly faster mode. On this note, I must say a word about the importance of cultivating silence, and peaceful or quiet surroundings. Over the years I have withstood much good-natured teasing (and the occasional "good for you!"), because I have so few home and personal electronics, and have opted to stay clear of the social media frenzy.

During the years spent writing the journals and this book, at home I had no television, no mobile phone, no Internet connection, not even a CD or DVD player. I acquired a tablet when I started KYTT, so that I could play the music and chants which accompanied the sets. I bought a laptop in order to write this book. I use these devices with pleasure – but always selectively, on my terms. This is all to say, the vibrations in your home, and your dependence on them, will affect how open you are to hearing or sensing unseen guides. If you wish to invite Presence, then it is worth experimenting with the practice of Absence – an absence of electronic devices in your designated peaceful spaces.

I can only offer you this gentle proof: these preferences and practices yielded the book in your hands. I wish you joy as you experiment with your own practices, and learn what is possible.

And this wild personal journey all started by asking one, little question, listening deeply, and writing down the answer.

As I shyly shared this manuscript with trusted family, friends, neighbors and fellow yogis and yoginis who were willing to read it in its early stages, some questions came up repeatedly:

"What will the reader get out of it?"
"What is the theme, center, or focus?"
"Why did you write to the angels?"

I had no answers for these questions. The book, the manuscript, simply was, it was my lifework, which exuded from me like honey over a four-year period. The answers were embedded in the text. I could not understand this need to cram it into a format for others, when it was my baby, my creation. Wasn't it obvious why it had to come into being?

These questions came up so often that I realized I had attracted them to myself. It became a thorn in my side. More remnants of Good-girl-itis had to be flushed out and rinsed away.

Then I read a beautiful line on a blog: "A bird does not sing because it has an answer. It sings because it has a *song*."

With that, I gratefully realized what the problem was – I was still projecting outwardly and draining my power away to imaginary outside readers, editors, and critics who didn't exist yet, and warping my writing to fit some external standard.

A talented tarot card reader told me, "Treat this book like a work of art." And so I went back to my deepest core values. I solidified this creation as my voice, my work of art, gently yet firmly impervious to outside influences. This sealed the power leak, and I moved on.

The key to transformation is to shift what *was*, into what *is*, by using the momentum of faith, hope, trust, and deep inner knowing of what *will* be. In other words, subtly manipulating components of time, and using this deep inner knowing to change the experience

of the past in *this*, the present. To go from being a flailing skater
on the ice of time, with windmilling arms, to being a speed-skater
gracefully powering through the curves, leaning into each moment
with heart-joy, each pressing stroke of the blade a fused triumph
of mastery and grace. Yet at the same time, remaining keenly aware
of the potential of a humbling fall, ready to reach for the willing,
unseen energies that will lift you back up into balance.

As I prepare to go to press in the early months of 2019, I am poised
between my old world of traditional 9-5 employment, and the new
one opening up, of being a self-published author. And in that,
I find myself right back where I have always been, at the point of
balance, in charge of my equilibrium, my sanctuary, and my story –
and I am still the little girl on the see-saw.

Appendix

Pocket Wisdom (from both sides of the See-Saw)

Entry Date

3/10/11   *Write, lass, write. Strange to say it is your challenge to overcome the sadness, the weariness of trying so hard, the discouragement — when you conquer these, you feel ease. When you feel ease, it all flows.*

11/28/11   *You **know** what you **know** —don't expect others to understand or agree, but get stubborn about pursuing it. This will always serve you.*

12/3/11   *You will read back over these writings and marvel that you ever felt so desolate.*

12/27/11   *It is in the overcoming that you are healed.*

12/30/11   *We took your blessings and magnified them - so you see, we needed your help on earth to work the miracle.*

1/4/12   *Do please keep praying and blessing. You have these proofs of how effective we can be when you have the courage to practice all the spiritual disciplines consistently. Yes, it is miraculous! You are our agent of miracles. What else can we accomplish with you, sweet friend, beloved child, our searching sister?*

2/7/12   *And so much goodness and abundance is a little terrifying when one is used to lack and self-limiting thoughts.*

2/29/12   *You are million-faceted, therefore you might do well to practice million-acceptances.*

2/28/12   *Awareness only expands, it does not contract.*

3/31/12   March 29, 2012 entry from the Angels, containing nine clear tools on how to shift a situation:
1. *Use EFT for your anger,*
2. *use acceptance for all your states of mind and heart,*
3. *ask us to transmute anything else,*
4. *please go for a long walk if you can*
5. *— or go sit in a church —*
6. *and rain blessings on your challenge.*
7. *Then turn it over to us — don't forget to ask! Grumbling is fine, but don't indulge —get rid of that mind-set, move on.*

8. Make the active choice about whether or not you want this situation to drain you, and act accordingly. You get stuck in, and loop in, the emotions which pet the ego.
9. Ask us to help you disrupt that looping, and we will.

This is a pattern you have been repeating for years. It is your choice, to change it or not. We can help you become unstuck. You will never do a more courageous thing in your lifetime than this. You do have it within you.

4/18/12   *We bring you the power to understand your power.*

4/23/12   *All will become much easier as you start to heal your heart, and operate your awareness out of your heart rather than out of your brain.*

7/12/12   *Taking action dissolves doubt, dissolving doubt builds trust, building trust helps you open yourself to miracles.*

7/17/12   *Bless them and bless the problem.*

10/1/12   *When you write, you are always clear, even if you think you are not, because the single-pointedness of the activity forces you to articulate the issue you need to know about most.*

1/24/13   *There are iron bands across your heart and it is safe now to undo them.*

8/31/14   *Your linear mind has not caught up with your intuitive one. Every time you experience the feeling of bafflement, look to this discrepancy, and resolve it.*

9/14/13   *…So many miracles and mysteries…at this point I just smile and say, "thank you."*

10/7/14   *But the deeper you go, the grittier it gets, and so it is understandable that people drift away or fall back, the closer they get to the source of the pain.*

11/26/14   *Soul is the rainbow which reaches from side to side, from Earth to Ether.*

12/23/14   *We send you the Harmony card as a reminder that states of conflict do not need to last long to achieve their goal, the friction to create the spark to light and ignite. Once achieved, do not stay in conflict! There is no need. Use the igniting power and move on.*

12/23/14   *Bless those years of pain and searching, dear one, they are your treasure hoard.*

11/18/18   *You do not feel it, you do not know it, you do not even sense it, but the room is now quite full of angel presence, for you have invited us here with your heart, your searching questions, your need for resolution, and—yes! These finely complex human situations which we so dearly love to assist with. For this we live.*

The Joy of the Journey:
A Prayer, a Poem and a Blessing for the Road

April Morning Prayer

Wake up, little soul!
Wake up, little soul!
Wake up, little soul!
I need you.
Wake up, little soul!
Wake up, little soul!
Wake up, little soul!
I love you.
My brain cannot think these rhymes
My heart cannot beat these times
My hand cannot write these lines
And I am weary of these mimes
Without you
Without you
Without you
Wake up, little soul!
I want you.
Arise, little soul, and expand
Guide the pen within this hand
Lead the heart with sweet command
Give the mind to understand
It's safe, little soul!
It's safe, little soul!
It's safe, little soul!
To fill the corners of my being, now
Until, again, we become Thee-Thou
And hearing sparrow-song, we bow.
In Joy we dwell, in the ringing Now.

April 16, 2016

A Very Barbara Poem

I'm going to spend the morning in bed
In order to fight this sense of dread
I'll work on writing this poem instead
To banish the darkness inside of my head.
I'll lie in the dawn's light and listen to rain
Knowing the metaphor cleanses my pain.
I'll laugh at myself for how clever this is
And feel simple hope surge back with a fizz.
I'm me! I say, and I am back once more,
It's so nice no longer to be on the floor.
I'm me! I say (and question this grammar) –
It's so nice to be out from under the hammer
Of thinking and thought, ideas, and emotions
Concepts, opinions, preferences, mental commotions,
Head-stories, narratives, mind-movies, agendas
Egos and Ids, and all their addendas.
Projection, dejection, and mental infection
Now divinely transmuted by angelic injection
Of blessings, love, faith, hope, trust and light
It takes all of these, and more, to turn back the night.
It's nice to lie in my bed when it rains
Using paper and pen to break mental chains.
Liberation! she cries, as she chants affirmations –
The angels are listening, with sweet exultations.
All's well once again, she's sleeping, she's versing
She's happy, she's feeling, she's no longer cursing
The book is written, it's *en route* to its birth
With prayers and blessings for joy on this earth.
The angels — and John — on rafters celestial
Are escorting our tears...*to laughters terrestrial*.

December 2, 2018, 6:00 am

May the long time sun shine upon you,
all love surround you,
and the pure light within you,
guide your way on.

Sat nam.

Acknowledgements

Dear reader, thank you for reading this book.

By now it is apparent to me – and I hope to you – that the angels have surpassed themselves in sending blessings to me in material and metaphysical form, weaving their divine timing and circumstance into an impeccable, glowing tapestry of manifestation. My job is to put down the words and watch with awe and humility as everything flows in.

The gift of help in writing this book has humbled me. Many people have responded with kindness, time, thoughtful comment, enthusiasm, and artistic contributions. The occasional loving kick in the seat of the soul-pants was especially necessary to jump-start my inertia.

I was continually astonished by the support system of willing, caring, involvement from friends, family, and the yogic community as I hesitantly asked for help, and people said "yes!"

This astonishment was heightened when I emerged from an intensive period of dealing with only non-physical energies, and began to approach, as my collaborative editor Rebecca Polan humorously put it, "beings with a central nervous system." In other words, I deeply appreciated and needed to work with living, breathing humans after so much time spent in the realms of angelic communication. It is my turn to pay forward these gifts.

I would like to thank the core group of friends who knew the strange and intimate nature of this book, and who always believed in me. They listened patiently to my doubts and fears, gave loving, sensible feedback, and grounded me when I was flying high in mental realms: Lale Ahkrass, Carla Borsotti, Patrice Carroll (Patwant Kaur), Lisa Lewenz, and Anni Mackay. When I struggled to explain what this book was about in concise terms, Nina Biddle-Luna's compassionate listening and journalistic skill drew the extraordinary "A Letter From the Angels" from me.

I thank all those who supported me with loving enthusiasm: Shantia Anderheggen, Joan Andersen, Flinda Behringer, Patricia and Marco Belda, Carol Brumer, Prim Bullock, Morgan Devlin, Kerry Cunningham, the Cotter, Dunning and Biddle-Luna families, Sylvie Deruy, Steve Elliot, Leah Rosin-Pritchard, Aynsley and Brian Schopfer, Jerry Scott, and Rene Stawicki. I am deeply grateful for the joy, innocence, and openness of Liddy Cotter and Isabelle Dunning, whose participation threw the pebble which started the angelic avalanche of this book.

And in my study of this lifelong human curriculum with its truly strange syllabus, I thank the many professionals and teachers of the yoga and wisdom-tradition communities where I found sanctuary and transformation. Like the angels, you are legion. Thank you and bless you, Heidi Doyle, Stephanie Marisca, and Wolf Moon Eduardo.

The experiences in this book were forged by the teaching grace of the kundalini yoga community: Reinette Fournier, Tom Speare, my KYTT classmates, Mary Brakenhoff, Kyla Maher, Mary Mohler, Margaret Trezza, and Sat Siri Kaur. I am eternally indebted to Hari Kaur Khalsa, Dharm Singh, and Sat Kartar Kaur Khalsa for their pure transmission of kundalini yoga teachings.

I am especially grateful to the following individuals, and offer my profound gratitude to:

Guru Singh Khalsa and Guruperkarma Kaur Khalsa: Your powerful blessings transformed me. There is no greater gift. Thank you.

Gurunater Kaur Khalsa, who created and blessed the rose quartz mala mentioned in this book, which gave rise to the name for RQM Press. She graciously and promptly re-strung it and blessed it again for me after it broke following a physical and spiritual heart-crisis in June 2018.

Foster Perry and Kristos T. Perry, whose teachings, presence and healings uncoiled a major energy snarl in my system, and cleared the way forward so that I could see the solutions.

The poet, yogini and author Danna Faulds, whose beautiful book *Into the Heart of Yoga: One Woman's Journey*, inspired me and illuminated the path forward.

Rebecca Polan, whose intuitive editing became like a mind-meld – thank you for making the journey such a joy. Your patience, talent, loving clarity, comprehension, integrity and professional focus, were the saving grace of this book.

Judy Kinzel, whose luminous, artistic vision created the beautiful cover art for this book, and whose kind, humorous wisdom was astutely in sync with all things angelic.

I thank the talented team of Carrie Chatterson and Haley Cwynar of Carrie Chatterson Studio, for the artistry of their graphic design of this book, and patient guidance through the technical shoals of layout, fonts, and formats.

The many spiritual authors, teachers, and workshop leaders whose books and teachings have led the way, sparked internal change, and kept me company on the path.

I give special thanks to the staff, administration, and board of trustees of Kripalu Center for Yoga, for sustaining this miraculous sanctuary of spiritual hospitality over the decades. May we all ever be held in such safety and grace, in our lifetimes.

I acknowledge the lineage of Ascended Yogic Masters for the generosity and legacy of their teachings.

If there is anyone whom I have forgotten to mention here, know that I carry you in my heart.

About the Author

Barbara E. Schlubach was born in New York City in 1960. Her education and varied careers have included fine arts and non-profit administration. A mid-life excursion into studying horticulture and training as a professional gardener became one of her most joyful personal achievements.

She has been a seeker and student of spiritual practices for over fifteen years. Her private experiences led her on a path of healing, the main focus of which has been Kundalini Yoga as taught by Yogi Bhajan. She is a KRI certified (Kundalini Research Institute) Level I instructor. Her lifelong love of reading literature, correspondence, and journal writing, fused with her spiritual searches and cultivation of silent, peaceful environments, led to her ability to transcribe unseen guidance in written form. Currently her primary contact is with angelic energies.

Barbara lives and works in coastal Rhode Island, where she enjoys gardening, tai chi, teaching and practicing yoga, and time spent in nature. This is her first book.